PRAISE FOR

Dreams and Shadows

"This beautifully crafted autobiography is a testament to the resilience, courage, and boundless compassion of an individual who turned her immigrant journey into a life of service and inspiration. Through its pages, readers witness the transformative power of education and advocacy, as well as the unifying strength of a heart dedicated to binding cultures together. This is not just the story of Emma's remarkable achievements; it's a blueprint for how compassion and determination can create lasting change in our communities and beyond. A must-read for anyone seeking inspiration to make a difference."

—Congressman Don Beyer, Eighth District, Virginia

"Beautifully written, *Dreams and Shadows: An Immigrant's Journey* chronicles Emma's remarkable life, from her childhood in embattled Bolivia to her immigration to the United States, arriving in the nation's capital as a young teenager. As an international student at a Virginia college, she begins her acculturation to American life during one of the most challenging periods in history—the Vietnam War—which would ultimately claim the life of her beloved husband.

"Through her descriptive prose, Emma draws readers into her journey between the two countries she calls home and reveals the profound influences that shaped her life of service and purpose. As she reflects, 'The dictators I have worked to overthrow are ignorance, low expectations, and the ways they suppress the human spirit. . . . I still believe that education is the path.'"

—Irma Becerra, PhD, president, Marymount University

"*Dreams and Shadows* is inspiring and compelling reading; but even more, it is a powerful rebuttal to the false and malicious rhetoric that surrounds the issue of immigration today. Emma's story turns that narrative on its head. It begins with her childhood in Bolivia, the warmth and strength of family that sustains her through unbearable heartbreak, and betrayal. In spite of devastating loss in her adopted country, Emma emerges as a prominent educational leader who makes a significant contribution to [our] understanding of the bicultural experience. A contribution that only an immigrant could make."

—Frances Payne, PhD, author of *They Make Us Dangerous, Bolivia 1964-1980*

"You are so lucky if there is someone like Emma Violand-Sánchez in your community. Emma, an inspiring teacher, found students in her county who desperately needed help—and a uniquely effective way to help them. Her life story is truly beautiful, truly American—and one of a kind. You will love meeting Emma."

—Donald Graham, former publisher, *The Washington Post*

"*Dreams and Shadows* is a story of one woman's remarkable life, a life characterized by passion, commitment, and resilience in the face of grief and struggle. Emma Violand-Sánchez's beautiful and powerful memoir recounts an immigrant's exceptional journey, not just in becoming an American but in becoming a force of change and progress and compassion in her community—all while continuing to cherish her roots and her culture. *Dreams and Shadows* is, in fact, a moving and uniquely *American* story, told with heartfelt (and at times, heartbreaking) honesty. It will inspire and open hearts, a desperately needed antidote to the times in which we live."

—William Mark Habeeb, PhD, author of *Venice Beach* and *Understanding International Negotiation Theory and Practice*

"This is a deeply personal account of one woman's remarkable journey from Bolivia to Northern Virginia. Emma Violand-Sánchez has lived a life of service, and her story is a reminder of how much we are all enriched by the presence of immigrants in our midst."

—Cecilia Muñoz, author of *More than Ready: Be Strong and Be You . . . and Other Lessons for Women of Color on the Rise*

"This is an inspiring book by an inspiring woman; necessary reading for anyone who cares about the lives, suffering, and dreams of immigrants. At a time when attacks on immigrants are escalating, Emma Violand-Sánchez reminds us that each of us is born with an intelligence that matters, and every person who comes to [the United States] with a dream deserves the chance to flourish."

—Debora Seidman, playwright, writing instructor, and author of *The Lilac Minyan* and *Writing the Prayer of Your Life*

"From the halls of a German convent school in Bolivia to the front lines of educational justice in America's capital, Dr. Emma Violand-Sánchez stands as a living testament that dreams transcend borders and determination reshapes destiny. Her memoir reads like a sacred text of immigrant resilience, where each page pulses with the heartbeat of a mother, educator, and warrior who transformed the impossible into pathways of possibility for countless dreamers. . . . With her founding of the Dream Project, she has not merely documented history—she has [created] a new future where every child's potential finds its wings."

—Zamilan, Dream Project alumnus

"*Dreams and Shadows* by Emma Violand-Sánchez presents a deeply moving and personal narrative, tracing her journey from her early years in Bolivia to her current life in Arlington, VA. Through this evocative memoir, Violand-Sánchez delves into profound themes such as family, abandonment, cultural displacement, resilience, identity, suffering, spirituality, and the transformative power of acceptance, culminating in an enduring sense of joy."

—Ann A. Kennedy, PhD, president, National Capital Area Chapter of the Fulbright Association; Dream Project board member

"This is a remarkable memoir of the long and winding path, beginning more than half a century ago when a teenaged girl came to the United States from Bolivia, equipped only with amazing courage and resilience. Through shadows and difficulties, Emma Violand-Sánchez would never give up her mission to help other immigrants."

—Carolyn Clark Miller, author of *We Also Served: Three Generations Grow Up in the Military*

"Emma Violand-Sánchez's *Dreams and Shadows: An Immigrant Journey* tells of a life anchored on four important pillars: family, service, education, and the author's bicultural identity. From a very young age, Dr. Violand-Sánchez [was aware of the struggles] of others less fortunate than herself. This is the story . . . of a woman of open mind and heart, who understands that once you leave your home, you will not return as the same person and you will not return to the same place. *Dreams and Shadows* is a book about the promise and the failures of the American dream. It is a book that speaks of resilience and the power of love."

—Barbara Gitenstein, president emerita, The College of New Jersey, author of *Portrait of a Presidency: Patterns in My Life as President of the College of New Jersey*

"In *Dreams and Shadows*, Emma Violand-Sánchez shares an incredible story of her struggle to avoid losing her Bolivian identity while trying to fit in and succeed as a woman and immigrant to the United States. Despite the shadows of family crises, early widowhood, and the grief of additional losses, she finds her calling as an educator and community leader, and she succeeds beyond her dreams, changing the lives of countless young people also struggling to find their way in an unfamiliar culture. . . . [A] beautifully written, candid, and inspiring story!"

—Teddi Ahrens, author of *Painting Joy: The Art and Life of Fernando Llort*

"With *Dreams and Shadows: An Immigrant's Journey*, Dr. Emma Violand Sánchez has written a warm and inspiring story of hardship, trauma, faith, and resilience. She has turned personal challenges and uncertainty into triumphs in a career dedicated to affecting the lives of decades of public-school students in Arlington County, Virginia. Dr. Violand-Sánchez wrestled her life's journey from the shadows, and with passion and determination she has lived the life of a public servant with purpose and humility."

—Diane Kresh, director, Arlington Public Library

"As an educator, I found this to be a compelling story with many valuable lessons. . . . It delves into the intricacies of founding and navigating nonprofits; the challenges of advocating for students, immigrants, and their families; and the complex politics of gender. It highlights the resilience required to survive and break through the glass ceiling, the profound love and support provided by family and close friends, and the spirituality inherent in human nature. A must-read!"

—Evelyn E. Fernández, educator, writer, editor, and author of *Inspired by Joy After Loss*

"This memoir of a life between Bolivia and the United States . . . reminds us that global events and political climates heavily impact individuals and our educational settings. . . . *Dreams and Shadows* is relatable to immigrants who have a unique identity of not being from here nor there. . . . [It clearly shows] how we as a society can better support our children by creating more cooperative education settings where everyone's intelligence and talents are fully realized."

> —Atif Qarni, former secretary of education for the Commonwealth of Virginia

"Emma's memoir takes [readers] on an inspiring journey that rekindles the hearts of those who carry multiple cultural identities. The twists and turns of her story made me cry, laugh, and, most importantly, remember some truly empowering moments in our fight for immigrant rights. [Her book] is like a big hug filled with *consejos* [advice] and wisdom."

> —Lizzette Arias, immigrant rights advocate and Dream Project cofounder

"[*Dreams and Shadows*] is a poignant exploration of love, loss, and resilience in the face of unimaginable grief and transformation. Emma's story invites readers to reflect on their own capacity for healing and to find strength amid [their own] lifequakes. . . . It is a groundbreaking exploration of bicultural identity and educational equity and an inspiring call to embrace cultural diversity as a strength and to reimagine education as a path to belonging and success for all."

> —Giancarla Rojas, Dream Project alumna

"Emma's story is a breathtaking journey of resilience and transformation, weaving together the raw emotions of immigration, loss, and advocacy. With incredible honesty, it tackles topics often considered taboo, making it deeply relatable and profoundly moving. This inspiring narrative is a must-read for anyone seeking a reminder of the strength found in family, community, and the unexpected turns that shape our lives."

> —Milenia Rojas, PhD candidate, Stanford University, Dream Project alumna

"The best biographies tend to feature lives that have gone very right or appallingly wrong. *Dreams and Shadows* embodies both. As an educator, the life of Emma Violand-Sánchez has gone very right. She achieved one pathbreaking success after another, with major widespread positive impacts on students—especially (but not exclusively) those facing some of the toughest learning challenges. She accomplished this despite coping with disruption, tragedy, and daunting setbacks and challenges in her personal life from childhood until well into middle age. . . . How she managed all this makes for a rich, eventful, and inspirational story."

—Michael Crosswell

"Emma is a remarkable person who has led a remarkable life. May her weaving of dreams and shadows illuminate your life as it has mine. She taught me the true meaning and loving power of community."

—Lisa Ling, author of *Dragon Fly* and *Love Tank Parenting*

"Emma Violand-Sánchez's very moving memoir, *Dreams and Shadows: An Immigrant's Journey*, proves that real life is far more intriguing than fiction. Hers is an amazing story of overcoming incredible challenges and finding the will, strength, and determination to carry on. Motivated by a need to serve, her life of accomplishments—coupled with terrible losses—are a testament to the human spirit of resilience. At the center of her story is the formidable undertaking that she, and others immigrating to the United States during an era of much social and political change, have endured. I am so inspired by her story."

—Toni M. Andrews, author of *The Road to Second Chance*

"There are many reasons to read Dr. Emma Violand-Sánchez's *Dreams and Shadows: An Immigrant's Journey*, beautifully cowritten with David Bearinger. At the deepest level, it is a meditation on the interior life of someone who will always be a bicultural immigrant in her new country, contrary to the myth of 'assimilation.' [It also shows the many ways that] honesty, courage, determination, and the support of her many beloved communities, along with her Buddhist practice and Catholic faith, helped her integrate all those parts of herself and [create] a life of service for others."

—John Mooney, PhD, former assistant county manager of Arlington County, Virginia

"*Dreams and Shadows* chronicles Emma Violand-Sánchez's personal, professional, social, and political development over a long and productive life as a Bolivian immigrant morphing into a hyphenated American. In this strikingly open and honest, well-written and developed narrative, she . . . recounts her work as a teacher in two countries, and her struggles and progress as an educator, program innovator, scholar, community activist, and political leader. . . . [A] compelling portrayal of a full life well lived."

—Robert G. Smith, former superintendent, Arlington Public Schools; associate professor emeritus, George Mason University, coauthor of *Striving for Equity: District Leadership for Narrowing Opportunity and Achievement Gaps*

"*Dreams and Shadows* is a deeply moving testament to resilience, service, and the unwavering strength of the immigrant spirit. Emma's powerful and deeply personal narrative offers rich insights into the transformative power of education, opportunity, and collective effort in the face of adversity. This book is both a celebration of immigrant resilience and a poignant reminder of the profound impact that compassion and leadership can have in driving meaningful change."

—Karen Vallejos Corrales, JD, Dream Project executive director

"In *Dreams and Shadows: An Immigrant's Journey*, Dr. Emma Violand-Sánchez shares moments of her life in a flight of stories as she lives between Bolivia and the US. Beautifully written, this book is a quest of love, faith, and commitment to making learning systems better for everyone."

—Hareth Andrade-Ayala, poet

"A powerful and deeply resonant exploration of identity, belonging, and adaptation. *Dreams and Shadows* offers an inspiring journey for anyone who has navigated new environments, embraced change, or sought to reconnect with their sense of self."

—Ingrid Guerra-Lopez, PhD, dean and professor, College of Education and Human Development, George Mason University

Dreams and Shadows:
An Immigrant's Journey
by Emma Violand-Sánchez
with David Bearinger

© Copyright 2025 Emma Violand-Sánchez

ISBN 979-8-88824-646-7

All rights reserved. No part of this publication may be reproduced, stored in a retrieval system, or transmitted in any form or by any means—electronic, mechanical, photocopy, recording, or any other—except for brief quotations in printed reviews, without the prior written permission of the author.

Published by

◣ köehlerbooks™

3705 Shore Drive
Virginia Beach, VA 23455
800-435-4811
www.koehlerbooks.com

DREAMS AND SHADOWS

An Immigrant's Journey

Emma Violand-Sánchez

With David Bearinger

VIRGINIA BEACH
CAPE CHARLES

This book is dedicated to the memory of my husband
Lieutenant Albert Hugh Giddings

TABLE OF CONTENTS

Foreword by David Bearinger ... 3

Preface ... 7

Prologue: The Journey Begins ... 9

Chapter I: Childhood in Bolivia ... 11

Chapter II: Roots ... 22

Chapter III: Moving to the United States ... 36

Chapter IV: Radford and Beyond ... 46

Chapter V: Love and War ... 68

Chapter VI: Lifequake ... 84

Chapter VII: Where Have All the Flowers Gone? ... 93

Chapter VIII: Starting Over in Bolivia ... 97

Chapter IX: Politics and Turmoil: It's Complicated ... 105

Chapter X: Shadows and Light ... 111

Chapter XI: Returning to the United States ... 128

Chapter XII: Welcome to Arlington ... 142

Chapter XIII: The Shifting Landscape ... 157

Chapter XIV: Imagine a Child ... 163

Chapter XV: "That's It!"—How Do Children Learn? ... 177

Chapter XVI: Love Is Blind ... 191

Chapter XVII: Moving On, Starting Over ... 205

Chapter XVIII: Advocacy and Change:
The Question of Identity ... 221

Chapter XIX: Service in Politics: Working in a New Arena ... 241

Chapter XX: The Dream and the Shadow ... 253

Chapter XXI: The Faces of Love and Loss ... 276

Chapter XXII: Spiritual Journey ... 292

Epilogue: Transformations, Lessons Learned ... 305

Acknowledgments ... 310

Photos ... 313

FOREWORD
By David Bearinger

When Emma asked me to collaborate on the writing of her memoir, I already knew something about her accomplishments and the broad outlines of her personal story. I'd interviewed her for a publication years earlier, and we'd worked together on a half dozen or more public events and programs, several of them aimed specifically at the needs of teachers.

I'd also developed close friendships with members of the Bolivian community in Virginia, visited the Valle Alto region and the city of Cochabamba where Emma spent her early years, and been closely involved with the Dream Project, which became a major focus of her life's work after she retired from Arlington Public Schools.

In some ways I was well prepared for the journey we were about to take together. I knew Emma's lifelong commitment to service. I knew her passion for education and social justice and about the fruits of her decades of advocacy on behalf of immigrants and refugees. I knew the value she placed on family and that she was a practicing Catholic *and* a follower of the Buddhist teacher Thich Nhat Hahn.

What I didn't know was the depth of her inner life; the trauma she was carrying, hidden even from her family and closest friends; and the resilience that kept her from succumbing to a succession of personal challenges, any one of which could have crippled the life of a less courageous person—or derailed it altogether.

In short, I knew that Emma was a strong, resourceful woman. I just didn't understand what those words *really* meant. Until I learned her story.

We were just a few weeks into the work of writing *Dreams and Shadows* when Emma opened the door to her life and invited me to walk freely there—to look deeply and write what I found. This is no small thing, to open your life to another person. I was still naive about the rigors of the journey ahead, and maybe she was too, but the gift of her trust and her courage in bestowing it weren't lost on me even then.

We spent the first six months in conversation, sometimes virtually; but as often as we could, we met in person. The more we talked and the more we delved into the back pages of her life's story and dug below the surface of her many accomplishments—beneath the barebones chronologies and facts of what happened when—the more my admiration for this woman grew.

Gradually, I realized that being an immigrant had not merely shaped Emma's life and given it coloration—I'd expected that. Instead, I came to understand that being an immigrant is her story's molten core.

Emma's life has been exceptional, but her journey, its inner *and* outer dimensions, is one I think every immigrant will recognize, regardless of background or circumstance. But *Dreams and Shadows* isn't only an immigration story. It's a story about glass ceilings and what it takes to break (and not be broken by) them, and about the extra challenges and hurdles that women face, whether they live in Bolivia or the United States. It's a story about human relationships, the power of faith and family; about love and loss; and about the simple joys of life, like being a grandmother, an *abuela*.

It's also about acculturation as a lifelong process, creating and nourishing a bicultural identity, and staying clear of the vortex of the "melting pot," which is still the image many people have of what immigration to this country entails.

The deeper we went, the more vivid the pictures became: pictures of the Vietnam War; of the waves of immigration from Southeast Asia and Latin America that were transforming the communities of Northern Virginia at warp speed; the convulsive shifts in federal and state education policy; and the emergence of public schools as a battleground in America's culture wars.

I saw many ways that Emma's story is also a story of the times she lived through. But first and foremost, her story is a journey of the heart, recounted by a woman whose powers of observation are exceptional and whose achievements are themselves an affirmation of the American Dream; a proud immigrant for whom "every thread of my identity is wrapped around that core."

Some lives are relatively poor in terms of external events but rich in reflection and wisdom. Others are defined by worldly accomplishments. Their richness is in experience, with less time and energy given to the search for meaning. The life of Emma Violand-Sánchez overflows with riches on both sides of the coin.

The pain of being invisible in a story you spend your life and energy helping to create is real. So is the anguish of trying to hold on to pieces of who you were and where you came from while becoming a new person in a new land. But the joys and rewards of adapting, growing into a new culture, are also real, and so is the gratitude that most immigrants feel in being here—for the sweet breath of freedom and opportunity, for themselves and their children.

In that respect, the experience of being an immigrant in 2024 is the same as it has been at other times in our nation's history. Because except for those whose ancestors were here for thousands of years before the waves of colonization broke across the shores of the Americas, all of us have come here from someplace else. It's who we are as a people—a nation of immigrants and refugees who have come in search of something, each walking his or her own path of shadows and dreams.

The words that describe Emma's life—trauma and resilience, service, faith, family, resourcefulness, hard work—and her desire to contribute and give back, her longing for acceptance and to step from the shadows, to embrace and be embraced by the dream of America, could just as easily describe millions of other immigrants, past and future.

But we can't *really* understand what those words mean. Until we learn their stories.

David Bearinger
Palmyra, Virginia
July 4, 2024

PREFACE

I'm an immigrant. Every thread of my identity is wrapped around that core.

I became a citizen of the United States in 1973 and have lived in this country for most of the past sixty years. I've immersed myself in the life of my community and my adopted country, but even now, I see myself as a person whose roots lie somewhere else, not here.

Like most other immigrants I know, I've wrestled and wrestle still with the question of identity: Who am I? It's a question most people ask themselves at some point in their lives. But for immigrants, the stakes are higher *because* our roots are elsewhere.

There's a saying in Spanish: "No soy de aquí, ni soy de allá," which means "I'm not from here or from there." Ask anyone who has come here from another country what that saying means to them, and especially if you ask it in the language they grew up speaking, most will tell you, "Yes, it's the truth." It's a truth that almost all immigrants share, no matter where they come from or how they came here.

Every immigrant and refugee I know wants to belong, to shed the label "them" and become one of "us." The melting pot is part of the American myth, but those who step into it pay a heavy price, laying aside pieces of their identity to become someone they are not. I never wanted to make that choice. Instead, my quest has been to embrace my bicultural identity as a Bolivian American and encourage others to embrace theirs.

When I was very young, I received a gift. That gift was the feeling in my heart that I was not separate from those who were suffering. I understood then, in ways I still struggle to explain, that I am "them," and "they" are me.

And so I became a weaver, not of cloth but of dreams and shadows. The threads on my loom are family, education, faith, opportunity, service, and the love I have for my two countries, Bolivia and the United States.

We are searching for community. I believe that God calls us to work not in isolation, not by ourselves or for ourselves, but in service to others. In the Catholic Church, community is literally the body of Christ. Which means that we are called to serve in community where it exists and to *build* it where it does not.

The great Vietnamese Buddhist teacher Thich Nhat Hanh said that community is an organism, and we are like living cells within a body whose life depends on each of us in the same way that each cell in a body depends on every other. As Jesus said: "Even unto the least of these . . ."

When I was in my mid-seventies, a dear friend wove a tapestry and called it *Emma, weaver*. She attached notes to the threads, naming what she saw as my various accomplishments. I didn't know she'd done this until after she died. But I've kept it ever since as a reminder of what my life has been: a weaving of the dreams and shadows of my immigration story so that others will know and understand that we are not separate. There is no "them," only "us."

PROLOGUE
The Journey Begins

I remember the white dress, the warm sun on my face, palm trees that seemed a hundred feet high, yellow and pink hibiscus, and the jacaranda branches heavy with purple flowers. I remember the bright clicking sound my shoes made on the stones of the Plaza Colon.

I'm in Cochabamba, a city in the Bolivian central valley where I was born. It's 1950, and I'm six years old. It is Sunday afternoon.

At the doorway of the Templo del Hospicio, women and children are begging. I've seen these women and children often on Sundays when my family goes to church. After church we have a homemade lunch and maybe go for a ride in my father's car. There are few cars in Cochabamba. Most people can't afford one, but my father works in a family import–export business, and he loves cars; they are one of his passions.

I'm aware that my family has many things other families don't have. I'm aware of a system that enforces these differences. I don't know where it came from or why it exists. But I've decided to do something about it. Yet what can a six-year-old girl do? What can I do?

I want to attend catechism with these children, even though I take religious instruction at a private Catholic school called Santa Maria. So I ask my mom if I can go to church by myself today. After all, I can walk myself to school. She says yes. Cochabamba is like a garden city. Our house is behind an iron fence with a locked gate, but I feel safe and am not afraid.

I don't tell my mother why I want to go to church this afternoon. I simply feel a strong need in my heart to connect with the children who are begging, and to pray with them. My prayers to the Virgin Mary always make me feel reassured and strong. I want them to feel strong too.

I'm keenly aware of injustice. *Why can't women be priests?* It seems so unfair, the way girls and boys are always treated differently. My school is just for girls, and the nuns are always saying that boys can't be trusted. I don't understand why this is, but it's the reason we, the girls, have to wear our long hair in braids, never in a ponytail, and why we're not allowed to wear sleeveless dresses.

I have three sisters. Another child is on the way, and my mother is praying constantly that it will be a boy. I also pray to the Virgin Mary that she will help my mother and send me a baby brother. My mother and I don't know that the sex of the baby is already decided at the moment of conception—by the father.

My father wants to have a son so that he can carry on the name Violand. He is the only person in Bolivia with that name. His father had one sister but no brothers. His sister died when she was very young, and he is an only child. He worries that his name will be lost.

Even now, with my whole life ahead of me, I see that the world is not fair. It's hard to watch children just like me begging in the street for money. And it's hard to be seen by my church—and even by my own father—as having less value because I am a girl. Is this what God wants for me?

I must find the answer.

CHAPTER 1

Childhood in Bolivia

The table in front of me vanished—plates, cups, flowers, *pollo, puré de papas*, all of it. Gone, dissolved like it was made of sugar and the world had suddenly become a thunderstorm, the rain falling so hard around me that I couldn't see.

"You are going to live in the United States."

When my mother spoke, we all knew better than to question her—at least, not then. But why? Why now? Why us? Why me? Why was I being sent away again? The old feelings of abandonment came roaring back.

My sisters Julia and Susy were thinking the same thing. First our father stayed behind in Cochabamba while we moved and had to start a new life in a strange city nine hours away, and now this. It wasn't fair.

"I want to stay in Bolivia."

I was the one speaking, but the words sounded like they came from inside an iron bell. I felt like I didn't belong in my own body—like a great hole had opened up inside, filled with blazing-hot lava that would scald me out of existence if I fell inside it. I was scared and confused and angry. I wanted to be a little girl again, so young that my mother couldn't send me away.

"What about my friends?" I asked. "What about Jaime?" Jaime was my boyfriend.

I could see my mother was unhappy too, even though she was calling this an opportunity. Later, I understood how hard it was for her, this decision—how she'd prayed day and night, asking God to show her another way, so her three oldest daughters could stay with her in La Paz.

But *Tía* Mecha had explained it well, and my mother was right: It was an opportunity. Julia would go to Michigan. Susy and I would finish high school in Virginia. My three youngest sisters, Maria Eugenia, Anneliese, and Paty, would stay with my mother. The solution made sense. Besides, there wasn't a practical alternative. My mother had mostly hidden her struggles with money from us, but we all knew.

I think deep down I understood the decision even then, and I loved her for it. Some part of me knew this was what I was supposed to do. And for a split second, I also felt a thrill: *I'm going to the United States.*

Then it was like a heavy curtain had dropped, and I was back in Argentina, looking out across the schoolyard at the boarding school in Quilmes, Buenos Aires, with the other girls in our beige-and-green uniforms, cotton frocks covering our knees. Feeling alone.

I don't remember anything else that happened that night, but in the morning, the thunderstorm was gone. The table was there like always, a bowl of papayas and bananas in the middle; it wasn't made of sugar after all. The hole with the lava in it had closed up overnight. And my sisters and I began our preparations for the journey ahead.

My first memory:

It's twelve years earlier, and I'm three years old, playing with my sisters in my favorite place, the patio outside our house in Cochabamba, with its high stone walls, well-tended beds of flowers, and peach trees all around.

It feels safe. The walls throw long, cool shadows in the morning and late afternoon. I'm eating peaches off the tree branches and a piece of freshly baked bread while my nanny Jesus—which can be a woman's name in Bolivia—toasts coffee beans.

I love that smell, of roasting coffee, and the taste of peaches on my fingertips.

It troubles me that the gate to our patio is always locked. I'm curious. I want to explore our neighborhood, to see what's out there, especially the army barracks next door. Why can't I go there?

Somehow, this afternoon, the lock on the gate is open. It's my chance, and without asking anyone, I go.

My sister runs to tell my mother, who is frightened. She goes to the barracks and brings me home. She spanks me. I'm crying. She says the soldiers can't be trusted.

But why? Why should I be afraid of these soldiers?

Four years later, there's a revolution in Bolivia. It's 1952. There are soldiers outside our house with pistols. They're looking for my father. My father hides, but weeks later they find him, and he is taken to jail. Now I understand, about the soldiers.

For a few days, we hide too, at the house of my uncle, Luis Alcazar. When the city is calm again, we go back home. The locked gate and the high walls of the patio feel safe like before, but it's not the same. Something is lost, and for the first time in my life, I feel alone.

As a small child, I was already well aware of differences in Bolivian society. Poor and Indigenous people were not treated the same as we were, even by the church, and our family and friends enjoyed many privileges other people did not have.

In those years, more than 70 percent of the people in Bolivia were Indigenous. They were identified by skin tone, eye color, or last name. Most spoke Quechua, some spoke Aymara. Many spoke only rudimentary or broken Spanish, enough to get by, like immigrants in their own country, which was how they were often treated.

The men worked in construction, as bus or truck drivers, or in other so-called service occupations. The women, known as *cholitas*—a term mostly used by the upper- and middle-class Bolivians to describe Indigenous women who had come to the cities to live—dressed in wide, usually pleated knee-length skirts called *polleras* and white felt hats. They wore their hair in heavy braids.

In cities like Cochabamba, many of the cholitas worked as housekeepers and cooks or sold goods in the markets. They carried their babies in hand-loomed cloths called *aguayos*. Their children, even toddlers, played in the open streets, and the older children attended public schools if they went to school at all; many didn't, especially in the rural areas. Riding in my father's car outside the limits of the city on a Sunday afternoon, I would see whole families, even the smallest children, tilling the soil. These farmers were known as *campesinos*.

Our family had a cook, a nanny, and a gardener, and while my parents insisted that we show them respect, they never ate with us. They served our table, and then they ate in the kitchen after we had finished. They washed and ironed our clothes. I remember that Jesus—our nanny, not the Son of God—told us scary stories at bedtime, which I loved. And I loved *her*.

What disturbed me most was the poor children begging for food, knowing they didn't go to school and seeing how hard they worked. Many years later, I learned that my DNA is about 40 percent Indigenous, but no one in our family spoke Quechua or Aymara, and my father would surely have hidden this genealogical fact if he'd known it.

In Cochabamba in the 1950s, it seemed like it was always spring. There were plazas and markets filled with fruits, vegetables, and colorful textiles and few cars; people rode bikes, and when I was old enough, I walked to school.

In the early years, our family life was full of happiness.

My grandmother Julia lived with us. I remember her in the

kitchen, teaching my mother to cook; and I remember looking through the open door to her room, seeing her in prayer, dressing for Mass, or saying the Rosary. The sight of her praying warmed my heart. Her faith was at the center of everything she did.

My mother was very attractive and one of the few women in Cochabamba who drove a car. She loved fresh fruit. Bowls of bananas, oranges, and papayas—and, of course, peaches—were always close at hand. She would break into song at any moment, usually a song from Tarija where she'd lived as a child; and she sometimes sang as a trio with her brother Alberto and her sister Mercedes ("Mecha"). She also played the guitar.

My father was handsome and charming, and my mother always wanted to please him. There's a story she used to tell, about a time when I was two years old and she was driving through the city with me, and we had a minor accident. The damage was slight, but she didn't want my father to know about it because he was so protective of his new car. So she had the repair work done and never told him what happened. I was sworn to secrecy, but for months afterward, every time we drove through that intersection, I'd shout, "Boom, boom." My father asked repeatedly, but no one ever told him the reason for my outbursts, and somehow, I managed to keep my oath of secrecy.

Both my parents were protective, my mother especially, and we had strict rules and schedules but not many responsibilities beyond school and church. We would visit friends, celebrate birthdays and holidays, go to the swimming pool, or ride our bikes. We each had our own peach tree to climb, personal territory that we guarded closely. We played hopscotch or marbles, sang *rondas* like "Arroz con Leche," or played "store" or "school" with our dolls. In "school," I was always the teacher. We had no television, but my parents had the latest music, so if we couldn't be outside, we'd listen to 33 rpm records and dance.

But behind Cochabamba's veil of happiness lurked darker parts of the story. Unpaved roads outside the city quickly turned to mud when it rained. Politics broke through the walls keeping us safe, and the day my father was arrested, they forced their way into our peach tree garden.

I was eight years old, and I went with my mother to visit him in jail in the plaza. We took him soup my mother had made and blankets. I remember a large room with many men inside. I hugged my father, held him as tightly as I could. The other men were watching. It was scary, and I'd heard my mother tell Tía Mecha that the *milicianos* of the socialist Movimiento Nacionalista Revolucionario (MNR), which had captured him, were sending prisoners to concentration camps. I didn't know what a concentration camp was, but I could tell from the way my mother said the words that it would be much worse and far more dangerous than this jail.

Bolivian politics, especially in those years, divided along complicated lines. Even though my father was a leader of the conservative political party, Falange, some members of the MNR were family friends. My mother negotiated and pleaded with everyone she knew to gain my dad's release. She later told me that one man had said to her, "I will get your husband out of jail, but you have to sleep with me." I don't know what she promised him, but my father was freed, and I'm sure she never did what he demanded.

Her fear of soldiers and the military ran deep, maybe all the way back to an incident when she was a young girl, in Tarija. She went to the river, probably to bathe, and saw a band of soldiers from the Chaco War, a bloody conflict in which Bolivia lost substantial portions of its land to Paraguay. She never told me what happened there at the river; maybe it was nothing. But it made a strong impression that she carried with her all her life.

As a young child, I was pious and devout. I prayed often. Prayer gave me a feeling of rootedness and connection, of having someone—God, Christ, the Virgin Mary—who was protecting me, loving me, and would always be there in times of need. I loved confession, the veil and the Rosary; I loved the idea of being released from sin. I wanted to have Christ in my heart always. I wanted to be a nun. My father even gave me the nickname Schwestita, meaning "Little Sister" or "Little

Nun." It was not entirely a compliment. But my grandmother Julia praised my piety, and that was reinforcement enough.

I went to Mass, came home for lunch, and then went back to church again for catechism. Once, I entered a Protestant church, which was forbidden. I heard music and I was curious, so I slipped in. Later I had to confess it as a sin. When my sister Julia was preparing to take her first Communion, she wrote all her sins in a green notebook, which I found and read out of curiosity. But I was filled with guilt afterward, and when Julia got her first period a few weeks later, I thought it was my fault.

In school, the nuns all said the boys couldn't be trusted: "You know what they want." I *didn't* know what they wanted; but by the time I was in the fourth or fifth grade, I started noticing boys in a different way. I was pretty, and they would drop by the house to visit.

I liked them and wanted to be around them, but the nuns at school said we shouldn't have boys as friends. They said we should never bare our arms when boys were around, but if I couldn't bare my arms in public, how could I go swimming in the public swimming pool? Once again I thought, *This is not fair.* Maybe I didn't want to be a nun after all. But I never lost my faith, at least not then, and when I was at boarding school in Argentina and was lonely or confused, going to Mass and saying prayers gave me comfort.

When I was four years old, I was very shy. I cried a lot and hated the spotlight. My mother enrolled me in a children's theater program to build up my confidence. We had to recite poems and stories, and eventually I lost my fear of public speaking. Looking back, that early training paved the way for a career that would not have been possible if I hadn't conquered my fear early on.

My parents sacrificed to send us to the best schools, meaning private, not public schools. My first was Santa Maria, a German all-girls school in Cochabamba run by nuns. I was a good student and loved learning, but the teachers were all very strict. My first-grade teacher, Sister Maria Bernarda, was kind, but she instilled in us the fear of hell. She said that Protestants and communists would go there if they didn't repent and become Catholic.

When I was twelve, my mother decided to send her two oldest daughters to a private boarding school in Buenos Aires. Argentina was known for its first-rate bilingual boarding schools based on the English model. They attracted mostly upper-class students from Argentina and the surrounding countries, including Bolivia.

I didn't want to go, but I wasn't given a choice, and so in February of 1956, Julia and I found ourselves in Quilmes, wearing our green frock uniforms, trying to fit in. We had classes in English in the afternoon and Spanish in the morning.

Being in a new country was hard, but I loved learning and tried to make the best of it—until Julia was hit by a bicycle, suffered a concussion, and started having headaches so severe that my mother decided to bring her back to Cochabamba, leaving me at Quilmes alone. I felt abandoned, and those feelings of abandonment, of being left or sent away, have surfaced again and again throughout my life. But I went to Mass on Sundays, and I felt lucky because one of the other Quilmes students was a good friend from Cochabamba, Ana Maria Parada. We went to classes and studied together, and she was an excellent piano player. I went home for the summers, my parents were rebuilding their marriage after my father had an affair, and all seemed to be well.

And then the bottom dropped out. My dad had another affair, and a month before the school year ended in November, there was a failed attempt by his party, the Falange, to overthrow leftist President Hernan Siles Suazo. As a result, my father's business was in trouble, money was tight, and when I came home for the summer, expecting to return to Quilmes in the fall, we were told that my mother and we five girls would be moving to La Paz. I would not be returning to

Quilmes after all. To top it off, my mother was pregnant again, with child number six.

Julia was the one who told me about the affair. I'm not sure how she knew, because my mother never told us until much later. The move was explained to us in terms of money and politics, not marital issues. Julia and I both overheard a conversation between our mother and Tía Mecha about how my father was having financial problems, the house would have to be mortgaged and rented out, and that he and my grandmother would get a small apartment in Cochabamba.

So my mother packed the five of us in the car and drove us the nine hours to La Paz, moving into a house Tía Mecha had found for us. I enrolled in a new school called Saint Andrew's, a co-op school established by parents—the same school where I would be hired to teach many years later.

It was the first co-ed school I had ever attended, and I loved it. Any worries about my father's infidelities, my parents' marriage, or the political situation in Bolivia were soon behind me, despite another failed coup in April 1959 that sent my father into exile two years later, in Peru.

I savored my adolescence. I was a flirt with the boys, an excellent student, and a class officer, and I had an active social life outside of school. My sister Paty was born. My father came for visits, but he slept in a room separate from my mom. I was curious about the arrangement but too preoccupied with my own life to worry about it. Neither of my parents mentioned that they were planning to divorce.

By age fifteen, I had a boyfriend, Jaime Vargas, who was two years older than me. He was handsome, so much so that even though I was pretty and vivacious, being with him sometimes made me feel insecure.

His best friend had a car, but my mother didn't want me to go out alone with him, especially not driving. Looking back, she must have been aware he was pushing to have sex with me. Fortunately, I said no. Years later, after I moved to the United States, Jaime moved to New York and joined the US Air Force. He came to visit, said he wanted to marry me. We went together to my senior prom at Mount Vernon High School in Virginia.

The relationship never went any further, but at the age of sixteen, it felt like a serious romance. Because my mother wouldn't let me drive with him, Jaime would come to my house, and we'd walk to get *salteñas*, a traditional Bolivian pastry filled with spiced meat and vegetables, or to see a movie. He was a member of a loose-knit fraternity that called themselves the Country Club.

There were other groups too, with names like Jets, the Top Hats, Splendid. Each one had its own colors; the Country Club's were red and white. Only boys could be members. This was Bolivia, after all. Girls were admitted through their boyfriends.

It was an exciting time. American popular culture was finding its way into the country. We saw American movies, anything with James Dean—*Rebel Without a Cause, Giant, East of Eden*. We listened to American music: Elvis, the Platters, Neil Sedaka. My favorite was Paul Anka, especially "Put Your Head on My Shoulder." I memorized the words to all his songs.

I loved my life. I was doing well in school, involved in sports, and comfortable in my world. But the political crisis in Bolivia was closer than I knew. This was also a time of hyperinflation, devaluation of the Bolivian peso. My mother was renting out rooms in our house, feeding twenty people at lunchtime to earn extra money, and still not making ends meet.

And then, as she would do so often over the years that followed, Tía Mecha opened the door. It was not a door I wanted to walk through at first, but it was the door to the rest of my life, to everything that followed.

Mecha was the first in our family to emigrate and had been living in Washington, DC. She taught Spanish at the Foreign Service Institute for the US State Department, where she met John (Jack) Powelson, a Quaker from Fairfax County, Virginia, who was currently in La Paz on a Fulbright Fellowship.

Jack and his wife, Robin, were looking for a young Bolivian high school student to live with them, babysit, and teach Spanish to their daughters, Cindy and Judy, when they returned to the States. Their next-door neighbors, Ed and Edie Bierley, were a Catholic couple who were looking for the same thing.

Mecha's idea was that my mother would send the three oldest girls—Julia, Susy, and me—to the US. Julia, who was finishing up her senior year at Saint Andrew's, would go to Detroit to live with Albert Defezzy, my father's cousin, who had a job at General Motors. Susy and I would go to Fairfax, Virginia. We wouldn't be paid, but we'd have free room and board and go to school. I would spend my senior year there.

My mother spoke with officials at the Ministry of Education and got permission for Susy and me to take our final exams in August instead of at the end of the school year, in November. A dinner was arranged. Mecha and the Powelsons were there. So were the Powelsons' daughters.

We sat at the table, and my mother welcomed them. The food was delicious as always, and a bowl of fruit was on the table for dessert. The Powelsons seemed nice but a little strange. It was July 17, 1961.

"You are going to live in the United States."

CHAPTER II
Roots

There is no way to understand my life's journey without knowing something about my family's roots in Bolivia, and about the lives of my parents, my grandmother Julia, my aunt Mecha, and my five sisters.

Family has been and remains my rock, my root system, my safe harbor, and the source of whatever strength I possess. Families are also complicated, mine included.

My parents are Adalberto Violand-Alcazar and Emma Sánchez-Rossel. Adalberto's grandfather emigrated from Innsbruck, Austria, to La Paz at the end of World War I, part of a wave of immigrants from the former Austro-Hungarian Empire seeking refuge and a new life.

My mother's family was from Tarija, the southernmost state of Bolivia, near the Argentine border. Her mother died when she was a year old and her father when she was three. She was the youngest of eight children.

My parents met in high school and married young, and for many years they were deeply in love. My father was the most charming, charismatic man I've ever met. Women adored him. I still do, and my mother adored him most of all—even after infidelity, after their divorce and his remarriage, twice, and after decades living apart. And I believe that in his way, he still loved her.

It was complicated.

Abuelita Julia

My father's mother, Julia Alcazar, *mi abuela*, was the first child of a large family from the Yungas region of La Paz. Yungas is on the eastern slope of the Andes and includes the westernmost reaches of the Amazon. Parts of it are densely forested even today. It's also an agricultural region of deep valleys and steep, terraced hillsides, famous for growing coffee.

Her parents owned a farm, called Cocayapu, where they grew mangos, oranges, papayas, tangerines, bananas—and coca, a medicinal plant considered sacred by many Indigenous people in the Andes region, who used it as a mild stimulant and to help them live and work in the high altitudes. It wasn't until the 1950s that coca was processed and exported in large quantities as cocaine. The farm also grew cocoa, for making chocolate. The family had a big farmhouse.

Most of the workers who farmed the land were Indigenous, and my grandmother learned to speak Aymara so she could communicate and understand what they were saying. I remember the smell of coffee and sugar roasting at Cocayapu and the songs the workers sang when they were packing fruit and coffee beans for shipment to the markets in Cochabamba.

The nearest town, Ocobaya, was within comfortable walking distance. It had freshly painted white buildings and a cluster of small stores around a little plaza with a church at the center. There was a school nearby named for Julia's father.

A great-uncle, Luis Alcazar, had an even larger farm in the nearby town of Chulumani. Luis also owned an import-export business, Alcazar y Compañía, with offices in La Paz, Cochabamba, and Potosi.

Growing up, my grandmother was my spiritual guide, my role model. It felt like my heart was glowing with a warm light whenever Abu Julia was nearby. I loved her deeply. She was kind and patient and had a calming influence on whoever was around her. She adored my father, and she loved her daughter-in-law and all her granddaughters, me especially, as if we were all simply part of her, no separation between us. She was the matriarch of our family in those early years, but in a gentle way. I can still see her getting ready for Mass and Communion, which she took every day, or at work in the kitchen. The kitchen was her domain. She was an exceptionally good cook, and her meals were joyous occasions, especially for me as a young child. She was also a patient tutor for my orphaned mother, who had never cooked a meal before she married Adalberto.

I picture Abuelita Julia with white hair, usually tied up in a bun, and a loose-fitting white shirt, a long black skirt, and soft shoes. The softness of my grandmother's shoes made a deep impression on me, and I can still hear the swishing sound they made as she cooked or crossed the stones of our patio on her way to the garden and peach trees outside.

Alongside her spirituality and strong Catholic faith, Julia's worldly accomplishments were exceptional for her time and place. She was one of the first two girls from Yungas to graduate from high school—in her case, from the Sacred Heart Boarding School in La Paz. It took two days to make the journey from her family's farm to the city by horseback, which she did multiple times, starting at the age of six. Later, as a young and comparatively well-educated woman, she managed a store in Potosi owned by her brother.

Potosi once held the richest deposits of silver found on earth. A conical mountain called the Cerro Rico—the "Rich Hill"—was its epicenter, but veins of the precious metal ran through the surrounding hills like filigree, in every direction. For more than two centuries, the mines in and around Potosi generated vast wealth for the Spanish conquerors, wealth that surged through the economies of Europe, building churches, financing wars, and enriching aristocratic family and state coffers. This was the story of conquest in Bolivia and throughout Latin America. It set up those patterns of injustice based on social class that I first felt in Plaza Colon.

From the late sixteenth to the early eighteenth centuries, Potosi was one of the largest and wealthiest cities anywhere in the Americas, with theaters, bullfights, gambling houses, and scores of magnificently decorated churches. But eventually the silver was exhausted, and a process using mercury to extract the lower grades of silver devastated the land and water and the health of the mostly Indigenous men, women, and young children who worked in the mines.

Even in the 1930s, Potosi was still a center of business activity, and the store my grandmother managed was owned by Alcazar y Compañía. She would travel at night by truck from Cochabamba or La Paz to bring back supplies. In those days, it took courage for anyone traveling alone to make this journey; and for a woman, the risks were greater.

My grandmother married late. My father, her youngest child, was born when she was thirty-eight. Most of her family's land in Yungas was confiscated and redistributed in the 1950s during the agrarian reforms. Both of her other two children died at an early age; and then her husband, Paz Eduardo Violand, died when she was in her early sixties, three years before I was born.

In most ways, my grandmother was a traditional Bolivian woman. She was a devout Catholic. She wanted her granddaughters to dress modestly. She never wanted us to walk barefoot, which she probably associated with poverty, or to be in the sun, darkening our skin. The cloud of class division based on race hung over all of Bolivia, and over our family too.

But in other ways, Julia pushed the boundaries, especially the low glass ceiling and the narrow walls surrounding most Bolivian women of her era—and of mine. She believed strongly in the importance of education, for women as well as men, and she worked hard to instill this belief, first in her son and later in her granddaughters. This attitude was extremely rare among Bolivian women of her generation.

When the time came, my grandmother strongly supported my parents in their decision to send Julia and me to Quilmes in Argentina to get the best education possible. And later, she also supported my mother's painful decision to send her three oldest daughters to the United States, agreeing with my aunt Mecha that this was an opportunity too good to pass up.

Even now, almost fifty years after her death, I still feel my grandmother's presence and the ways that presence nourished my inner life, both as a child and for decades afterward. I think about the farm girl from Yungas riding for days on horseback to do something no other young girl she knew had ever done. I think about her driving alone on those treacherous unpaved roads at night, the courage that must have taken, and about her managing the store in Potosi, breaking new ground in her world a second time.

I think about the sorrow she experienced in her life, the losses, and about her gentle nature. And most of all, I think about the years when she was growing old, when she lived in our home, the matriarch of the family, helping to care for her granddaughters, loving and caring for my mother.

Courageously, at age eighty, my grandmother came to the United States to care for my niece Angie, the oldest of all her great-grandchildren. She was always ready to help with childcare responsibilities, to do whatever needed to be done. She is my role model in that way too, as an *abuelita* who loves her grandchildren beyond measure—and will until the final days of my life.

I think, too, about my grandmother's devotions, her prayers, the way she dressed, the way she moved and spoke, and the countless ways she inspired me just by being who she was. The forces this exceptional woman set in motion have shaped my life and given me strength in ways I can still only begin to understand.

Adalberto Violand

My father was born in La Paz. His two siblings died in early childhood, and my grandmother spoiled him, while his father was known to be very strict. He attended the German school in La Paz, and his fluency in both German and Spanish would be an asset later, both as an entrepreneur and when he was named ambassador to Germany.

When my father was in high school, the family moved to Tarija. His charisma already at work, he instantly became very popular. There's a story of young Adalberto inviting all his high school friends to the social club and charging the expenses, which were considerable, to his parents' account. Partly as punishment, my grandfather decided to send my father back to La Paz, back to the German school; but he and my mother had already met and fallen in love, and he begged my grandfather not to send him away from his beloved Emma. And so, his parents promised that if he finished school in La Paz, he could come back and marry her.

Which is what happened. They married and moved to a single room in Cochabamba, and my father got a job in a hardware store owned by his uncle. My oldest sister, Julia—called July and pronounced "Julie" in Spanish—was born, I followed two years later, and my father proved to be adept at business—and at politics. By the time I was six, he owned his import-export business and was becoming active in the community, in service clubs like the Lions and as president of the Cochabamba football league; and at some point along the way, he joined the Falange Socialista Boliviana.

The Falange was established in 1937, and by 1950 it had become the second-largest political party in Bolivia. It was far to the right, grounded in a strong anti-communist ideology, and it espoused the virtues of private enterprise and leadership in young people. The party was strong in places like Cochabamba and Santa Cruz, but it failed in the Andean region of Bolivia, a stronghold of the socialist MNR.

Bolivian politics, rarely stable, was moving into a decades-long period of almost constant turmoil, and over the next twenty-five years I would see my father move from the epicenters of political power into exile and back again several times.

As a child and up until his death in 2005, one of the qualities I loved most about my father, and sought to emulate, was his leadership. He had a joyous spirit and was always optimistic, even in the face of adversity. His kindness extended to people of all classes, not just to the elite.

Even now, I try to imagine my dad in meetings with right-wing dictators like the Chilean President Pinochet when he was ambassador in Chile or President Hugo Banzer, who cracked down hard on student protests in universities, suppressed leftist movements, and imprisoned or even killed dissenters, including priests. And I can't help but wonder: What did he say in those meetings? Did he urge restraint, tolerance? Did he support the growth of democratic institutions in Bolivia? What was his role?

It's hard to reconcile that this man I loved for his kindness could have supported or at least remained silent as these plans and decisions were being made. But whatever mystery surrounds my father's political life, I know how much he loved his country.

In the early years, political questions were still far away, beyond our locked gate.

I remember watching from the second floor as my parents hosted dance parties for their friends. My dad had a gift for making people feel comfortable and at ease. But he also had the air of a *persona*—impeccably dressed, elegant in his bearing, proud of his new car, and slightly untouchable. It's hard to imagine my father changing diapers or reading to his daughters, and as far as I can remember, he never did. I never saw him lift a hammer or do manual work. Once, when I had a flat tire, instead of helping me, my father called a taxicab and paid the driver to change the tire.

In those years, Bolivian culture prescribed strict gender roles where men were dominant and always in charge. And yet my father encouraged my mother to learn to drive. Conservative as he was, my dad seemed to have no difficulty breaking what was then one of the cardinal unspoken rules of his time and place by empowering his wife in a way that people all around couldn't help but see.

My father's family lost their land in La Paz when the MNR took power in 1952, and he was briefly jailed. In 1959, my parents separated. That was when my sisters and I moved with our mom to La Paz, Paty was born, there was another revolution, and my father became the target of persecution once again. He lost his business and went into exile in Peru, where the only work he could find was as a door-to-door salesman, selling car parts. My mother supported all six daughters on her own, taking in boarders and preparing lunch for *pensionados* to make enough money to live.

I was in college in the United States when I realized that my parents had divorced and my dad was remarried. It felt at the time like the worst kind of abandonment, but just a few years later I would come to know another, far more grievous kind.

Even as he aged, my father's charm never left him. Once, when he was visiting Washington, DC, my sisters and I took him to a restaurant where there was dancing. After he took a turn or two on the dance floor with his daughters, another woman, a stranger, came to our table and told us she wanted to dance with him and that she would take him home. She wasn't joking.

My father was a complicated man. But I learned many of my early lessons about love and empathy from him. And his dedication to and sacrifice for Bolivia is an example of service I have tried to follow in my own life.

Emma Sánchez-Rossel

The lessons I learned from my father about leadership and service are mixed with lessons from my mother about resilience and strength.

My mother was blessed—and she blessed everyone around her—with a gentle and forgiving heart. But her spirit was made of high-tensile-strength steel. She was unbreakable. Like my father, she lived her life in service; but in her, the spirit of service took a different form.

Her life story is a repeating cycle of adversity and overcoming poverty that affirms, again and again, the power of her faith and the love she had for her family and her homeland. In so many ways, she embodied the soul of Bolivia, and her story weaves through my own life journey like a silver thread, dancing and singing all the way.

My mother wasn't perfect; she was not a saint. But whenever I've needed an example of a strong and forceful woman who refused to buckle or succumb to hardship, I've looked to Emma Sánchez-Rossel to show or remind me of the way.

Mi mami was born in 1918 in Tarija, the youngest of eight children. Both her parents died by the time she was three, and she lived her earliest years in poverty. She drew eyes on a stone so she could have a doll.

When she was six, a grandfather who was blind returned to Tarija from Chile to help care for the children, and she remembered that he sang to them and gave each one a small piece of bread at night, before they went to sleep. As long as she lived, my mother never threw away bread. She said that, for her, it was the face of God.

As a young woman, she enrolled in a school for teachers in the department (Bolivian state) of Sucre, but she left to marry Adalberto. She learned to cook from her mother-in-law, Abu Julia, who also taught her how to serve her husband in the ways traditional Bolivian society prescribed. They were unusually close for a mother and daughter-in-law, perhaps because they were both so devoted to him.

When my parents separated after seventeen years of marriage and we left my father for La Paz, it was a time of revolution in Bolivia, of armed factions in the streets. There was a curfew, and people were forbidden to leave their homes, but my mother left anyway, walking several miles to a clinic to deliver my sister Paty, who was born two months premature.

My father was at best inconsistent in his child support payments and paid no spousal support. At least twice, my mother had to take out high-interest loans to avoid foreclosure. She had no money for her own medical care, no insurance, and she lost sight in one of her eyes permanently because of an infection. It was a preventable loss that made the rest of her life far more difficult, but I never heard her complain. Throughout her life, she dismissed concerns for her well-being and downplayed whatever health issues she was having. She kept her attention, and her prayers, focused on the needs of her daughters.

In 1995, my fiftieth birthday was approaching, and my mother called from Bolivia to say she was coming to celebrate. I wasn't even planning to acknowledge the occasion—it was a difficult time for me personally, and I wasn't in the mood to celebrate anything—but she insisted on throwing a party, complete with a disc jockey and, of course, dancing. She was seventy-seven.

When she turned ninety and was living in the United States, we celebrated in a Bolivian restaurant in Arlington with live music, and my mother danced *cueca*, a traditional dance form common to parts of Chile, Argentina, and the region around Tarija in Bolivia.

In her long life, my mother struggled with poverty, betrayal, abandonment, a litany of serious illnesses and health concerns, and with the loss of her youngest daughter, Paty. But her faith sustained her. She never lost heart; she never lost hope. She knew what she wanted. She kept her dignity and independence. And she remained a forceful presence in the lives of her family, to the end.

I think about Emmita and Adalberto when they were young and in love. I think about the qualities that sustained each of them. I wonder what life would have been like had they stayed together. I know it would have been different. I might have never left Bolivia; and none of what transpired in the years since would have happened.

Of the two, my father was by far the more complex. But I think my mother's strength exceeded his. Her love was more constant. His grace and charm carried him across many borders. Her faith carried her.

I imagine the joy, in heaven, when my mother finally met the parents she never really knew. And I wonder if she and her beloved Adalberto are dancing *cueca* somewhere now.

Mercedes Sánchez

My aunt Mercedes (Tía Mecha) was tall and strong-featured with a wide forehead and broad shoulders. Her gaze was so sharp at times that it felt like it could cut through a brick wall. She could freeze you in your tracks. When Mecha talked, you listened. She was a woman who demanded to be taken seriously.

She could be kind and loving too, but in a no-nonsense way. She had a force field around her that was impossible to ignore. Her posture telegraphed the message even before she spoke. She presented herself to the world with a confidence that was rare for a Bolivian woman in those days.

All her life, Mecha opened doors no one else could open. She also saw the doors no one else could see—or created them herself if they didn't already exist. She was my mother's oldest sister and the first person in our family to emigrate to the United States. As a young woman in Bolivia, she taught physical education in the Normal School in Sucre, which meant she was a teacher of future teachers, and she had that way of interacting with people, like an instructor, even with my mother and with us, her nieces.

She could be critical, even judgmental at times. You didn't want Tía Mecha to see you not looking your best. When Mecha was coming, my mother always rushed to clean the house, to make it spotless, and she reminded us constantly to stand up straight and be polite.

Mecha was distrustful of men. She didn't want her nieces to be in the company of boyfriends—or any other men, for that matter—without close supervision. If she was there when boys came to visit us in La Paz, she made sure the doors were open, no privacy; and if she thought they were staying too long, she'd tell them bluntly, "It's time for you to go." They were all afraid of her.

Later, when I was a young woman living in the United States and eager to feel "liberated" by smoking cigarettes, I hid the ashtrays and other evidence when she visited. For her, smoking just wasn't something a woman did—not an educated woman with "prospects." Her dream was that her nieces would marry "appropriate" men. When my sisters and I visited her in Washington, she'd take us to Georgetown to meet young foreign service officers, telling us, "These are the kind of men you need to know."

Mecha got a scholarship from the UN to study French at the Sorbonne, learned the language quickly, and when she came home, she got a job teaching French at the Alliance française, also in La Paz. This was in the mid-1950s. A few years later, she came to the US to teach Spanish at the Foreign Service Institute in DC. She got her green card and eventually became a US citizen, the first member of the Sánchez family to do this. I think it's fair to say that Mecha cut the trail for all of us. The connections she developed with Americans working in Bolivia created both the means—and the passageway—for my two sisters and me to come to the United States as teenagers and be educated here.

She was there in La Paz the night in 1961 when it was announced we would be moving to the United States. That moment was her handiwork. And years later, when I got the news that my first husband had died in Vietnam, her first words when I told her what happened were "I'll be there." She was on the plane within hours.

Mecha married once, briefly, when she was teaching at the Normal School in Sucre, but she was divorced six months later and never discussed what happened or the reasons why. After that, she focused on her work and on her family in the United States.

When she retired, she moved back to Bolivia, to Tarija, and was elected to the Bolivian senate. She worked with women in prison and with the elderly. I once went with her to a center in Tarija where low-income *ancianos* met, and she brought refreshments and encouraged them to sing songs from Tarija. There's a statue of Mecha in the Plaza del Maestro in Tarija. She was named "*la mujer distinguida*" ("woman of distinction") for her work as an educator and civic leader.

I owe so much of the life I've lived to Tía Mecha. Many doors have opened for me across the span of more than sixty years because of her. We were close in some ways, but in other ways, Tía Mecha remains a mystery. What did she feel as a Bolivian immigrant in those years when there were few Bolivians—and few Latinos—living in the DC area? Did she feel lonely? Was she happy living alone, without a life partner? Without children? When she went back to Bolivia, did she struggle, as many returning immigrants do, to reintegrate?

My aunt's successes in life are undeniable. So are the gifts she gave to me and to others simply by what she represented as a woman who excelled, who achieved, who moved effectively across borders and inside them. One who, like me, devoted so much of her own life to teaching others.

Mis Hermanas

My five sisters—Julia, Susy, Maria Eugenia, Anneliese, and Paty—have been close companions throughout my life's journey, and I'm blessed and grateful that we remain close to this day. We've lived apart, sometimes continents apart; our lives have diverged, then reconnected. But the bond of love that holds us together has only grown stronger as the years pass.

My sisters are all strong, brilliant women, and when I think about our lives together, and about our large extended family of children, grandchildren, great-grandchildren, the image that comes to mind is of a beautifully crafted stone foundation, each stone unique in its shape and coloration, each one holding the others firmly in place.

My life has been built on that foundation, and I know that theirs have too. Paty left us early, but she remains a strong presence, through her spirit and through the lives of her children.

I think this is my mother's greatest achievement, the keystone of her legacy: having held our family together through immense personal challenges and across great distances. My mother taught us always to be there for each other, and we have been. Out of the richness of her love, sheer determination, and the power of her example, she created for us bonds of trust, affection, and mutual support that have held firm, especially during difficult times.

CHAPTER III
Moving to the United States

What does it mean to migrate? To leave your country, your family and friends, everything familiar? To stare into a vacuum where your language, culture, and identity have disappeared? To start anew? To become someone else?

These questions have followed and haunted, sometimes terrified, and sometimes inspired me since the moment I stepped on the plane in La Paz, bound for a new life in the United States. Twice—once then and once seven years later—I looked at my time in the US as an episode, a detour, a temporary landing. Bolivia was my home, and sooner or later, I'd be back home to stay.

What I found instead was that Bolivia traveled with me. Bolivia lives with me and within me, here and wherever I am. But the pain of separation is real. The feelings of dislocation and being lost in an unfamiliar place are also real. Even now, more than sixty years later, I remember what it felt like landing at the airport in Washington, DC, and on that first day of school in Virginia.

The myth of assimilation has power. For a long time, it was the story of America, the "melting pot": the story of people coming and laying aside the burdens of what had been for the promise of what could be. They gave up their languages but not their accents. They became Americans, not whoever they were before. Some even changed their names, or their names were changed for them.

I think about the waves of immigrants who came to this country in earlier times, across the ocean—about sons and daughters saying goodbye to families they knew they would likely never see again, stepping on the boat, and looking back, or not looking back because the pain of leaving was too great.

That was not my experience. I thought I was coming to the United States temporarily. Like many other immigrants, I left home because of economic hardship, but I was not a refugee. Money worries aside, I was still leaving a life of relative privilege in Bolivia. Yet when Mecha said it was an "exceptional opportunity," coming here, she was right.

I was coming to a place that was safe and comfortable, certain that my basic needs for food and shelter would be met. I'd have my aunt and my sister nearby. And if things went terribly wrong, I could always go back home. I was also bringing with me a strong sense of personal identity, eleven years of first-rate formal schooling in Bolivia and Argentina, and a solid grounding in my native language, Spanish. I came by plane; I didn't wade across the river at night or spend months or years in a refugee camp or detention center. I wasn't traumatized. I was loved.

But still, it wasn't easy.

The acculturation process begins at the moment of arrival, but it plays out in stages over a lifetime, and much depends on what the migrant brings with them. Experiences *before* migration, age, education, family structure and support, cognitive development, and many other factors unique to the person who's coming all play a role. And while there are predictable stages in the process of acculturation or integration—books have been written on the subject—it's still not the same for everyone. Even close siblings will experience the acculturation process in different ways, as my sisters and I have done.

Julia left first. Then Susy and I flew from La Paz to Lima, Peru, to Miami. There were some problems with our student visas, and the officials in Miami—all men—asked us so many questions about why we were going to Virginia. Our English was practically nonexistent, and I didn't always understand what they were asking; but eventually, they let us go, and we made our connecting flight from Miami to DC without any problems.

The Powelsons met us at Washington National Airport. I was in awe of the airport and Interstate 395. There were no roads like that in Bolivia, and there were so many cars. Every street was paved.

The scenery was gorgeous: trees and grassy fields along the George Washington Memorial Parkway, the view of the Potomac River and the city, the Washington Monument off in the distance, the Lincoln Memorial, people sitting on the grass or riding bicycles. It was so beautiful I couldn't stop looking. I felt like I was falling in love.

I don't remember what we talked about on the drive home, but Jack Powelson was fluent in Spanish, so I'm sure he was explaining what we were seeing, asking us questions about the flight, about our mother and sisters back home. One thing I noticed right away about the Powelsons was that being strict Quakers, they always addressed their family members—and each other—as "thee" and "thou." Coming from a boisterous, passionate, expressive family and a world where affection was shown openly, it took me a while to get used to the formality.

The Powelsons' house was on a man-made lake in Lorton. It was beautiful, simply furnished but spacious, and Susy would be right next door. That August was sweltering the way it always is in Washington in August, and we'd only brought fall and winter clothes, so Robin Powelson gave me a pair of shorts to wear. They didn't fit well, but I didn't care. The next day, we went shopping to buy clothes and shoes for school.

I was in awe of the stores—so many choices. At home, we only got one new pair of shoes a year, my mother made most of our clothes, and we were happy with what we had. It seemed like everyone we saw those first days in the US was happy and well dressed, like the wealthiest people back home.

We didn't have a television in La Paz or in Cochabamba, but I'd seen movies and photographs, so I'd had a pretty good image in my mind of what the United States would look like. So far, I wasn't disappointed.

One of the things that separated my sisters and me from many other Bolivian women was our parents' high expectations for us. They didn't want or expect us to believe we had no choice but to accept the role assigned to most Bolivian women our age, that of housewife. Our parents both pushed us to excel academically. The message they conveyed was that studying was our first responsibility, not household chores. This message was ingrained in me especially because I seemed to have been born with a desire to learn.

The Powelsons were both highly educated, and they shared our family's belief in the power of education, for women as well as men. They encouraged me to believe in myself. Robin was kind, with a loving and generous spirit, but I admired Jack especially for his intelligence. He taught economics at Johns Hopkins, and he tutored me every Sunday when I had problems keeping up in school.

I loved the Powelsons' children from the first. Cindy was five years old that August, and Judy had just turned three. They later had an infant brother named Larry. I was responsible for putting the two girls to bed at night, babysitting when the Powelsons went to meetings in DC, and teaching the children Spanish. Apart from the formal lessons, I was encouraged to speak Spanish to them every chance we got, which I was more than happy to do.

The whole family loved being outdoors. There was a large deck overlooking the lake and a covered porch where they sometimes slept during the summer. They also had a small cabin they could use when it got colder. Little Larry would sleep outside in his porta-crib, even in the winter. At first I couldn't believe it, but no one seemed to mind, not even Larry.

My room was in the basement. I slept on a sofa bed and watched TV at night after the girls had gone to sleep. I wasn't making a salary, but my mom gave me a little money, and I would buy myself potato chips and chocolate to eat late at night. I gained some weight as a result. The supermarkets were amazing to me, especially compared to the corner stores and the open-air markets I was used to seeing in Bolivia.

After a while, I began to enjoy the way the Powelsons spoke to each other. It was formal but always firmly grounded in respect. I appreciated the simplicity of their clothing and the way their home was furnished, without frills or decorative flourish. I was less fond of the diet and their musical tastes. The food they ate was very bland, and the grandmother was vegetarian. I had to learn to eat poached eggs and spinach. Sadly, the Powelsons only listened to classical music—no rock and roll, no Elvis, no Paul Anka, and no songs from Tarija in the morning the way my mother used to sing.

That was not true of the Bierleys' home, where Susy lived. Their home was joyous. Edie was an extrovert, warm and lively—she would have fit in well back in Bolivia—and Ed was an artist. The meals there were delicious, which made me a bit jealous of my sister. The Bierleys were Catholic, so I went to church with them on Sundays, and I always hoped they'd invite me to stay for lunch, but they never did.

After a few weeks, I was getting used to my new surroundings; and then the time came to enroll in school. Robin accompanied me to Mount Vernon High School to help me register for classes. She chose the classes for me: 12th Grade English Literature, 11th Grade American Literature, Civics, French, Typing, and Physical Education (PE).

I accepted the schedule without question. In Bolivia, you don't have a choice; all the students in a grade take the same courses.

On the first day of school, I wore my best clothes. I was scared and excited at the same time. As soon as I got there, it hit me like a giant wave crashing that I didn't understand anything that was going on. The building was so huge I got lost in the halls, and there were hundreds of students. Back at Saint Andrew's, there were only sixteen students in my grade. When the bell rang and we had to go to the next class, I had no idea what I was supposed to do.

Walking into the cafeteria at lunchtime was a nightmare—seeing all the other students sitting laughing and talking with their friends, and *I had no friends*. I didn't know where to sit. My English was poor, and I was too shy to ask or speak to anyone. Robin had given me a lunch box packed with a peanut butter and jelly sandwich. It was a little kid's lunch box that drew everyone's attention. I cringed with embarrassment.

Most students bought their lunch. I only had enough money to buy chocolate milk. It was obvious from the first that I was "different." I felt invisible and like I was in the spotlight at the same time. It was a horrible experience.

Besides that, I soon found that I was in over my head in every class except Typing and PE. I didn't know what the US Constitution was, and I'd never heard of the Declaration of Independence. I had no idea what my Civics teacher was talking about.

Taking French turned out to be a huge mistake. If I didn't understand English, how was I supposed to understand French taught by an English-speaking teacher? But my literature classes were even worse; *torture* wouldn't be too strong a word. Only the top students were enrolled in 12th Grade English Literature. It was very competitive, and the teacher offered no support. Imagine trying to read *Beowulf* if you can only speak a smattering of English; *The Canterbury Tales*; Shakespeare. These are hard for most *American* high school students. I was instantly lost.

Another embarrassment was PE. I was expected to take a shower at the end of class with all the other girls, and some of them walked to the shower naked. It was too much for me, a bone-rattling culture shock. Nothing like that would ever happen in a Catholic country like Bolivia. Where was I? What was I doing here?

Weeks went by. I failed most of my tests. Some teachers were kind and gave me no grade at all; others just gave me a D. Susy was having the same experience, and we'd talk every day on our way to the bus stop, which was about a mile from where we lived.

The US had so many luxuries, so many choices, but I was homesick for my school in Bolivia where I knew everyone, had many friends, and excelled academically. I knew I was smart; I'd had eleven years of proof of that in Bolivia. I just didn't feel smart in these American classrooms. Trying hard wasn't enough. I felt like an infant, a small child starting over, working harder but still falling behind. Yes, my school was modern, but it was overwhelming. Yes, we had good textbooks, but they were confusing. Yes, I had good teachers, but I often couldn't understand what they were saying. Yes, there were athletic fields and school buses and a nice house on a lake to come back to. But it wasn't home.

I wished I could talk to my mother, but in 1961, long-distance calls to Bolivia were expensive, if they were possible at all. Besides, my mother could not call me from our house phone. So I wrote letters. I visited Aunt Mecha some weekends. She had an efficiency apartment in DC by DuPont Circle, no separate bedrooms, so Susy and I slept on the floor. There was no air-conditioning; it was very hot.

Being with Mecha was comforting up to a point. But except for her and Susy, I didn't know any other Latinos, and certainly no one from Bolivia. I was always different; I always stood out. It was the loneliest feeling I had ever known.

My experience as a new immigrant facing high school with limited English proficiency and no friends and being far away from home opened painful wounds that did not heal. The wound of being different. The wound of feeling silenced, of being unable to make myself understood. Of not being able to show others how smart I was. The wound of knowing that all I'd learned and absorbed at home about my culture and the ways of my country didn't matter.

Yet my year at Mount Vernon laid the groundwork for almost everything that has motivated me in my career as an educator and as an advocate for immigrants and refugees.

There's a kind of "cultural capital" that immigrants like me bring to our new lives in the United States, to the situations in which we find ourselves, however challenging those situations might be. Mine included family history, the values of respect and reciprocity, my love of learning, a strong work ethic, and—perhaps most important of all—a strong command of my native language. In other words, my identity.

I also had the resilience I learned from my mother, the faith I absorbed from my grandmother, the support from Tía Mecha, mentorship from the Powelsons, and a self-confidence nurtured by my parents and teachers back home. Not every immigrant or refugee who comes here is so lucky.

Still, the experience of losing ground despite my best efforts left a lasting imprint. At best, these feelings of inadequacy are a drain on a person's vital energy; at worst, they cause debilitating stress. This is what I call the "sting of assimilation." Being ignored; being silenced. But I was determined *not* to be silenced, and I saw that the antidote to silencing is empowerment, so I began looking for ways to feel powerful and to express myself.

It helped that I never met anyone who was telling me, "You shouldn't be here." This might be one reason why, even though I was discouraged at times, I never lost hope.

After several weeks of struggling, I asked Robin if I could drop French and take Spanish instead. She said yes, and the school counselor agreed. That's when things began to change. Finally, I felt like I knew something. I excelled. I loved my teacher, Mr. Julca, who was from Peru; and my classmates could see how smart I was. I joined the Spanish Club.

I also joined the Keyette Club, sponsored by the local Kiwanis, an international service club. The Powelsons encouraged me to attend a Keyette/Key Club convention in Virginia Beach, and it was there that I began to feel accepted. I rode the bus with the other Mount Vernon students. At the convention, there was a dance. My English wasn't fluent, but I spoke the language of dance, of movement; I could express myself. The other girls were impressed. The boys were interested. And when we got back home, things felt different. I was finding my way.

Even my literature classes got better. At some point, I realized I could read the CliffsNotes, and that helped a little when test time came. In the spring semester, we read books by Ernest Hemingway—*For Whom the Bell Tolls* and *The Old Man and the Sea*. Hemingway had lived in Cuba, and *For Whom the Bell Tolls* is set in Spain. These connections opened doors that helped me understand what I was reading. Plus, Hemingway has an easier, simpler style than Mark Twain, whose books we had been reading in the fall. I was tired of reading books that meant nothing to me, that were disconnected from my own experience. This felt much better.

At home, the Powelsons encouraged me to think beyond high school. They took me on college tours at Georgetown, Trinity College, and the Washington School for Secretaries. I went to "college nights" and met the representatives from colleges across Virginia. I took the SAT, and though my score was low, I began submitting applications anyway. Jack Powelson urged me to apply for financial aid and helped with the application process.

I took the achievement test in Spanish and got a perfect score, showing that even though my grades and other measures of success were not impressive, I had strong academic potential. Apparently, Radford College noticed, and one day in April 1962, I got a phone call from the director of admissions, Dr. Shelley, whom I'd met at one of the college nights and who'd urged me to apply.

He said I had been admitted and awarded two scholarships, one for foreign students and one work-study, which meant that all my expenses would be covered. I was overjoyed but refused to believe it until the letter of acceptance finally came. Then I knew it was real. I was on my way.

CHAPTER IV
Radford and Beyond

August 1962

I was awake most of the night last night, but I don't feel tired. Instead, I'm looking out the window, thinking about how far I've traveled since that dinner in La Paz a year ago and dreaming of the new life that will soon begin. What will it be like? I'm scared but so excited I can barely keep still.

My mother is asleep beside me on the train. We left the city of Alexandria behind us hours ago, and now we're rolling past horse farms with stone fences and large, white-columned houses plucked right out of a storybook, or from a different kind of dream.

There are smaller houses too, and shacks with broken porches and cardboard in the windows, hogs in muddy pens. I see cattle standing on the banks of a narrow creek and an old man and a boy with dark skin herding goats with sticks, just like back home in Bolivia. We cross a swollen river, but I don't know its name.

The scenery changes, and now we're passing fields of tasseled corn, well-tended pastures, orchards, and little junction towns—Culpeper, Orange—places I never knew existed, so different from the landscapes of Cochabamba and La Paz.

Everywhere I look, the land seems lush and fertile. I see mountains in the distance, bluer than Lake Titicaca and so beautiful I can't stop staring. We get closer, and the Blue Ridge—that's what a woman sitting across the aisle calls it—turns into a hundred different shades of green.

But it's late August, and already higher up on the mountainsides there are patches of yellow and red. I can feel myself changing inside, like the leaves.

We roll through Lynchburg, Bedford, across a gap in the mountains into Roanoke. Then we're in the upper reaches of the Valley of Virginia and on the Great Wagon Road that once carried throngs of immigrants from Europe and the British Isles into Appalachia, across the Cumberland Gap, into the Ohio River Valley and beyond. Now that same road is carrying me. But in 1962, those stories I will eventually learn about Virginia and the United States are still a mystery waiting to be discovered; and besides, I have other things to think about today.

Because our final stop is in a place called Radford, home of an arsenal where the US Army makes and stores its ammunition—and of Radford College for Women, which is where I'm going.

My mother made the journey from La Paz to Fairfax so she could be with me for my high school graduation in 1962. I hadn't seen her in almost a year. She then stayed with Tía Mecha through the summer, partly for a surgical procedure that would keep her blind eye from drying out and partly so she could make the trip with me to Radford College on the train.

There were permission forms for the parents to sign, but I think she mostly wanted to see what an American college looked like. Neither of us had any idea. She never told me what she was picturing, but I'd imagined something like a convent or the boarding schools I knew back in Bolivia and Argentina.

This was different. I was in awe. For weeks, I was in pure discovery mode. There was good food in the dining hall and lots of it; there were tennis courts, a swimming pool, a soda fountain, people walking everywhere, laughing and talking. It was like a dream but so much better.

I was assigned to a corner room in the Russell Dormitory with two roommates: Alice Anderson, who'd brought her sewing machine with her—this seemed strange to me at the time; and Nancy Moran, who'd been in my Civics class at Mount Vernon High.

My English was still far from perfect, and my mother spoke barely any English at all. Though my roommates were friendly and eager to help, I recognized the differences right away. I'd come with two suitcases. They had lamps, rugs, notebooks, pictures to hang, room decorations, everything they needed.

Radford in those days was the "women's division" of Virginia Tech, which is located fifteen miles away in the town of Blacksburg. Tech was still an all-male college in the 1960s, and during freshman orientation, Radford president Dr. Charles Martin told us: "Most of you will marry someone from Virginia Tech."

In the end, that's what Nancy and Alice both did, and I did too. But I wasn't thinking about that then. I was adjusting to living with so many other people, to the steady stream of guys from Virginia Tech coming to the campus to pick up their dates and go downtown to see a movie or just hoping to meet Radford girls.

It would be ten years before Virginia Tech and other state-supported schools in Virginia opened their doors to women. And it took even longer for some of them to admit Black students. Radford in the early 1960s was about as far away as one could get from "diverse." There were no Black people on the campus except for those who worked in the dining hall or in custodial positions, cleaning dorm rooms or cutting grass. In a student body of almost 2,000, there were two women from Puerto Rico, and there was me. Otherwise, the campus was entirely White, and some of the students were from well-to-do families in Virginia.

So, I was a novelty right from the start, the object of curiosity but not overt hostility. I was a "foreign student," the same as I'd been in high school. People asked where I came from, but I didn't feel rejection or fear. I didn't experience that kind of negativity. My only explanation is that it must be different when you're one of a very few; then, you're unusual, maybe a little bit exotic, but you're not seen as a threat. Which doesn't mean you don't feel lonely sometimes. I remember walking to the Cove, a coffee shop on campus, just hoping to meet someone, *anyone*, who spoke Spanish.

Like many other small and midsize schools at the time, women's colleges in particular, Radford adhered to the doctrine of *in loco parentis*, which means, literally, "in the place of a parent." The assumption was that parents had entrusted their daughters to the college, and the institution would assume full responsibility for a student's safety and conduct in her parents' absence.

Radford's rules about dating were strict. Every incoming student had to sign an agreement promising that she would not date someone from another race. The first date—with anyone—had to be on campus. Students were not allowed to drink alcohol within a sixty-mile radius of the college, not even a glass of wine at dinner. We had to fill out other forms saying who was coming to pick us up, where we were going, and when we would return. We had to wear dresses to class. No pants or shorts allowed. We wore white gloves to formal events, like receptions at the college president's home.

Beyond these basic requirements, which were *not* negotiable, there was some flexibility. If a parent was willing to allow the student to use her own discretion (to a degree) and make her own decisions (up to a point), the college would allow those same freedoms, giving a young woman as much—or as little—responsibility as her parents wanted her to have.

My parents lived 4,000 miles away in Bolivia, and it would have been difficult, almost impossible to reach them by phone on short notice, and back then, even a letter took three weeks to deliver. So when the time came, my mother checked the boxes giving me the maximum possible degree of independence, freeing me from the kind of strict control that many of my fellow students experienced.

But what the form said hardly mattered: I'd always been inclined to follow the rules anyway, I couldn't afford to lose my scholarship, and besides, my mother's moral and emotional control was always right there, in my head. I carried the authority of my parents and their expectations within me, and I exercised that authority for them.

Which made things easier, in a way. My friends complained about the strict rules, but to me they didn't seem so bad, having grown up in Bolivia. Still, this was the 1960s, and the world was changing, social mores were shifting, old assumptions were being questioned, and it wasn't long before I experienced my own struggle with the rules about dating and sex. But for now, I was happy to be where I was, rules or no rules, even if my roommates did think it was strange when I knelt beside the bed each night to say my prayers.

What seems strange now, looking back, is how Radford's leaders—much like their peers in other colleges and universities, especially in the South—regarded their women students, the roles these students were assigned and expected to play in society, and the reasons for educating women at all.

Two years before I arrived, Radford celebrated its fiftieth anniversary. I found and saved a copy of a special anniversary publication in which the president and dean of women each wrote an essay. What they said is revealing, to say the least. Their ideas seem backward in retrospect, but they were commonplace at the time, as comfortable as old slippers and totally expected.

President Martin wrote:

> [Radford] has tried never to lose sight of the fact that this college is primarily engaged in teaching WOMEN [emphasis his]. We have tried in all our planning to remember that these young women, after they teach or have been for a time in industry or research, will marry, establish homes, and rear children. It is our women who, through their role as mothers, shape America. For this reason we try . . . to lead our young women into a gracious way of life. . . . We try to inculcate graciousness.

The dean of women, Ann McDowell Trabue, agreed but took it a few steps further:

> Conduct which is proper is conduct which makes other people feel at ease. Attention to the social amenities, then, stems always from the desire to provide [our] students with the social graces which make human relations easier. . . . The Navy now rates its wives; aspiring executives must bring their wives for interviews. If the female half of the team is not able to extend the professional image which is desired, the masculine half may lose out.

Those attitudes feel like insects frozen in amber now.

Even in the innocence of that freshman year, from 1962 to '63, the tremors that would soon shake the world could be heard if you listened hard, like thunder in a distant but approaching storm.

While I was still a senior in high school, the United States began sending military "advisors"—most of them Army Green Berets or CIA operatives—to work and sometimes fight secretly alongside the anti-communist government forces in Vietnam.

Barely two months after I arrived at Radford, American forces started spreading herbicides and defoliants over large sections of the Vietnamese jungle for the first time. Then, in June 1963, a Buddhist monk set himself on fire in the middle of a busy street in Saigon. The image of this man sitting cross-legged in flames spread like a fire of its own around the world. It was one of the first images to "go viral," more than half a century before that expression entered common use.

Five months later, President Kennedy was assassinated. I will never forget that day. Kennedy was my hero, the first Catholic president. I cried in class when I heard the news.

At Radford, we were not oblivious to what was happening. We all read the headlines, and there were conversations after class and late at night in the dorms. It just seemed remote and far away. We were dancing to the Platters, Otis Redding, Sam Cooke, and the Everly Brothers, but the songs coming out of the storm had a harder edge, particularly those from Bob Dylan: "Blowin' in the Wind," "The Times, They Are a-Changin'," "With God on Our Side," and "The Lonesome Death of Hattie Carroll" are a few examples. It would be another year before the Beatles made their first appearance on the *Ed Sullivan Show* and two years before the first US combat troops from the 3rd Marine Division arrived on the airstrip in Da Nang, in March 1965. But even in that first year, there were people who saw and felt what was coming.

I wasn't one of them. Radford was protected; in those early years it was all white gloves and *in loco parentis*, and for the time being, I was immune. Or thought I was.

My grades were good, I was making friends, and my social life was exploding, in a good way. I ran for secretary of the freshman class and won, even though I had no idea what the secretary of a college class was supposed to do. I went to Mass on Sundays and joined the Newman Catholic Club, which made regular trips to Blacksburg for "mixers" with the boys at Virginia Tech. I started dating a Tech junior named Frank Lev after meeting him at a Newman Club mixer. We went to basketball and football games. To parties and dances. It was an exciting time. But it was a time for asking questions too.

Frank had an apartment in Blacksburg, but Radford's rules didn't allow me to visit, much less stay there overnight. He invited me to a "spaghetti dinner" with his roommates, and I went, but I struggled with the decision. I could lose my scholarship if anyone found out. So I went to see a priest and asked him what I should do—and he refused to tell me. He said it was up to me to decide.

Frank's roommates thought my anxiety about that dinner was funny. They laughed about it. Meanwhile, some friends were already spending nights with their boyfriends.

Looking back, it seems like I was standing exactly halfway between that six-year-old girl in Plaza Colon asking, "Is this what God wants for me?" and the woman I would eventually become. The times were changing, and so was I, but slowly.

During freshman year, my father went into exile in Peru. He stopped sending me money, and I struggled financially, even more than before. Somehow, the school's administrators learned about this, and one day President Martin handed me a check for $50, which was a lot of money in the spring of 1963.

It was a gift made from a fund set up by then US Senator Harry Byrd of Virginia, the architect of "massive resistance" to school desegregation in the South. The funds were to support a "deserving student." In the decades since, I've often wondered if the old puppeteer, the man who created the infamous Byrd machine, would think he'd made a wise investment if he knew who this "deserving student" turned out to be.

I learned about my father's exile in a letter from my mother and wept for what seemed like hours. I was worried, but I also knew that exile was better than a Bolivian prison. I prayed for him multiple times every day. That is, until I learned that my parents were divorced and my father had married another woman.

I was shocked and confused. I was angry. Why hadn't he told me? I knew my father had been with other women, but I thought he and my mother were living apart for financial reasons. Now I understood why he always slept in another room when he visited. Now I understand many things I'd never thought about before.

I wrote him a long, angry letter. I told him, "I don't know you. You're not the man I thought you were," which must have been hard for him to hear. I know it wasn't easy for me to write; and it took a long time to forgive him, not because of what happened but because he'd kept it secret from us, most of all from me.

It was a low point, a time when I had to go deep inside myself, reassessing everything I thought I knew about a man I loved so deeply—a man I looked up to and adored. I also developed ulcers worrying about my mother and our financial struggles.

In the months leading up to this revelation, I'd become friendly with Dean Trabue, who was also my psychology professor. Despite what she wrote in that fiftieth-anniversary publication, she believed strongly in empowering young women. She understood what I was feeling and was quick to offer support.

I soon landed a job in the Foreign Language Lab as part of my work-study scholarship. I'd started out shelving books in the college library, but I was taking French and Spanish, and when the chair of foreign languages asked me if I'd be interested in the "lab," I didn't hesitate to say yes.

From the start, I loved the work. At times the lab became a refuge, a place to hole up and recharge. I had a pleasant voice, and I recorded tapes in Spanish. My job was to welcome students and give them tapes so they could practice whatever language(s) they were studying.

When my sister Susy came to Radford in the fall of 1963, she also had a work-study scholarship but ended up working in the dining hall. I think she was jealous, sometimes, that I had this plush job at the lab, where I could also do my homework. Sometimes I think she still is.

In my sophomore year, I broke up with Frank and started dating a Tech football player from Tennessee named Jim Secrist. We were introduced by a mutual friend. He was not a star player, but he was a nice guy, polite, respectful, and very handsome. Though we enjoyed each other's company, it was never a serious relationship.

I also pledged to a sorority, Alpha Sigma Tau. It was not an elite sorority. The emphasis was on service and leadership. One of the service options was to work with African American communities in the city of Radford. I'd had very little contact with Black people since I got to the United States, and I knew almost nothing about Virginia's racial past. But you couldn't escape the realities of segregation in the South no matter how hard you tried, and I'd witnessed the race and class divisions in my home country. I also knew about poverty, which was common in Bolivia—impossible to miss or ignore.

My "service" task would be to take books to these African American children, to read with them in their homes. I embraced the opportunity, and most of the families were welcoming, at least on the surface. But I also had deep, instinctive reservations then, and I still do, about the kind of "service" where nurturing and sustaining personal relationships is not part of the bargain. It's not what's expected in those situations, and it's not what usually happens.

For me, I felt like I'd been dropped out of a helicopter whenever I arrived with my books at one of these children's homes. I didn't know what to make of my feelings at the time; I didn't have the tools or the experience to question the assumptions I was making in any meaningful way. Instead, I thought, *Well, this must just be the way things are here.* But before long, it dawned on me that this is one of the pitfalls of a service mindset.

The intentions may be good, but good intentions are not enough. In fact, they're barely helpful as a starting point, and sometimes they just get in the way. What seems at first like service can turn out to be condescension in disguise. People want their human struggles to be recognized, but they don't want to be pitied or made the object of other people's concern, *especially* when that concern has no anchor, no connection, no long-term commitment to those who are supposedly being served.

It took me a while to understand this, but understanding it has opened the door to work I might never have been able to do otherwise and to some of the richest, most fulfilling relationships of my life.

Sometimes, you end up being as grateful for what you *didn't* know as for what you did; and this experience, brief as it was and as limited as its impact might have been on the families I visited, did turn out to be a gift. Just not in the way I expected.

My sorority sisters and I thought we were bringing something of value to the families we served, and in a way, we were. But ironically, the *most valuable part* of the transaction for me was the cringing I did during and after those home visits, and the questions I took away from the experience.

Junior year was a watershed. A door opened, and the rest of my life was waiting for me on the other side. It started with an infraction, a careless breaking of the rules that resulted in the only punishment I ever received in my time at Radford.

It was January 1965, and one of the women in my dorm, Dianne Carter, was dating a famous Virginia Tech football player named Sonny Utz. Sonny played fullback and went on to have a brief but stellar career in the Canadian Football League.

Sonny had a car, but he was going out of town that weekend, so he said Dianne could use it while he was away. Harmless. But for some reason that I never understood—maybe it was the lack of parking space or an excess of *in loco parentis*—Radford students weren't allowed to have cars on campus, and the school was serious about enforcing the rule, even for borrowed vehicles.

Dianne was adventurous, confident, a little bit rebellious, and she invited a group of us to a basketball game at Tech. It was a Friday night. We drove to Blacksburg, saw the game, and drove back to campus. All seemed to go well. I never was a rule-breaker, but I remember thinking that I'd finally gotten away with something, like my sister Julia always seemed to do.

What we *didn't* know until later was that Dianne had parked Sonny's car right in front of the dean of women. Dean Trabue was watching us as we pulled in, and a few days later, all of us, not just Dianne, had to appear before the Honor Court for violating the no-cars-on-campus rule. Our punishment was that we were "campused" for a month, meaning that we couldn't leave the college except to walk downtown.

Two or three weeks passed, and one night in February, another friend, Sally Jenkins, was getting ready for a blind date with a Virginia Tech student named Al Giddings. The way this worked was that the girl would wait upstairs until her date arrived, and then whoever was staffing the desk in the lobby would call and say, "Sally, you have a caller in the parlor." Very stiff and formal. The boys were always "callers," and the lobby downstairs was always "the parlor."

On this night, Sally was still getting dressed and fixing her hair when Mr. Giddings showed up. She asked me, "Emma, can you tell him that I'm running late and talk to him until I get there?" Being "campused," I didn't have a date that night, and so I did.

I was taken aback. He was handsome, tall, and sandy-haired with a winning smile and kind eyes that sparkled even in dim light. I told him I wasn't Sally, that she'd be downstairs soon, and to my surprise—his too, I think—we hit it off immediately.

The conversation was great from the start, and he seemed interested in me. I was flattered. I was intrigued. I thought he was charming. I wanted to know more. We talked for maybe half an hour, and then Sally showed up, we said goodbye, and off they went.

I stayed up late that night waiting for Sally to come home. I wanted her to tell me about her date with Al Giddings. She said he'd talked more about me than about anything else, asking her who I was, what I was majoring in; and at one point he asked her directly if she thought it would be okay to call me.

I guess she must have told him yes, because a few days later, a Wednesday, Al called. It was on the public phone in the hall between dorm rooms, and he asked me out.

I was excited and jittery. I felt something warm inside me and couldn't stop smiling. It felt like my heart was dancing with my brain. It was a feeling I had never experienced before. I said yes but had to explain that I couldn't leave campus except to go downtown. He told me it was alright, he didn't mind, and that he'd see me on Friday night.

Friday night came—"Emma, you have a caller in the parlor"—and we walked downtown. It was cold, a February night in the mountains, but I barely noticed. We went to see a movie and then for Coke floats afterward. We talked nonstop.

Al told me he had a sister who was six months younger. Six months? He said they were both adopted; that his parents lived in Richmond; that he was in the Tech Corps of Cadets and also something called the Cotillion Club. I didn't know what that was, and he told me they had formal dances. I said I loved to dance.

It was a beautiful evening, simple and straightforward like the man I was just beginning to know; but there was a magic in it too. Straightforward magic, if that makes sense. There was no pretense to Al Giddings. Right away, we had a special connection. He didn't even know where Bolivia was, but I didn't care. *Maybe someday I will show him*, I thought. We walked back to the dorm, and he asked if he could see me again. I'm sure I said it quietly, but I wanted to shout: "YES!"

Al and I began dating. He wrote to his parents about me. When my punishment was lifted, he borrowed a friend's convertible, and we drove about a half hour to the Mountain Lake Resort, where the movie *Dirty Dancing* would later be filmed. It was a Saturday afternoon, a warm day in the early spring, and the sun was shining. I remember the breeze on my face. We held hands, and he asked me to be his date for the Ring Dance, which was a major event at Tech, very formal.

Of course, I said yes. I was already falling in love with Al Giddings; and besides, it was the dream of every Radford woman to be invited to the Ring Dance.

The day came. Al wore his white dress uniform. I wore a white dress with white gloves, and he gave me a spray of red roses. We danced, and the song I remember most is "Unchained Melody" by the Righteous Brothers, which ends with the words "God speed your love to me."

That night, I felt like Cinderella, like my dress was made of gold and I was walking on a silver cloud. But I was in a quandary. On the soles of my silver slippers was the dread of sin.

Al and his friends had rented a cabin for an after-party at Mountain Lake. They'd hired a band. Al begged me to stay the night. They'd be heading straight to Mountain Lake when the dance was over and be drinking when they got there. How would he take me back to Radford? And if he did, he'd be the only one alone without a date once the party started. He told me not to worry and promised me nothing would "happen."

I agreed to stay. But I was breaking all the rules; I could lose my scholarship. I said yes because I knew, even then, that I loved him. But I also took precautions. I rented a room in Blacksburg for the night so that, if challenged, I could "prove" I'd been sleeping there and not partying at Mountain Lake.

I was still a good Catholic. I was still my mother's daughter. The hold of the values I grew up with remained strong, as did the tendrils of my mother's trust. What would she say if she knew? What was God saying?—because He *did* know. What would I do if I lost my scholarship and was sent home to La Paz or back to Mecha's cramped little studio apartment in disgrace?

The Ring Dance was on Saturday; and on Sunday, I prayed, asking God for forgiveness. It was true that nothing had "happened"; Al and I hadn't slept together the night before. But I still had to confess that I'd lied. And I worried for a long time afterward that someone back at Radford—the president? the dean of women? a dorm counselor?—would learn the truth and I would be expelled.

I went to summer school that summer, taking courses I'd need to be certified as a teacher. Around the time I met Al, I'd made the firm decision that education was my path. Radford started out as a "normal school," teaching the "norms" of pedagogy, and in 1965 a high percentage of its students were still planning to become teachers. Now I was one of them.

At first, my plan was to become an interpreter working for an organization like the United Nations. I even made a trip to Georgetown, thinking I'd enroll in their program for training interpreters. But when I got there, I was asked to read and interpret the *Federal Register*—a tedious and difficult document to read, even in English. Trying to interpret it in Spanish was a nightmare.

By that time, I was also thinking that if Al and I eventually decided to marry, I could find a job teaching French and Spanish almost anywhere. I was getting ahead of myself as far as marriage plans were concerned, and I knew that, but it was an easy decision in the end.

That summer, I met Al's family in Richmond. His family lived in a very modest home with a wood stove and no air-conditioning. A nook in the kitchen was stacked high with old magazines. Mr. Giddings was in his early sixties at the time, and Al's mother was in her late forties. He worked as an accountant, and she was his secretary.

Mr. and Mrs. Giddings were polite, sincere, and down-to-earth, like Al. Al's sister, Mary Lou, was funny and warm, and I stayed overnight in her bedroom. They were Presbyterians, and we all went to church together on Sunday. While most Catholic churches in the US were less stringent than the churches in Bolivia, I had to confess that transgression too. It made me think about the time in Cochabamba, long ago, when I was drawn inside a Protestant church by the music and had to repent for my sin afterward.

Al's friends in Richmond were heavy drinkers—beer and bourbon. There was a rhyme about which one to drink first and second; one was "pretty risky" and one promised "never fear," but I could never remember which was which. I was a little concerned about Al's drinking, but I shook it off. He was more of an introvert than I was, and when he drank, he loosened up. I just felt happy when he danced with me.

In the fall of my senior year, I did my student teaching—in Spanish and French—at the Andrew Lewis High School in Salem. It was a heady, wonderful experience that assured me I'd made the right decision about my future career. I found out I could integrate aspects of Bolivian culture to make learning the language a richer, more meaningful experience. I taught my Salem students Bolivian dances, which made me even more popular. To put it simply, I loved what I was doing, and I was good at it.

Salem was a long drive from Radford, and I didn't have a car anyway, so I rented a room in the home of a woman named Celeste. Celeste was a blatant racist, extreme in her prejudice toward Black people and about what was happening in the country—desegregation, the Civil Rights Movement. She hated Martin Luther King Jr.

She was also physically handicapped and a binge drinker. She worked at the local post office and would come home on Friday night with a bag full of bourbon bottles, start drinking, and keep going until late Sunday. I hated staying in her house on weekends. Al would invite me to football games, and I was more than happy to go, but he was becoming more insistent about sleeping together.

He and his friends would rent a room in a barn not far from Salem, book a band for the night, and drink and dance. All his friends spent the night with their girlfriends, but I wasn't ready to take that step. We'd been dating for months, and Al still hadn't told me he loved me. Naturally, I wanted to please him and for our relationship to work. I was so conflicted about it that I developed new ulcers from the stress. The other women at Radford didn't seem to have the same fears I did—not just of becoming pregnant but also of sinning, of breaking the rules, losing my scholarship, disgracing my family, or losing Al.

It was dangerous for Al to drive me back to Salem after a night of heavy drinking. I remember one night in particular: Al and his friends had rented a house at Dixie Caverns, with several rooms. I didn't want to stay there overnight, and I insisted he drive me back to Salem. He wasn't happy about it, and when I got back to Celeste's, she was awake. She started cursing, raging about Black people. I thought, *Maybe I should have spent the night with Al after all.*

Because of this tension, the relationship cooled a little as the fall wore on. Over Christmas, I got a ride to Tía Mecha's in DC with another Tech student named Tim. He was handsome, charming just like Al, and over the holidays we went out together several times. Al invited someone else to be his date for a friend's wedding. But I still loved Al Giddings.

Then he had a serious car accident—while he was drinking, as it turned out—and a short while after that, he came to see me in DC.

I don't know if it was the accident or if he'd heard I was going out with Tim, but I think Al must have decided he had something he didn't want to lose. When we got back to Tech and Radford after winter break, he asked me out several weekends in a row. In February 1966, we celebrated our first anniversary, on Valentine's Day. I waited for him to tell me he loved me, but the night went by, and he never did.

Though we were seniors, we'd never discussed marriage or plans to continue our relationship after graduation; this seemed strange. But I decided to hold on and keep waiting.

When it came time for the Spring Cotillion dance, Al asked me to go with him, and again I said yes. He and his friends rented the cabin at Dixie Caverns, just like before. This time, I drank. I stayed at the cabin with him, and we made love—for the first time in my life; and when I woke up in the morning, Al's pin was there on my nightshirt.

It was understood: A pin was the prelude to engagement. We were engaged to be engaged. At last, he told me he loved me, and I felt like I was floating. I was so happy. It seemed that we had a future together after all.

My heart became like a coin spinning in midair. On one side was pure joy. On the other side was fear and guilt. Guilt because we *weren't* married and we'd had sex. What would my mother say? Tía Mecha? My little sisters? The church? God?

And what if I was pregnant? I'd had irregular periods all my life, and now I had to wait, to live for weeks with the anxiety, the doubt, the questions, until I could know for sure.

It turned out I wasn't pregnant. Graduation came. Because Al was in the Reserve Officer Training Corps (ROTC), after graduation he would have to serve for two years in the Army, as a second lieutenant. I was planning to return to Bolivia to see my family for the first time in almost six years. We talked about our future and what that would be. Al promised he would come to Bolivia for Christmas, but first he had to earn enough money to pay for the trip. His parents couldn't help him.

It was hard to think that we'd be separated for the next six months. But neither of us had money to spare, Al was waiting for his orders, and it seemed like we had no choice. I had a job waiting for me at the American School in La Paz, teaching Spanish to students in grades two through twelve. There was no backing away from that, and I missed my family so much.

So, we said goodbye in Richmond, I stepped on the plane to Bolivia a few hours later at Washington National Airport, and that was that.

Sitting on the runway, waiting for takeoff, I remembered how it felt being on the train to Radford back in August 1962, gazing out the window at the blue mountains in the distance, scared but excited, wondering what awaited me.

It all seems like such a long time ago.

It was summer in Virginia, winter in La Paz. But I felt incredible joy stepping off the plane. I was all dressed up, wearing a light-blue suit and a hat. When I left, my sister Paty was one year old, Anneliese was five, and Maria Eugenia was ten. They'd changed so much in five years; and so had I. My mother looked older but so beautiful, wise, and strong. The house was filled with love, familiar food, with questions and joyful conversation—in *Spanish*. It wasn't long before I felt at home again.

But it was an adjustment. I'd been free in Virginia in so many ways. I'd lived on my own at Celeste's, traveled by myself and in the company of other women my own age—and of men. Here, even though I had a good job with responsibilities, I was still expected to follow the cultural norms, to live with my mother and obey a different and unwritten but still very powerful and unbreakable set of rules.

Cultural adjustments aside, I loved being home with my mother, sisters, and grandmother.

I missed Al. We wrote letters, but Al was not an intellectual, expressive person. I knew he felt deeply, and I knew he was missing me as much as I missed him, but his letters were simple and unadorned, with news about everyday events but rarely anything that went beneath the surface of things.

I was welcomed by my friends from high school and the old "Country Club." I spent long hours with Abuela Julia. But I was confronted once again by the poverty in Bolivia, the rigid distinctions based on class, and the treatment of Indigenous people. I thought I'd become a different person during those years in the United States—that somehow I would be immune to these things. But seeing the discrimination and poverty hurt as much as it ever did.

At Radford, I'd mostly been protected, except for those drop-ins at the homes of Black families. Radford was many things, but it was not a place where students—women in white gloves with "callers" waiting for them in the parlor—felt or would even notice the sting of racism. Those things could seem abstract and far removed. But not here. Soon, I was counting the days until Al arrived.

In late November, Al sent me his flight schedule. I was ecstatic. My father took me and my sisters to the airport in La Paz to meet the plane. When I saw Al walking toward me, I must have jumped ten feet into the air to hug and pull him close to me. We kissed, and I introduced him to my father and sisters. My mother stayed home preparing a welcome dinner.

We were lucky. At almost 12,000 feet (11,893 to be exact), La Paz is the highest capital city in the world, but the altitude didn't affect Al much. We went straight to my mother's house in the Sopocachi district, and she'd prepared a fabulous meal to celebrate his arrival. My father stayed for dinner, and the mood was happy and relaxed.

Al spoke only a few words of Spanish, but my parents and sisters all liked him instantly. I think they sensed his openness, his basic goodness. He was welcomed and accepted right away, and it didn't seem to matter at all that he was an American, that he wasn't Bolivian, that he wasn't even a Latino. If he were a different kind of person, it could have been a lot more difficult.

My father's chauffeur took us to Lake Titicaca. My dad had a car, so he drove Al around to see the city and the school where I was teaching. I invited friends to the house to meet him. He was fascinated by the clothing of our cook, a cholita, and he asked me to take a photo of the two of them together. He seemed curious and comfortable everywhere we went. I still marvel at how easily he adjusted to a world so different from his own.

In Bolivia, New Year's is a major celebration. There was a party at a friend's house, so, according to the custom, we waited at home until midnight so we could wish a happy New Year to my family and then went to the party, which lasted into the next day.

We were in our best clothes, we danced, and some of my friends spoke English, which made things easier. But language barriers aside, Al was comfortable with everyone, and they were comfortable with him. The visit was everything I'd wanted it to be and more.

I was hoping, but I don't think I let myself expect it: Al had bought me a diamond ring. Two rings, actually. One was very inexpensive, and that was the one he brought with him. He'd wisely left the "real" diamond at home, just in case I'd changed my mind in the months between June and December. I hadn't.

We went to a happy-hour party at the home of a US marine named Kurt. Al explained the situation and asked Kurt if he could send him the "good" ring later, in a diplomatic pouch. Which is what happened.

The price of the ring he brought with him didn't even cross my mind. Al was asking me to marry him. But first, he had to ask my parents. I told my mother I'd like to have a special family dinner and invite my dad and grandmother. She said yes, of course.

My father understood English, but my mother and Abuelita Julia did not, so it was my job to interpret for them. This was going to be more of a challenge than interpreting the *Federal Register*, and in a much different way.

The conversation started slowly. We were all sitting down, facing each other after dinner. Al told them he wanted to marry me, and he asked for their blessing. He said we would live in the United States and that he'd be serving in the Army for two years as an officer. By that time, he'd been assigned to a post at the Yuma Proving Grounds in Arizona.

My father and mother quickly agreed; Abuelita Julia started crying. My sisters were so happy. They hugged me and they hugged Al, and they gave us their blessings. We toasted with champagne. It was a moment of pure joy and happiness. Al and I were both readjusting and realigning our worlds to fit each other. We were opening our lives, our perspectives, our futures, our families.

Al accepted that we would have to get married in the *Catholic* Church. He promised we would raise our children Catholic, even though his family were Presbyterians. It didn't matter. We were not sure where we'd live after Yuma; that didn't matter either. Our hearts were young. We were in love. My father poured another glass of champagne.

No one gave a thought that night to Vietnam.

CHAPTER V
Love and War

February 6, 1968

"Emma, you have a phone call."

The phone is down the hall in a booth on the second floor of Russell, the dorm at Radford where I'm living this semester as a counselor, working on my master's degree.

It's Al; he's calling from Saigon.

"How? Where? Al, where are you? Are you hurt, are you okay?" He tells me that he's fine and not to worry; but what does that mean, "not to worry"?

A few days ago, the North Vietnamese launched coordinated, simultaneous attacks on every major city and military base in South Vietnam, breaking the war wide open when there was supposed to be a weeklong truce to honor the Lunar New Year. At first, people thought it was just fireworks they were hearing, not rockets and gunfire.

The Tet Offensive: Some called it the brainchild of Ho Chi Minh himself, designed to spark an uprising among the South Vietnamese and to stun the Americans and their allies with a show of strength: *General Westmoreland, you know that light at the end of the tunnel you've been talking about? It's an explosion.*

And now, Al is in the middle of it, a second lieutenant in a support battalion for the 199th Infantry Brigade, based in Long Binh. Long Binh is between Saigon, the capital of the Republic of Vietnam, and the American air base at Bien Hoa.

This much I know when he calls, but not much more. I do know that Al's unit does logistics and supply; he's not going out on long-range night patrols or fighting in the jungle or dropping out of a helicopter into a rice paddy under fire—what the press is calling a "hot landing." Thank God for that at least.

But he doesn't tell me that the Logistics and Command Center at Long Binh was hit hard on the first night. That there's an ammunition depot there, and a hospital—that it's the headquarters for supplying most of the American troops in that part of South Vietnam. Which means it's a prime target. And that it's also a place where they bring the wounded. What horrors has he seen? I don't know. He doesn't talk about that either. There is no time.

The past week has been hell. The pictures and the footage out of places with names like Khe Sanh and Hue made me shiver. Hue is where the fighting seems to be the worst right now, but the reports say it's spreading everywhere. We've been watching the news on television every night. I can't bear to look at what I'm seeing, and I can't look away.

Al's voice seems a little shaky—*Can a voice be wounded?* I wonder—but it's still the voice I love, my husband's voice. Most of all, it's proof that he's alive. He's not hurt. I can feel him on the other end of the line.

The connection isn't perfect. My breath comes in sharp, jagged bursts. I listen and the sound becomes a picture of his face. I close my eyes. I pray silently and hard; I try to tell him that I'm overjoyed and that I'm scared. "Please tell me what's happening, Al. Where are you? We've been watching the news. It sounds bad."

He says he can't talk long, that the attacks are still going on, but he's safe and he loves me. "Dear God, Al, I love you too. Please take care of yourself."

Then he hangs up, and he's gone, vanished back into the nightmare of a war happening 9,000 miles away from me. I want to touch my husband. I want to shield him from whatever he's seeing. I want him not to be afraid.

I'm crying. I'm so relieved, but it's strange: I feel emptier than I did before he called. It's like the sound of his voice is still here inside my head, but it's getting fainter all the time; and when I look at the walls of the phone booth, I see his kindness, I see his gentle smile. When will I hear him again? Where is my husband, my life partner, Lieutenant Al Giddings? Where is he going? Who is with him? Is he safe? It aches that I can't touch him. That I can't see his face. That I don't know.

The visit in Bolivia was going so well that Al decided to stay a week longer. My father agreed to loan us his car and the chauffeur—who was also his bodyguard—so we could drive to Yungas. We'd been with family and friends nonstop since Al arrived, with no time for just ourselves; and I wanted to show him Chulumani and Cocayapu. I wanted him to know where my abuelita came from.

In those days, Yungas was a natural place to take visitors on a weekend getaway, like Lake Titicaca. It's in the tropical area of Bolivia, parts of it are exquisitely beautiful, and in 1967 my father's family still owned some of the land they'd had there for generations. Al and I couldn't sleep together as we would have done if we were in the United States, but the chauffeur seemed to understand our need for privacy, and he gave us plenty of time alone.

But there was unrest in Bolivia. In June, government troops operating under orders from President René Barrientos attacked a group of tin miners who were protesting low pay and dangerous working conditions in the Siglo XX Catavi mining complex in Potosi. The attack came during the early-morning hours of the Night of San Juan, a traditional winter solstice festival. Elite units from two Bolivian regiments surrounded the celebrating miners and attacked with guns and dynamite, killing at least twenty men and wounding seventy more. The incident became known as the Massacre of San Juan, and it remains the largest massacre of its kind in Bolivian history.

Tension was high in the weeks following, especially in the south. Barrientos, who was receiving support from the US to fight communism in Bolivia, had also learned of a small guerrilla force operating out of the jungle. The guerrilla group was founded and supported by Che Guevara, who had come to Bolivia in secret in November. Guevara was trying to gain a foothold, laying the groundwork for an uprising of the poor—the campesinos—against the military government and the right-leaning elites. Naturally, Barrientos saw this as a threat, and the army was placed on high alert.

While my father had returned from exile in Peru, he was not formally a part of the Barrientos government, but he *was* serving as the president of a coalition of private entrepreneurs and businesspeople and was therefore a target of the communist insurgents. Kidnappings had become common, and Adalberto was on "the list."

Driving through Yungas, our car was stopped at a checkpoint set up by government soldiers. I don't remember being afraid. The chauffeur explained who we were, and Al was already aware of the political tensions, so the episode itself was not traumatic. But it did cause us to rethink where we were going and to cut the Yungas trip short. Al flew back to the United States a few days later.

Now that we had my family's blessing, Al and I began to plan our wedding day. Susy had also become engaged, and her fiancé's family was also from Virginia. Al's parents were in Richmond, and Julia was living near Lanham, Maryland, not far from Tía Mecha. So we decided to get married in the United States.

I had my dress made in Bolivia, and we set the date for July 22, 1967. Susy would be married a week later, in the same church. The same priest would officiate, the same food and drink would be served, and she would wear the same dress; my mother couldn't afford to buy two.

The weddings would be simple, traditional Catholic ceremonies, each with a small number of guests, mostly family and a few close friends. The plan was to have the reception at Julia's home. But Julia's husband withdrew the invitation at the last minute for an unknown reason, so I stayed with Tía Mecha in DC, Al stayed in Richmond with his parents, and we ended up having the reception in the church basement.

This was not the only source of tension. The day before the wedding, Al and I had our prenuptial meeting with the priest. Al had already made the commitment to me that our children would be raised Catholic, so it was no surprise and not an issue when the priest asked him to make that same promise. But Al's mother wasn't happy. She never understood why we couldn't get married in the Presbyterian church in Richmond, and the idea that her grandchildren would be raised Catholic was very hard for her to accept. This was only seven years after John F. Kennedy, as a candidate for president, had to promise the nation that his first allegiance would be to the Constitution and not the pope. Catholics were still viewed with suspicion by many Protestants, and while I felt totally accepted by Al's parents, I also knew that, deep down, they wished he hadn't made that agreement; and he and I both felt their disappointment.

The wedding was on Saturday afternoon. When you get married in a Catholic church, a Mass is always part of the ceremony; but Al couldn't take Communion, and neither could his parents or his sister, Mary Lou. It was awkward.

I was also conscious of the cost: My mother kept a close accounting of what she spent, which was understandable considering her circumstances. After all, she'd had to send three of her six daughters to the United States a few years earlier just to make ends meet. Knowing that we'd been as frugal as we could be didn't make it any easier for me, watching her reactions and thinking about the expense.

All of that aside, it was a day filled with the purest joy I'd ever felt. It was my dream to get married. It was my dream to get married to Al. I was going to be starting a new life in the United States. I had no hesitation about any of it, and my family had accepted Al completely. I was deliriously happy. I was also deeply grateful to Al for his willingness to be married in the Catholic Church. He knew how important it was to me, and he shifted his own thinking (and managed his parents' expectations) accordingly.

We'd be moving to an Army base in Yuma, Arizona, starting our new life there. But first, the honeymoon—brief because we had to be back in time for Susy's wedding a week later, but this was our time together.

We spent our wedding night at the Shoreham Hotel on Calvert Street in Washington, DC. It was everything I dreamed it would be. Sexual desire is one thing, but when it's mixed with the purest love for the person lying next to you, the whole world changes; it becomes a place of beauty and hope, without the need for caution or fear. Everything is possible. Every touch makes the light surrounding you grow stronger. Every murmur, every kiss is sweet.

After making love that night, we called for room service. I read the menu, and for some reason it seemed like a good idea to order Caesar salad. When the waiter came with a tray and started making the salad with raw egg, I wondered, *What was I thinking?* But we laughed about it, sitting at this fancy table in our hotel room and eating Caesar salad with real silverware, toasting with champagne.

A few hours later, we were on our way to Mountain Lake Resort, where we'd gone after the Ring Dance fifteen months before. We were starting our married life in the place that had brought us together. It all seemed so right, so perfect.

On the way back to DC on Friday, we stopped off at Radford for a meeting with President Martin. I introduced Al, and Dr. Martin asked if he was expecting to be sent to Vietnam.

Vietnam! It hit both of us like a stun grenade, a flash of blinding light.

For a long few seconds, I didn't know what to say or how to react, and neither did Al. Naively, we had never really talked or even thought much about the possibility of him going to war. I recovered and told Dr. Martin that we didn't know; we were waiting to see. But if Al *did* end up going to Vietnam—the standard tour of duty there was one year—I would probably stay in the United States.

Dr. Martin said that if that happened, Radford would welcome me back; I could pursue a master's degree and probably get a fellowship.

When we left his office, I felt disoriented, like I was not fully enclosed in my own body. I had to force my legs to walk, my hands to open the car door. But Al was practical—not the kind of person to get lost in worry or emotion. We agreed that if he did get sent to Vietnam, Radford would be a good place for me to be while he was away.

Still, it felt like a dark genie had been let out of the bottle and would not go back inside. A bucket of icy water had been thrown in our faces.

When I left the US after graduation, Vietnam had not yet entered every living room in the country. The reports out of Washington and Saigon were still optimistic. The US was winning the war. Yes, American soldiers were dying, but it was for a purpose that was good and noble, one that reflected and affirmed American values: fighting communism, defending freedom, helping an ally, patriotism.

In the summer of 1966, this still carried the ring of truth, not propaganda. And the government—the president, the secretary of defense, and commander of US forces General Westmoreland—were all saying it would be over soon anyway. Although some people, mostly on the political left, were asking serious questions and there were scattered protests, some of them well organized, the anti-war movement was just beginning to gather steam. Besides, we didn't have a television in La Paz.

Coming back to the US a year later, Vietnam had become a dark cloud hanging over thousands of military families. The enemy was no longer being "contained." The number of American troop deployments—the dreaded "call-ups"—seemed to be increasing by the week, and the country was splitting apart.

With my return to the United States and my marriage to Al, this was supposed to be the happiest time of my life. And it was. But now there was this twinge of fear, like a sound too low and faint to be audible—that "rolling thunder" of a war being fought far away in Southeast Asia; and I couldn't stop wondering how Vietnam would affect our lives.

I put the fear aside and celebrated Susy's wedding. We spent that night in a hotel, and the next morning we left for Arizona. I remember that I brought a tennis racket with me on the plane, and Al joked that the other passengers would think I was a tennis pro.

I had the same two suitcases I brought with me from Bolivia. Al's parents took our wedding presents back with them to Richmond and would send them to us later. We settled in for the long flight to Phoenix and our new home—the Yuma Proving Grounds army base, south of the Gila River in the Sonoran Desert.

We had a duplex on the base, with a table, four chairs, a small dresser, and a double bed provided by the Army. That was it. The kitchen had the necessities: pots and pans, inexpensive flatware, glasses, bowls, and plates. It was simple and unadorned.

Al's parents sent our wedding presents, and we bought a few small items to enhance the living space, but neither of us felt like we needed much in the way of material things. We were happy in our married life, and this was all temporary—two years of active duty at the most. We had a home of our own and each other.

Our duplex was within easy walking distance of the officers' club, which had a bar and a dining room, and there was a swimming pool on the base. There were lots of young military couples like us, but I was the only Bolivian. A few of them invited us for dinner.

There was always someone getting ready to go to Vietnam, and there was talk about it. Families were concerned, for obvious reasons.

But mostly it was seen as a fact of Army life in wartime. Some people got deployed almost right away; others waited months or years to hear the news, and for some, the news never came at all. You just didn't know; and sooner or later, you learned to accept that.

My cooking was rudimentary at best. Abuela Julia had taught my mother to be a wizard in the kitchen, but neither of them gave a thought to teaching me. So Al and I ate canned food—salmon, tuna casserole. I made some potato salad and experimented with a book on Bolivian cooking that my mother had given me. Fortunately, Al's culinary expectations were not higher than his young wife could reach. We made do, and I don't remember him complaining about it.

At first, I was happy staying home, seeing him off to work in the morning, and having lunch together when he came back in the middle of the day. Al was a joyful man, always upbeat, always smiling, gentle, and nurturing.

It was Al who suggested that I learn to drive, and he offered to teach me. We had a Nash Rambler with an automatic transmission, and the streets in Yuma were flat. The learning curve was easy and fast. I'd seen my mother behind the wheel, and I felt more excitement than fear when my turn came. Driving gave me a new level of independence and opened the doors of opportunity in other ways.

Al's pay was meager, even by the standards of that time, and I decided to look for a teaching job to supplement our household income. The school year was just starting, and most of the public school teaching positions had already been filled, so I applied to Arizona Western College, a two-year community college on the outskirts of Yuma.

The head of the Spanish department was Latino, and we hit it off right away. I was hired to teach two classes, Beginning and Intermediate Spanish, two days a week. Just like back in Salem, I wove aspects of Bolivian culture into teaching the language, and I was well liked by the students. I was also hired by the Yuma Chamber of Commerce to teach a class in Spanish for local government workers.

In September, Al and I made a trip to Tijuana to buy some living room furniture. We had a party for my birthday in early November. I cooked chili and tortillas for our guests and taught them Bolivian dances—*cueca*, *Taquirari*. We didn't have much money, but my life was rich and full, and we were content. I wasn't expecting luxury.

About a week later, Al came home for lunch as usual. He was standing in the kitchen when he told me he'd received his orders: He'd be leaving on December 27. For Vietnam.

The world wobbled on its axis. We'd just had a party. We were making friends. We had new furniture. I loved my work, my teaching. We had a good life. I was even learning to cook. I was only twenty-two. *Why us? Why now? Please don't let this happen.*

Just like before, Al was matter-of-fact about it. He started planning out the road from here to there. There was paperwork to be done—a will to be drawn, power of attorney. We would take a road trip for Thanksgiving and spend Christmas with his parents in Richmond. He said it was a perfect time for me to go to graduate school.

When a soldier is deployed to a combat zone, he (or she) must first have a complete physical exam to make sure he's fit. In Al's case, the doctors found a cyst in his back that would have to be removed before he left. He would spend two weeks in a hospital in San Diego. I couldn't leave Yuma right then because I was finishing up the semester, so he would have to go alone; but I did visit him once while he was recovering. For Thanksgiving, we took our trip—to Las Vegas, the Grand Canyon, and San Francisco.

Back in May, a singer named Scott McKenzie had released a song called "San Francisco (Be Sure to Wear Flowers in Your Hair)" that became a pop anthem and hit number four on the Billboard chart. In November, the song was still being played in rotation on nearly every top-forty radio station in the country. There was no way to avoid hearing it except to turn off the radio, and no way to separate the so-called flower children from the anti-war movement. What became known as the "counterculture" was emerging, gaining force, and San Francisco was its epicenter.

I don't remember that our trip took us anywhere near the notorious (and fabulous) Haight-Ashbury, but we knew the war in Vietnam was becoming deeply unpopular. Young men were burning their draft cards and fleeing to Canada to avoid serving, and those soldiers coming back from 'Nam were reviled as killers, not celebrated as heroes.

I think we probably gave that part of San Francisco a wide berth.

We were trying to live normally, but even by the time Thanksgiving came I wasn't over the shock. Hearing the news that day in our kitchen was like someone had dropped a beautiful heirloom bowl and broken it into a thousand pieces.

Al was part of the Adjutant General's Corps. His duties in Vietnam would be legal and administrative, logistics and supply-related, not direct combat. But in my mind, that didn't matter. Whether a soldier was doing paperwork or going out on patrol, he was still in a war zone; it was still a dangerous place. But Al took it in stride. His focus was on taking care of the details, the necessary business, and I don't think he spent much time worrying about the risk. If he did, he didn't show it.

Al's way of handling things, even difficult things, had a calming influence on me, but I still carried that fear, right up to the edge of the Grand Canyon, looking down. I carried it into the streets of San Francisco and to the slot machines in Las Vegas. I remember being especially anxious the day he left for San Diego. It was becoming real.

Al was right. If I went back to Bolivia while he was in Vietnam, it would be harder for us to communicate, so I applied and was accepted to graduate school at Georgetown and Radford. I wanted to go to

DC—Tía Mecha was there—but Georgetown was too expensive, and just like Dr. Martin had said, Radford offered me a fellowship, as a residential counselor.

So I decided to get a master's degree in counseling. Al and I would make decisions about the future when he returned.

The holidays were a challenge. We put the furniture in storage, and Al and I drove through Arizona, Texas, Louisiana, Alabama, Georgia, the Carolinas, and into Richmond. I remember leaning my head on Al's shoulder as he drove. I don't remember what we talked about, but I know I must have said, "I love you" a hundred times.

It was a joyless Christmas. Darkness suffused every conversation, the exchange of gifts. Celebrating was impossible, but I went through the motions for Al's sake—and for mine. Of course, Al's parents weren't happy at the prospect of their son going to war, but characteristically, they were calm on the surface and showed little emotion, even when they were saying goodbye.

I drove Al from Richmond to Dulles Airport on December 27. It was snowing. He was calm, and I still don't understand why I wasn't crying. I told him I'd be driving to Radford the next day with a friend, so he didn't have to worry.

His flight left in the early afternoon: Dulles to Oakland, California, and then from Oakland to Honolulu and Saigon. I went with him to check his duffel bag; he was wearing his uniform. I walked with him to the gate, where he would take a bus to his plane. We kissed, he boarded the bus, and then he got off to kiss me again. I watched the bus doors close, and I saw him waving goodbye through the window.

I waited for the plane to leave, walking around the airport dazed and alone, feeling a sadness I had never felt before in my life, all-consuming, pulling like a whirlpool. Once I knew his plane was in the air and there was nothing else I could do, I crossed the parking lot to the car so slowly that it felt like I was barely moving.

Nothing seemed real. I felt empty. I felt like one of those mechanical dolls.

I remember the cold and the heavy clouds that afternoon, and I remember opening the door of our little green Rambler and getting in; but I don't remember anything else. I'm not even sure where I slept that night. It must have been at Tía Mecha's.

The next day, Tammy, a friend from Bolivia, rode with me to Radford. It helped that I wasn't alone. I drove the entire way, more than 300 miles, the longest drive I'd ever made in my life. We stopped in Salem, and I spent the night at Celeste's house. Tammy had a date, and she left me there.

Even on a good day, being around Celeste was depressing. But this was almost unbearable.

The next five days felt like years, but New Year's Eve was the worst. There was nothing I could think about except our *last* New Year's Eve and how happy Al and I had been with my family in La Paz, getting ready for the party, staying out all night together.

But I was all alone now, and Al was on his way to Vietnam.

On January 2, I drove to Radford, to Russell Hall where I would be the resident counselor. I was supposed to be helping students, but I felt so empty, so drained of energy: What did I have to offer them?

It took a week or two, but, gradually, my outlook started to improve. I went out to dinner with girlfriends, played bridge. I met with students. I went to class. I settled into a routine.

Back in the summer (of 1967), General Westmoreland had said he thought US forces could begin to withdraw from Vietnam within two years; gradually we'd be turning the war effort over to the ARVN, the Army of the Republic of Vietnam. But that fall, there was heavy fighting in the northern provinces of South Vietnam, and the Marines set up an observation base on a high plateau at Khe Sanh, near the Ho Chi Minh Trail.

In December, just as we were preparing for Al's departure, Westmoreland was traveling through the United States, trying to shore up support for the war effort, saying he saw a "light at the end of the tunnel." But on January 21, what became known as the Battle of Khe Sanh began when the North Vietnamese Army launched a series of attacks against the American garrison. Ten days later, the Tet Offensive shredded most of what was left of the Johnson administration's credibility with regard to the war effort.

The coordinated assault on American positions across South Vietnam took commanders on the ground and officials in Washington by surprise. Westmoreland was said to be "stunned" by the scope and ferocity of the action, which included attacks on the US Embassy in Saigon.

On February 1, two Viet Cong battalions attacked the US Logistical Headquarters Complex at Long Binh, where Al was stationed.

His tour of duty in Vietnam could hardly have begun at a worse time. Tet began with mortar and rocket attacks, followed by massive ground assaults. American forces pushed back the attacks within a day or two, everywhere except Khe Sanh and Hue, but the damage was done.

Within days, Westmoreland asked for 200,000 additional US troops; and at Long Binh, the Army rushed to set up a perimeter defense that included almost 20,000 meters—more than twelve *miles*—of double-row, triple-strand concertina wire to help repel the ground attack they thought was sure to come.

I didn't know any of these details, but starting with the siege at Khe Sanh and in the aftermath of Tet, as public support for the war crumbled, its defenders became more strident. Images of Khe Sanh and the fighting at Hue filled TV screens, and even families who did not have a son (or daughter) in Vietnam were frightened. I was glued to the screen, terrified.

That's when the call came from Al, saying he was alright; but I could never be certain of that again.

Weeks passed, and I started to receive letters from Al. They came often, almost every day, and he was also writing regularly to his parents, as was I. The letters were cheerful, reassuring, although he did say in one of them that he would never wish what he had seen on anyone, not even his worst enemy.

For me, education was the rudder that kept me stable and on course. I told myself I was at Radford for a purpose, and although I was more and more skeptical about the justness of the war in Vietnam, I still believed that Al was there for a purpose too—and that he'd be okay and back home for good in December. We could start our life over again.

On March 31, President Johnson shocked the nation and the world when he announced on a television broadcast, "I shall not seek and I will not accept the nomination of my party for another term as your president" and that he would devote the remainder of his term to seeking peace in Vietnam.

Four days later, Martin Luther King Jr. was killed in Memphis, and on June 5, Bobby Kennedy was shot at the Ambassador Hotel in Los Angeles. He'd opposed the war and had just won the Democratic primaries in California and South Dakota the day before. He died the next day.

There were riots in several major American cities. The country was going through one internal convulsion after another, and the war in Vietnam showed no sign of slowing down. Peace negotiators in Paris spent months arguing about the shape of their meeting table.

Al's letters sustained me and kept me sane, and I was grateful that he seemed to be in reasonably good spirits. He talked about small details but didn't delve deeply. This was his way. There was no hint of depression, much less despair or hopelessness. He was looking ahead, and so was I.

In April, he wrote asking me to meet him in Hawaii on August 27 for a week of R & R. After that, he would have just four months left in his tour. I was overjoyed.

I bought my plane tickets and gifts for Al. The days ticked by, and I began packing my suitcases, deciding what to bring. I dreamed about our week together in Honolulu, about what it would be like seeing him again, to hold him at night, to see his smile, hear his voice—I hadn't heard it since that call back in February.

I would be flying out of DC and would stay with Mecha the night before. It was August 23.

That morning I was called to the main office at Russell Hall. A soldier was waiting for me there.

CHAPTER VI
Lifequake

"I regret to inform you that your husband, Lieutenant Al Giddings, died from a gunshot wound on August 22, 1968."

I shook my head. "No, you're wrong. This isn't real; it's a dream." At the same instant, I broke down crying. I never wanted anything more than I wanted in that moment to blink and wake up.

"No, please. It isn't . . . He can't . . . My bags are packed. I'm going to Hawaii to meet him. I have my tickets. I have presents I bought for him. I have his letter saying that he can't wait to see me. He signed it TQM, *Te quiero mucho*. I don't believe you. What you're saying is a mistake."

I turned inside out. My brain was on fire. My heart was breaking. It was like the walls of the room and everything in it had turned into lead. The weight was unbearable.

I asked the soldier, "How did he die?"

He said he didn't know.

I felt like I was going to vomit or pass out. I didn't know what else to do, so I asked the dorm director if I could make a long-distance call to my mother in Bolivia. She said yes.

I had to schedule the call to La Paz; there was no direct dialing. My appointment for the call was at noon. My mother answered, I heard her voice, and I started to cry again. I told her: "*Mami, Al se murió en Vietnam.*" She said, "*Vente.*" Come.

I don't remember what else the soldier said to me except that someone from the Army would contact me. He had such an impersonal face. He told me he was so sorry, and then he left.

I was sobbing and dizzy, but I calmed myself and called Al's parents at their office in Richmond. His mother answered the phone. Naturally, she wanted more details, but I didn't have them. All I knew was what the soldier told me. I said I'd be there as soon as I could and hung up.

What was I going to do now? My world had abruptly collapsed, as if there'd been an earthquake. I went back to my room in the dorm. I saw the suitcase open with Al's presents and my clothes inside. My dreams were gone.

A friend stopped by to see me. She'd heard the news and wanted to help. I asked her to go downtown with me so I could buy a black dress. She was surprised but agreed.

I walked through the door of the department store like a zombie. The salesclerk seemed shocked that I was looking for a black dress in the summertime, but she found one for me. We went back to the dorm, and I put on the dress. I needed to let the world know I was a widow now—that my beloved husband, Al Giddings, had just died in Vietnam.

The horror that the sudden death of a loved one brings has many faces. Your world has broken into pieces, but life still goes on all around you as if nothing happened, as if nothing has changed. Physically, superficially, you look okay; you might even look normal except that your eyes are puffy and red. But you have a sword in your heart. You walk like a robot. Voices sound like echoes in a cave. You go into a store in Virginia in the summer and you ask for a black dress: why?

If someone dies after a long illness, there are tasks to keep you busy before it happens, time to reflect. You try not to think too much about it, but on some level, you know the impact is coming. You have *some* time, at least, to prepare. But this hit full force like a collision at highway speed. I could never have prepared myself. How could I?

Which is why I began calling Al's death and its aftershocks

a "lifequake." It was an upheaval, a convulsion of the world. One moment, everything appeared normal. The next, nothing seemed real. It was the end of one world and the beginning of another one, but only for me. I felt so alone. So lost. Like going into permanent exile, leaving your home country, leaving yourself and everything you thought you knew behind.

A stone had been pulled out of the wall that was holding me in equilibrium, and now the other stones were falling all around me. I didn't know what anything meant anymore.

Summer school had just ended, and—thank God—there were no students in the dorm. I called Tía Mecha, and she arrived by plane the next day. I picked her up at the Roanoke airport. I remember feeling like a little girl when I saw her, but she took control of the situation. She said, "Let's do what needs to be done."

We packed a few things, Mecha took care of the suitcase with Al's presents, and we drove to his parents' house in Richmond. His remains would be sent there.

When we arrived, Al's parents were in shock, but they were stoic. I never saw them cry. And they were not wearing black. If we'd been in Bolivia, that would have been the first thing they did, to put on black clothes. I was shocked that they went back to work the next day.

Mecha had to return home to Washington, so she left me there. I was alone in Al's room. I slept in his bed. I felt him there beside me.

At twenty-three years old, with little experience of my own in the world, I had to plan my husband's funeral. Mr. and Mrs. Giddings were kind and supportive, but these were my decisions to make. Al could have been buried at Arlington National Cemetery, but I knew he'd come to hate the war, the war that had just taken him from me; burying him at Arlington seemed hypocritical. I didn't want that. I decided on Westhampton Memorial Gardens in Richmond. But it was all so surreal. How do you choose your husband's gravesite? I decided on a spot close to a tree. I was too numb to feel anything.

The next ten days went by in a slow-motion blur, as if time were crawling on its hands and knees. On September 4, the funeral home called to say that Al's body had arrived. Instead of the joyful reunion we were planning, full of life and passion and dreams about our future together, I was about to be reunited not with Al but with his lifeless body instead.

I asked the funeral-home staff to open the casket. Al was embalmed and I barely recognized him. It was horrible. I told them to close the casket and not open it again. I started to cry. I was frozen in pain. It was real now. There had been no mistake. Al was dead. This was forever. He wasn't coming back.

The next day I met with a priest. He talked about the Resurrection and told me we should celebrate Al's life, not mourn his death, and that I should consider not wearing black but white, a symbol of purity, innocence, and hope.

This rang hollow to me. My faith in God and the church was shaken. God took my husband. The priest was kind, but he had no idea what I was going through. I chose the music for Al's funeral. One of the songs was "Ave Maria," which was sung at our wedding. It had a different meaning to me then, but in the face of death it seemed starkly appropriate.

The funeral was held on a sunny day, September 7, 1968, sixteen long, excruciating days after the soldier delivered the news. Mecha represented my family. Al's parents and his sister were there; so were a few friends from Radford and Virginia Tech.

At the gravesite, there were military honors. A flag was given to me. The casket was lowered to the ground. I wept uncontrollably. After a while, Tía Mecha took my arm, and we left in the black funeral limousine. Life was unreal.

We drove back to the house. There was food, but I couldn't eat or make small talk. I went to Al's room to cry. After about an hour, Mary

Lou and some of Al's friends decided to go to a bar. They invited me to go with them. How? Why? What did they expect? Did they want me just to drink to feel better? I told them no.

The next day I drove to Washington with Mecha. I bought a round-trip ticket to La Paz. I needed to be with my family. I returned my ticket to Honolulu at the same time. I remember going to the office of United Airlines on K Street to ask for the refund. They asked the reason, and I told them why. It was all I could do to keep from sobbing. Another reminder, another shard of grief piercing my heart like shrapnel. How long could I keep going like this?

When I arrived in La Paz, my mother and sisters were there waiting, all of them wearing black. We cried and we hugged, and I held on to each of them for a long time. I wrapped myself in their love and support—but it was only for a week. I had to go back to Radford to finish my degree. Al would have wanted that.

As short as the time with my family was, it was healing. The world seemed real again and not so barren and bleak. I came back to the United States stronger than when I left, which was a blessing. But when the new semester started, I had a hard time settling back in.

I was depressed. A dullness hung over everything. I would find myself crying in class. I had no interest in what I was reading, no motivation to study. Friends tried to lift my spirits; they invited me to the coffee shop, a football game, a movie, but mostly I declined. I preferred to be alone.

Looking back, it's clear I needed help. I needed some kind of intervention, but that was not a term people used back then. It was ironic: Radford was training me to be a counselor, to help others through difficult times; but there was no grief counseling available to me through the college, no one in a position to offer professional help and advice. Instead, I was left to work through the grief and the shadows surrounding me on my own. It would take another twenty years before I found the help—the therapy—I needed.

One day in late September, a package arrived from the US Army with Al's wedding ring inside. It seemed so impersonal, almost cruel. I thought at the time, *Well, now this is the end of it; it's over.* But it wasn't. The lifequake was building for a second massive temblor, with even longer-lasting consequences.

On October 16, Al's official death certificate arrived in the mail. I opened it, and it was like the gates of hell swung wide. It said that Lieutenant Albert Hugh Giddings, my husband, the man I had been on my way to meet in Honolulu in just a few days, died on August 22, 1968, "by a self-inflicted gunshot wound while mentally unsound."

Self-inflicted? Al shot himself? How? What does it mean, "mentally unsound"? In his last letter, as in all the ones before it, he sounded fine. How could it be that the love of my life took his own life with no warning just five days before we were to be reunited?

I called the Army officer who'd been assigned to help me through the first stages following Al's death. He had no explanation; all he knew was what was in the death certificate. Like all my other interactions with the Army, this one was cold, bureaucratic, maddening. I gave up trying to get more information from them. It was all I could do to manage the here and now.

Reading the death certificate, over and over again, cut a hole into my heart. I was shattered, lost—and silenced, too, because how could I share this news with Al's parents when they were already suffering? How could I tell my family, my mother, my sisters that Al took his life, *our* life, without giving me a chance to help him? I wanted to shout: "No, we buried Al weeks ago. I was working my way through the grief. And now I get this notice in the mail, I'm *completely* alone with the information, and I can't tell anyone?"

People die in war. I understood that. But how could he have done this? Why did he do it? *Did* he do it? Nothing made sense.

Suicide creates the worst feelings of abandonment in those left behind. It's an ugly ball of emotions with venom inside. Shame. Guilt. Anguish. Confusion. Rejection. Stigma. Anger. Loneliness. Desperate questions with no conceivable answers. And a pain that is so much deeper than grief. Unbearably deep.

It was a blessing that, out of courtesy and respect, most people would never ask *how* Al died. As far as the rest of the world was concerned, Al was a casualty of war. I would leave it at that. I would have to carry this by myself, which made me a casualty too, even more than dealing with his death itself.

As a counselor, I knew the reasons why a person might decide to end his life. But Al's letters to me and to his parents were always positive. He never showed signs of depression, although he did express anger sometimes about being sent to Vietnam, and about the war. War is a horrific experience. I knew that too. Al had said as much. But what had he been hiding from me? What was his turmoil? What was his hell?

Mine was that I didn't know and might *never* know.

Dear beloved Al Giddings, my lover, my husband, my life partner, my friend, please tell me why?

A few weeks later, I got a letter from a soldier who knew Al in Vietnam, someone in his platoon. He wrote to say that Al had been drinking heavily in the weeks before he died, but that was all he said. Was Al drunk when he shot himself? Once again, there were no answers, only questions that cut like broken glass when I asked them.

Lifequakes like the one I experienced in the summer and fall of 1968 cause massive disruptions. They can push people past the limits of their endurance. They can twist things. I've been fortunate that in all the years since, I have never felt more than momentary anger toward Al. Disappointment at times, but not anger. I think I loved him too much for that.

Trauma can be hidden and suppressed. For a while. But it finds a way out. It expresses itself in subtle and not-so-subtle ways, especially in moments of severe stress or when a memory is triggered by a sound, a smell, a dream. Most of what I eventually learned about trauma and the effects of trauma took years, decades to comprehend. I do know that my feelings of abandonment as a child were like small tributaries flowing into a roaring river that grew and overflowed its banks after I learned the truth about Al's death.

Peace came with time. Years later, I found a way to even be grateful—not for Al's death or for the way he died but because the trauma I experienced helped me to better understand the pain of the people I was working with, of immigrants and refugees, including war refugees from Southeast Asia, from Laos, Cambodia, and, yes, from Vietnam.

I still feel the pain of my lifequake, but I'm grateful for this too: that the love Al and I had, for the brief time we had it, was pure. It was simple and direct, uncomplicated; and it was never damaged by the kind of anger that invades many marriages and tears them apart from the inside. Although I would experience this too, later in my life.

Who knows what Al would have been like, coming home after a year in Vietnam. Would we have spent decades cleaning up the wreckage and maybe failing even then? Maybe he didn't want me to see how damaged he already was. Maybe he thought he was protecting me from something. Once again, I'll never know.

Al Giddings was present in my life for less than three years, from the time I first met him in the dorm at Radford in February 1965 to the day he left for Vietnam, on December 27, 1967. In many ways, in the time we had together, he *was* my life.

In death, he gave me a secret I carried alone for decades: a silent, invisible wound that I had to bear the way some veterans carry a piece of shrapnel inside their body until the end of their days.

In therapy eighteen years later, I would learn that my task was to remove Al from my body, to let the trauma of his suicide go. In the winter of 1968, I only knew I had to finish my degree; and once that was done, I would go home to Bolivia, with no plans ever to return to the United States.

CHAPTER VII
Where Have All the Flowers Gone?

After reading Al's death certificate that morning in mid-October, the feelings of isolation became much, much worse. At night, I'd lie on the bed listening to Joan Baez. The insistence in her voice matched my grief. It was clear and pure like water from a timeless spring. She sang about earthly things, like sorrow and loss, but from a place that seemed high above the pain of this world, detached from it. I listened to her sing Pete Seeger's "Where Have All the Flowers Gone," which is one of the most powerful anti-war songs ever written, its refrain so deceptively gentle with the question "When will they ever learn?"

For weeks, that voice was the only medicine I had. The same purity that made it otherworldly made the woman behind the voice seem lonely too—lonely and unreachable, just like I was. But whatever threads of relief her songs offered were too thin to last; they broke as soon as I opened my eyes the next morning.

And then, there was the Beatles' "Eleanor Rigby." That song, too, touched my loneliness like icy fingers. Like it had been written about me. What was this dream I was living in? What was this face I was showing to the world? Who was it for?

I wrote letters to Al's parents and visited them a few times. They were kind, but we rarely talked about Al's death. By then, my sister Maria

Eugenia was a freshman at Radford (Susy had graduated), but I don't remember that we had any conversations about what was really going on. The isolation deepened. Meanwhile, my professors knew my husband had died in Vietnam, but they didn't make accommodations. My grades went down. I burst into tears at odd times. The dean became concerned about my welfare and recommended I see a psychologist on campus. The psychologist asked if I'd done anything that could have contributed to Al's suicide. He said there was a danger that my next partner might do the same. Was he serious? I gave up on counseling. I also stopped going to church. I felt abandoned by God. So I talked to Mecha; she was stoic and not much help. Besides, she didn't know my secret, and I couldn't tell her.

I would have to do this alone.

Friends continued inviting me to football games, to dinner out. A young man from Spain asked me on a date; I couldn't even consider it. I had no energy, no desire. It was like I was inside a black hole, pressed down by a black weight that was pressing from the inside too, and from every direction at once.

In the fall of 1968, the war in Vietnam was everywhere, on every street corner, every television screen. You couldn't escape it. I couldn't. The horrific photographs and footage. The grim firsthand reports. The body counts. The rhetoric about winning the "hearts and minds" of the Vietnamese. The growing intensity of the anti-war movement at home.

And it seemed like the presidential campaign only threw gasoline on the fire. Richard Nixon vs. Hubert Humphrey, with Alabama Governor George Wallace, an avowed racist, running as an independent. That fall, the first African American woman was admitted to Radford. Her roommates immediately moved out.

As a candidate, Richard Nixon said he had a "secret plan" to end the war, but there was no plan. Young men continued burning their draft cards. Less than a week after Al died in Long Binh, anti-war protests outside the Democratic Convention site in Chicago exploded in violence.

Pro-war "hard hats" were holding counterdemonstrations, Nixon's running mate, Spiro Agnew, was calling for the return of "law and order," and soldiers coming home from Vietnam were being spit on in airports. My feelings were divided between loyalty to Al, a hatred of the war that he had also come to hate, and a growing mistrust of the US government.

At twenty-three years old, I looked at my life and felt like I'd been left stranded in the worst land, unable to watch what was happening around me but incapable of looking away. I saw American soldiers not much different from Al being airlifted into battle, and I saw them killing Vietnamese. I saw dead and wounded soldiers, Al's age or even younger, carried from the battlefield in trucks—or, in one famous photo, sprawled on the top of a tank, covered in bloody bandages. And I saw other young men, also not much different from Al, being beaten by police on the streets of US cities for protesting a war they believed to be immoral.

I felt pain for the soldiers, as if I knew every one of them. I felt pain for the demonstrators in the streets. And I felt pain for the returning soldiers who were being treated like war criminals. Al could have been any one of them. I wanted to shake the people who were spitting on these soldiers, calling them baby killers. I wanted to scream: "You don't understand what's happened to them over there. They were innocent, like my husband. They didn't want to be there. They didn't think they had a choice. They were never prepared to see what they saw there, to face what they had to face. My husband was not prepared physically or psychologically, not for a war like this. My husband was innocent. My husband died in this war. I'm innocent too."

I also felt sympathy for the Vietnamese people; and much later, I came to understand more than I ever dreamed about how complicated the war was for many of them: how much pain and loss *they* suffered;

that many of them *did* believe, and many still do, that the Americans were there to help; and that the Vietnamese who came here as refugees *because* of the war were not nearly as angry as they could have been—and maybe should have been—about their shattered country and their broken lives.

I would eventually be blessed with the chance to serve and work closely with many of these refugees, people who, like Al, were also casualties of senseless war. But in those final months at Radford, I was still searching for the strength to do what I had to do, wondering where all the flowers of my life had gone, and struggling even to find my breath sometimes, like a soldier with a chest wound.

All I wanted was for the time to pass so I could return home to my family and country and pick up the thread of my own interrupted life.

CHAPTER VIII
Starting Over in Bolivia

I don't know how I managed to get through that final semester at Radford. Those weeks are mostly a dark blotch now, an empty place in my memory, but I remember the feeling. It was like a heavy curtain had been drawn around the woman I'd once been, so full of life and hope. Only small flickers of light came through.

I graduated in December 1968, barely four months after Al's death, with a master's degree in counseling, but I was still reeling. Al's parents came to the graduation, and I was grateful for their support, but the stoic way they dealt with losing their son still mystifies me. It seemed as if the grief barely touched them; they simply went on with their lives. How was that possible?

What would the future be like now? I knew I couldn't stay in the United States, to live here alone without Al. I applied to the Sorbonne, thinking I'd go to Paris to study languages, but it didn't take long to realize what a mistake it would be to move to a new country with no friends or family support.

So, I went home to Bolivia instead, certain I could find work in La Paz—and that I'd be surrounded by the love I so desperately needed in order to heal. I was too young to know what healing really meant or what it would require. I just knew I craved it.

I carried the secret of Al's suicide with me, but the weight of it seemed to lighten the minute I stepped off the plane.

Like many other immigrants, I have two countries. I love them both, but my soul and my heart belong to Bolivia. They always will. Coming home felt like reentering a warm house after being outside in the cold. I'd prepared myself to live in the United States with Al, but now I knew—and everything that happened in those first weeks and months confirmed it—that *this* was where I belonged.

My mother and my sisters Maria Eugenia, Paty, and Anneliese met me at the airport and welcomed me with open arms. I was still wearing black, but there was nothing somber or mournful in our reunion. I was thrilled to be home.

My father had returned from exile and remarried. My mother was still renting out rooms in our house and cooking lunch for as many as twenty people a day to support the family. The world back in La Paz seemed just as I remembered it, and I immediately began reconnecting with the life I'd left behind.

I was returning to myself, to Bolivia, and to my family and friends; to the ways and customs I knew and understood so well; to the sights and smells, to the sound of Spanish being spoken all around me; to the open and loving way people in Bolivia have of expressing themselves. In short, I was home again.

At first, I thought I should wear black so the world would know and there would be no mistake: I was a widow. It seemed like the right thing to do, a way to honor Al. But that soon began to feel unnecessary, even out of place, and by Christmas I had set aside the mourning clothes, and my lifequake entered a dormant phase. I never forgot Al, and I hadn't finished with the grief either. I just covered it over.

Emma the widow? That was my life in the United States, 4,000 miles away, a chapter that was now closed. Many of my friends had met Al, but none of them really knew him, so they weren't feeling the loss. My family never pressed or asked questions, which made it easier to put my darkest secret under lock and key and to keep it there, separate and undisturbed.

———•••———

It was the holiday season, and La Paz was brimming with life. Poverty and hardship are inescapable in Bolivia, but La Paz is a magnificent, colorful city surrounded by beautiful mountains, and every neighborhood, every street and plaza, is unique.

The neighborhood we lived in, Sopocachi, is a good example. Just half a block away from our house was the Plaza Abaroa, named for Eduardo Abaroa, a Bolivian martyr who was killed defending a bridge during the War of the Pacific, in which Chile gained resource-rich territory from both Peru and Bolivia and Bolivia lost its access to the sea. In one corner of the plaza was a restaurant that sold salteñas. It was a social gathering place for the "Splendid" fraternity. On another street was a coffee shop called Quick where boys from the "Country Club" fraternity, the organization my onetime boyfriend Jaime was part of, would gather.

Sopocachi was alive with social interactions—a place to meet friends from private schools like the Colegio LaSalle, San Calixto, Colegio Alemán, which my father and sister Maria Eugenia attended, and, of course, Saint Andrew's. These social networks were important, their traditions ran deep, and the friendships made in school lasted lifetimes, shaping identities and often continuing down multiple generations. There were rivalries, but the lines between separate networks were easily crossed. The "Top Hat" fraternity had hosted the New Year's Eve party Al and I attended when he visited two years before; and the Tennis Club was a place to go for lunch (or to play tennis) no matter which private school or fraternity you belonged to.

The world I was reentering in La Paz felt like a cocoon filled with life and joy and friendly banter. I'd been away for almost seven years and was carrying a grievous wound inside me. But the world of La Paz awaited, wide open, beckoning me to enter. And I did. With enthusiasm.

For one thing, most people in Bolivia knew and cared little about what the US was doing in Vietnam. There were no television broadcasts from the war front, and most Bolivians, even upper-class Bolivian families, didn't even have televisions back then. Coverage of the war, the anti-war protests, the Civil Rights Movement, the images that saturated life at Radford, simply weren't part of my new life in Bolivia. Or the lives of anyone I knew. I was now free from the constant reminders of the horrific conflict that took my husband. Besides, it was summer in La Paz, and the days were warm and long, not like in Virginia in December.

Looking back, I see that in putting aside the black dress, I was also laying down my grief in exchange for an embrace. The enveloping arms of Bolivia were warm and strong. A bustling household filled with love; the markets and street vendors; the plazas and restaurants; friends dropping by for tea or to say hello; the excitement of the holidays—they all made it easier, not to forget the past but to sequester it. To become a new person very much like the person I was *before* I left for the United States.

It was the first Christmas without Al, and there were some difficult times. The memories flooded back at odd moments, uninvited, unexpected. But I didn't cry openly. No one knew. I immersed myself in the joy and celebration of the holidays.

In other ways, returning to Bolivia as a widow was difficult—more so than I imagined, having gotten used to life in the United States. This was especially true at holiday time. In Bolivia, the custom is to visit people in their homes. Friends came by to invite me to all kinds of social gatherings; but these same Bolivian customs actively discourage single women, including widows, from going out alone at night and especially from being seen at parties without a man. There was a stigma attached. Eyebrows would raise. People would talk.

Mostly, my friends treated me like in old times. A group of friends welcomed me back to join them for weekly teas, and I was living at my mother's home, so it was safe, comfortable. But there was that undercurrent, the reality that my options as a widow were strictly constrained.

One of my earliest visitors was a man named Gonzalo Ponce. I'd met him years before, when I lived in Cochabamba, and I went to school with his sister Annabelle. Gonzalo was five foot five, four years older than me, and the sixth of eight children. He had graduated from the University of Colorado in the United States with a degree in art and was working for Braniff Airlines. I knew his mother too, Señora Delfina, a wonderful woman who was living in a big house in Cochabamba and baking cakes to make extra money. His father had died years before.

Gonzalo was very attentive and started showing up often. I was mourning Al, but I tried to be friendly, and my mother encouraged me to socialize. After Christmas, my friends invited me to the Tennis Club for a New Year's Eve party, but I couldn't go without a date, and Gonzalo suggested I go with him. I didn't see any harm in it, and it was fun to see friends, dance, and welcome in the New Year, even though it was impossible not to think of Al and the way we'd celebrated the holidays—and our engagement—just two years before.

I remember thinking at the time how different the holiday celebrations were in Bolivia and the United States. In Bolivia, you don't shop for Christmas presents in malls; you go into the streets, like stepping into a street fair that continues day and night. New Year's is an all-night party running into the next day, filled with eating, toasts, and dancing: drinking *api* in the morning (a traditional Bolivian drink made from purple corn flour, cinnamon, and spices) and champagne at twelve; eating fried cheese empanadas and *fricase*, a pork soup, at 10 a.m. on New Year's Day.

That night we danced the *cueca* and the twist to traditional

Bolivian folkloric music and rock and roll. Several friends had recently come back, like me, from years spent at colleges in the US.

Rounding out the holiday season is Alasitas. Artisans produce miniature representations of daily life, and at the center of it all is the Ekeko, a little man, usually a campesino, who carries items that embody dreams and hopes for the New Year: money if the hope is to become wealthy, a suitcase if the dream is to travel, and so on. I was drawn further back into the world I'd left behind, as if the hard and painful memories were being covered over by season after season of leaf fall compressed into a few weeks' time.

After the holidays, I started looking for work. One of the first places I applied was at Saint Andrew's, my former high school. The campus was in a beautiful part of La Paz called La Florida. Father James O'Connor was leading the school at the time, and he offered me a job teaching psychology and English as a second language. I asked if I could also start a counseling department to advise students, and he agreed. Tragically, Father O'Connor was killed in an airplane crash that following September, and it was my job to console the students. I was surprised at how easily I stepped into this role, even though I hadn't fully dealt with my own grief and shock from the lifequake barely one year before.

But that remained in the future when I began at Saint Andrew's. Luckily, I had a car, a white Opal that my father had urged me to buy, though I first had to learn to drive a stick shift; the streets of La Paz are not flat like they are in Yuma. It took some work.

Living at home with my mother was a joy. She would cook my breakfast and take the car out of the garage while I was getting ready so I could be on time for school. I was happy at Saint Andrew's too. In Bolivia, the students stay in the same classroom throughout the school day, and the teachers switch. I developed close relationships with many of the students, who would visit me at home to talk about whatever was concerning them or to have coffee or tea.

A few weeks later, I got a second part-time position at the Bolivian Institute for Education and Social Action (IBEAS) as assistant to the director of their education department. Through this work, I would learn much about the state of rural education in Bolivia, especially about the needs of rural teachers and the lack of respect they received.

The woman who hired me was Dr. Ruth Payne, a Dominican nun. She offered workshops that served hundreds of rural teachers, most of whom were high school graduates with no college degree. I was responsible for administering something called the Barilla intelligence test, developed in Spain, and then for analyzing the results.

It didn't take long for me to realize that this method was deeply flawed, both culturally and linguistically. Most of the rural teachers were Indigenous men who spoke Aymara or Quechua as their first language. But the Barilla test was written in "high" Castilian Spanish. Not surprisingly, the results showed that most of these rural teachers were functioning at below-average intelligence, which was not true; they just couldn't fully understand what they were reading, and they responded to the questions from an entirely different cultural perspective.

Sister Ruth and I worked together to create a report for the Ministry of Education recommending that these kinds of tests *not* be used in the rural areas. Meanwhile, the workshops we offered were embraced enthusiastically by the teachers. They were eager to learn and to receive materials they could take back to the communities where they taught. We also coauthored two books, *Creatividad y Inteligencia* (*Creativity and Intelligence*) and *Guía Vocacional y Profesional de Bolivia* (*Vocational and Professional Guidance in Bolivia*), which was about the role of counseling in ensuring student success.

The work was rewarding; it was like having a foot on two perfect launching platforms. Both positions foretold important pieces of the work I would eventually do in the United States. I knew who I was again. I felt like I was sailing, like I'd been reborn.

It was not apparent yet, but I was about to enter a time of upheaval and crisis in my personal life, a collision between my lifequake and the reality that all Bolivian women of my generation had to confront.

CHAPTER IX
Politics and Turmoil: It's Complicated

In Bolivia, political instability is like a chronic disease. In the seven and a half years I lived there after leaving Radford, there were five presidents plus a junta. Four of the presidents seized power through military coups.

When I arrived home in December 1968, General René Barrientos was leading the country. He was a rabid anti-communist who had been trained at the infamous School of the Americas and was receiving support from the United States. He was also charismatic and popular with ordinary Bolivians, in part because he spoke fluent Quechua.

A year earlier, in October 1967, Bolivian Army rangers had captured and killed Ernesto "Che" Guevara, who led a guerrilla insurgency in the jungles and urged tin miners in the southwestern part of the country to revolt. It was no secret that Barrientos had directly ordered Che Guevara's death, and when the general's helicopter crashed on the way to Cochabamba in April 1969, many people thought he had been assassinated by Che's followers, although this was never proven.

Barrientos was succeeded by his vice president, Luis Adolfo Siles. Siles was a lawyer who wanted to move the country toward democracy, but his term in power was brief; barely five months passed before his government was overthrown by another general, Alfredo Ovando Candía.

Years earlier, Ovando had served as copresident with Barrientos, and he was the commander of the Bolivian Air Force when he took power again in September 1969. His term in office was marked by political violence that spilled into the streets of major cities across the country. He nationalized the operations of US-based oil companies and invited leftist intellectuals to join his cabinet. He also spoke strongly in favor of improving living conditions for the nation's poor.

His populist positions took conservatives both in and outside the military by surprise. In June 1970, a new Marxist guerrilla movement emerged in the lowlands of La Paz, driven in part by students and faculty from the universities who were aligned with the outlawed Ejército de Liberación Nacional (ELN). Ovando's response was relatively generous to the insurgents, unlike Barrientos, who had called for "heads on spikes."

On October 6, 1970, there was another coup, led by General Rogelio Miranda, but there were divisions within the military itself, and a considerable amount of blood was shed as garrisons from the opposing sides battled each other. General Miranda, a reactionary nationalist, ousted Ovando; but within hours he in turn was replaced with a triumvirate of generals.

It was chaos. Bolivian forces on the left eventually took control under the leadership of General Juan José Torres, who became de facto president on October 7 until August 1971. He appointed General Ovando as the ambassador to Spain.

Torres was openly hostile to US influence. He ordered Bolivian troops to occupy US installations and expelled the Peace Corps. He pardoned the guerrillas and tried to replace the elected congress with an *Asamblea del Pueblo*. He also closed IBEAS because of its connection to Chicago-based Catholic priests. All the IBEAS property was expropriated, all the work we had done destroyed—the buildings, the convent, the books in the library, all of it—and without paying a centavo of recompense. I was crushed.

General Hugo Banzer overthrew General Torres in yet another coup d'etat in August 1971. Under his regime, left-leaning priests were persecuted. The military moved against the progressive wing of the Catholic Church, leftist students were murdered, and urban guerrillas were kidnapping and killing executives of companies. My father was on the hit list of these so-called urban guerrillas.

Against this backdrop, the socialist Salvador Allende had been elected president of Chile in November 1970, and unrest and unease swept across Latin America, some of it very close to home. The situation was complicated, chaotic, bewildering, and dangerous because power changed hands so quickly and so often, with little warning.

This upheaval was not a distant fact that could be ignored within the halls of Saint Andrew's. One of the school's most admired teachers was a man named Nestor Paz, who left unexpectedly to join the armed resistance in Teoponte, a small rural village in La Paz Department where leftist university students organized a new insurgency after Che Guevara's death in 1970. Most of the guerrillas were Bolivian, but a few Chileans, Argentines, and Peruvians also took part, in a modest fulfillment of Che's dream that people from across Latin America would rise up together.

The insurrection in Teoponte was brief and bloody, lasting from July to November 1970, and it was easily put down by the military. The guerrillas were either killed or dispersed and went into exile. One of Salvador Allende's first acts when he assumed the presidency in Chile was to give asylum to the survivors of Teoponte—a step that probably contributed to his CIA-assisted overthrow three years later.

Nestor Paz's father was a general in the Bolivian armed forces and eventually became the governor of the department of Sucre. The family was from the upper class, well respected, and Nestor attended a prestigious Jesuit high school. He was handsome and charismatic, and after high school he entered the seminary, expecting to become a priest. But he soon changed direction, left the seminary, and enrolled in the University of San Andres in La Paz to study medicine. His direction changed again, and he began teaching religion at Saint Andrew's, which was where we met. He was brilliant and deeply spiritual, and so was his wife, Cecilia Avila. Both were Marxist Christians, proponents of what later became known as "liberation theology."

When Nestor left to join the Teoponte guerrillas in July 1970, the high school students at Saint Andrew's were in shock. I was too. Many of the students already sympathized with Che Guevara, and now Nestor Paz was their hero. I had to calm the parents who worried that their children were becoming socialists.

Nestor died of starvation eighty-seven days after joining the Teoponte guerrillas. Although he never became famous internationally like Che Guevara, he was seen—and is still seen by many people in Bolivia today—as a martyr for the cause of liberation and on behalf of Bolivia's poor.

He kept a journal, a diary, that he titled *My Life for My Friends*. When he knew he was dying, he wrote a farewell letter to his parents, saying:

> At this moment I am happy, for I realize that I am achieving the goal of my life: to do something meaningful for others, to put into concrete actions my desire to love. On the other hand, I am also sad because I have to be physically far away from those I love the most. I am at the end of my search now, it is simply a matter of realizing my dream, God willing. A big warm hug, a loving kiss for you both. Today I received Christ in communion perhaps for the last time. I have an unbreakable faith in the decision I have made because I am convinced that it is the path of the Lord. Goodbye. If Death surprises me, I will wait for you in the New Land, loving without fail . . . Victory or death.

Elsewhere, he wrote: "To be Revolutionary, we have to discover Christ, and once we discover Christ, we will be revolutionaries." After Nestor died, Cecilia became an urban guerrilla and was killed by the military along with other ELN members. Their deaths touched many of us in the Saint Andrew's community; and Nestor's life and commitment to faith in action touched me too.

The convoluted politics of Bolivia and the turmoil of those years had a direct impact on my own family as well as my professional life.

My father was a lifelong advocate for private enterprise. He opposed socialism in all its forms. The organization he founded and led for many years, Confederación de Empresarios Privados, drew the attention of right-leaning groups in the United States, France, and other "first world" Western countries: At times, he actively sought their aid. This brought him into conjunction with General Banzer and his regime. He became a close advisor and then chief of staff to President Banzer, and he later served as Banzer's ambassador to Chile from 1976 to '77. When Banzer was elected democratically from 1997 to 2001, my father was named ambassador to Egypt.

I know my father's patriotism and his love of the Bolivian people were unshakable. I know how much he wanted his country to thrive in the world, how tirelessly he worked to regain Bolivian access to the sea. We shared that love, and I respected him. But our political standpoints were at times very different.

It was complicated.

I also had a deep respect for Nestor Paz. Nestor's wife was a beautiful young woman who shared the same fires of idealism that were burning in my own heart, but she became embittered and embraced violence to a degree I could never accept.

It was not my way to support a guerrilla movement. Revolution and the overthrow of political dictators was not my path. But I've carried the seeds of inspiration that Nestor Paz planted with me all my life. The dictators I have worked to overthrow are ignorance, the low expectations people often have for one another and for themselves, and the ways—sometimes subtle, sometimes overt—that institutions, laws, and customs suppress the human spirit, denying opportunity to some while lavishing it on others.

Reentering the world of Bolivia as a young woman in my

mid-twenties, idealistic and full of energy, I wanted to be an agent of change. I wanted to correct what was wrong. I was not complacent. I believed with all my heart that the problems in my country could be addressed substantially, if not solved entirely, through education, especially for the rural poor. I wanted to create schools in rural areas, to hire and support qualified teachers, and to give those teachers the resources they needed to help lift poor and Indigenous children and their families up through the light that education brings.

I had a strong social conscience, but I was also young, and my family enjoyed privileges unimaginable to many of Bolivia's rural poor. Growing up, my mother struggled financially, but my sisters and I all went to private schools; we had a comfortable house, a car, a refrigerator, and I was a member of the Tennis Club. At what point does the social conscience of someone with the privileges I enjoyed slip into paternalism?

We can romanticize Bolivia, as many people do—especially those connected with international organizations on the political Left. But it's a complicated country with a complicated past. I was young and I didn't see it clearly at the time, but solutions to the stubborn and deeply entrenched problems I was confronting in Bolivia were not simple; they rarely are.

You do what is in your power to do. Injustice may be intractable, but that doesn't mean we must accept it, and I still believe that education is the path, the most effective guerrilla action anyone can ever take. This is true in both of my countries, as I came to understand eventually.

My countries are closely linked, and not just through my own experience. Over the past thirty years, so many people have left Bolivia for the United States, and they are still coming—looking for stability, economic opportunity, and the kind of education that is not available to them "back home."

For many of them, it's been a one-way journey. For me, the journey was more complex.

CHAPTER X
Shadows and Light

The holidays were over. School started in February, coinciding with the beginning of the Oruro Carnival season, and there was a steady stream of dances and other social gatherings. Gonzalo kept asking me out: We went to movies, parties, and a series of fundraising events for a nonprofit organization I'd recently founded with three other friends called Un Maestro Más ("One More Teacher").

He was polite, and we had several friends in common. But he wasn't interested in being just my escort; it was clear he wanted to be my boyfriend. I wasn't dating anyone else, so we settled—from my perspective, we simply drifted—into that relationship. My best friend advised me not to become engaged, and I knew I wasn't ready to be married again, but Gonzalo was insistent, and patient; he knew where the weak spots were.

Most of my friends from school were already married with children. We met as a group every Tuesday for tea and pastries, and the conversation always turned to children and husbands. I had neither, but everyone knew that I was dating Gonzalo. Some said I should marry him, while others told me to be careful.

One day, Gonzalo decided he would ask my father and mother for permission to marry me, and they said yes. My father said Gonzalo came from "a good family"—that he'd gone to an American university and would make a good husband. My mother was not impressed by these credentials, or by Gonzalo, but she wanted to see me married again. She knew it was hard for me, being in Bolivia alone.

In a moment of weakness, I suppose, I agreed to marry him even though I had reservations about it. I was never truly happy with the decision. As a young woman, I didn't recognize the impact that those feelings of abandonment—first by my father, then by Al—were having on my life. I thought starting a new relationship and getting married would help. I was wrong.

My sister Julia arrived from the United States with her future second husband. By then, I was dreaming about Al every night—dreaming he was still alive, that he'd return from Vietnam soon and we'd resume our life together. I cried with Julia one night, talking about Al, and she advised me not to marry Gonzalo; but by that time the wedding invitations had been sent, and there was no way I could back out. Gonzalo was not interested in hearing anything about Al, ever. He only wanted to talk about tennis and the next social event.

With the $10,000 benefit from Al's life insurance policy, I'd bought a house in the San Miguel neighborhood. It was furnished, and even though I was living at my mother's, Gonzalo asked if he could live there until we were officially married. I said yes. We set a date for the wedding: December 8, 1969. Since I was a widow and this was Gonzalo's first marriage, our marriage was sanctioned by the church.

For the wedding, I wore a long cream-colored dress, and Gonzalo wore a tuxedo, but otherwise it was a simple ceremony, with about forty invited guests, mostly family and friends. We had the reception at my mother's home. There was nothing fancy about it. It wasn't joyous, either, at least not for me.

After the ceremony, Gonzalo drove my car—he didn't own one—to the house in San Miguel. Sitting next to him, I felt like I was having a panic attack, like a voice inside was screaming, *What did I just do?!*

Our honeymoon was in Rio de Janeiro because Gonzalo had free airline tickets from Braniff, and things did not go well. We both got badly sunburned, but that was the least of it. We were newly married, and already I was having serious doubts. I was coming apart inside. I hadn't even begun to heal from the loss of my beloved Al Giddings, and Gonzalo was oblivious to what was going on inside me. I pretended everything was fine.

Coming home from the honeymoon, we moved into the San Miguel house and started life as a married couple. But it was a one-way relationship from the beginning. I brought everything to the marriage. He was happy just to drive my car and enjoy the benefits of having a wife who was financially stable.

He was insensitive, to put it mildly. We had a housekeeper, and he expected her to bring breakfast to our bed, wash the car, polish his shoes. He seemed to think that because his family was from the upper class, he was supposed to be served. It was so different from the way I felt and the way I was raised. We argued about this. Gonzalo insisted we build a small room with a cold shower onto the end of the house for the housekeeper, but I said no: She would stay in our second bedroom and use hot water when she bathed.

Not long after we got back from our honeymoon, all the furniture and household items Al and I had in our Yuma duplex arrived, sent by the US Army. I was crushed to see these artifacts of my former life, of Al's and my marriage, including all our wedding presents, which Gonzalo treated as if they were presents meant for *us*. The Army also sent Al's clothes. There was a beautiful blue sweater I'd bought for him, and Gonzalo started wearing it without asking my permission. I was enraged. He had no right. He had no sympathy. He had no understanding, no respect.

What do you do when you realize these things about the man you've just married? It dawned on me that in Gonzalo's mind, I'd simply been a "good catch." He was happy that I worked because he liked the income. He didn't much like the independence my work represented, but after all, I paid for his membership in the Tennis Club.

I played the role of wife without feeling the love a new bride should feel for her husband. It was not the kind of love I felt with Al. I tried hard to be a good partner, to support Gonzalo financially and emotionally. My friends encouraged me to have children, and I wanted to have children, but our sex life was empty. There was no emotional connection, and I had difficulty getting pregnant. My periods had always been irregular, so I never knew; and whenever I did have a period, disappointment followed.

We decided to visit a gynecologist for advice. I had to take my temperature every day and follow the doctor's orders about when the right time was to have sex. It was far from the romantic, passionate, and intimate connection I really wanted. Gonzalo blamed me, and as far as I can remember, he was never tested. I'm sure he never considered that the problem might have been with *his* body, not mine.

I'd had doubts about the relationship almost from the beginning. Even Al's parents, who wanted the best for me and hoped I *would* remarry someday, warned against taking that step too soon. They said they worried I was rushing into this. Now I understand that I did what I did partly out of loneliness and suppressed grief. I didn't give myself time to heal because no one, not even my closest family, knew the truth about what I was really dealing with: Al's suicide. But it's also true that the restrictions on women imposed by Bolivian society—even by members of my own family—pushed me into a corner that seemed to offer no escape *except* marriage.

I was resilient, far more so than I knew or imagined at the time, but I was a prisoner. And I was about to touch the bottom and glimpse a darkness even greater than the one I had already known. My life was becoming a battleground of shadows and light. Eventually, the light would prevail, and the doors of the prison would open wide again. But it took a while.

Fortunately, I loved my work. I had developed close relationships with the students and teachers at Saint Andrew's and was also coming to understand what their counterparts in the rural parts of Bolivia were up against when it came to securing a good education.

I was part of two social groups. The one that met for tea on Tuesdays was mostly classmates from Saint Andrew's. We were concerned about socioeconomic inequalities, especially in the realms of education and the empowerment of women. On Thursdays, I met with another group of friends, all married and with children. Many of them and their husbands were volunteers at Un Maestro Más.

Un Maestro Más was very close to my heart and began with the Tuesday group, one of whose members was Marcela Siles, the daughter of former President Siles Suazo. We had a friend named Roberto Gonzales who was doing research for the US Agency for International Development (USAID) in rural areas. Initially, the focus of Roberto's work with USAID was on funding for rural road improvements, but he quickly realized that many school-age children in the rural areas weren't even going to school—because there were no teachers. There were no salaries to support them because the government was only funding teachers in the urban areas.

I remember clearly what he told us: "I'm going to the rural areas where the children are all celebrating the independence of Bolivia, and they don't even have a school to go to."

So we started talking about the need to raise funds for rural schools to hire their own teachers; and from these conversations came the idea to form the nonprofit organization Un Maestro Más. The goal would be to provide a teacher to any community willing to build a schoolhouse and give the teacher free room and board. The nonprofit's founders—Roberto, Marcela, and I, along with several others—all believed that there was a natural desire on the part of those parents and communities forgotten or ignored by the state to see that their children receive an education. This is true everywhere; but in Bolivia especially, the time seemed right to build on this natural desire.

So, we took steps to create an organization and began raising money to support it by hosting social events.

After the founding, I served as a volunteer and advisor to Un

Maestro Más for most of the time I was in Bolivia. The work energized me as few other causes have, and it also prepared me for the work I would do later in life: empowering teachers and creating nonprofit organizations to support dreams for education, specifically among immigrant and refugee families.

By this point I knew that my marriage to Gonzalo was a mistake, but I was surrounded by family, friends, and colleagues I loved and respected and who returned that love and respect fully, in manifold ways. My own hunger for education was increasing, I was once again inspired by the work I was doing and becoming more attuned to the struggles of Bolivian women in particular.

President Banzer closed schools and universities when he came to power in 1971. With IBEAS shuttered and Saint Andrew's temporarily closed, I was lucky that the American School in La Paz offered me a job as a teacher and counselor, with a salary more than three times what I was making at Saint Andrew's. This was fortunate too because I'd lost my widow's pension from the US Army when I remarried.

Accepting the new position came at a cost, though. I had to explain to my Saint Andrew's students why I was leaving midway through their junior year. I knew some of them saw and felt this as abandonment, and given my own struggles with abandonment, I felt guilty. I would miss their senior prom, which they had already named for me, though they did invite me to join their senior trip to Argentina and Chile.

In the end, I attended the prom *and* their graduation. I also continued to work with Un Maestro *Más*, which was thriving. In less than three years, we had already raised the funds to support teachers in fifteen rural schools, which was a major achievement in Bolivia at the time.

In my first year at the American School, I was a full-time

teacher. Later, I was a full-time counselor, working with students from pre-kindergarten through high school. I enjoyed teaching, but the counseling work was even more rewarding. I held individual and group counseling sessions and developed guidelines for measuring student achievement, helping to diagnose learning disabilities. I also organized parent-effectiveness training and learning-disabilities workshops.

In addition to my on-campus duties, I served as the American School's representative to the National Ministry of Education. I'd been a strong advocate for Bolivian teachers who were receiving lower salaries than their American counterparts and no housing or travel funds. This kind of disparity was widespread in Bolivia, and I wanted to change it. My passion for education and for serving teachers effectively fused with my hatred of injustice. Another problem I was inspired to help address was Bolivia's 60 percent illiteracy rate and second-lowest per capita income in Latin America.

My resume was also growing rapidly. I joined groups like the Association of School Counselors and the South American Association of American Schools. Working from those platforms, I attended conferences in places like Rio de Janeiro and Montevideo. I started teaching at the university level, as a professor in the psychology department at the Catholic University in La Paz. There were few counselors or psychologists in Bolivia at the time who were qualified to diagnose learning disabilities and recommend steps for remediation and, in some cases, prevention. I was able to do both.

Meanwhile, my marriage continued to unravel. Gonzalo lost his job. He was unemployed and went to Argentina to buy leather goods to smuggle into Bolivia. He was caught and detained, and I had to go to the La Paz airport and pay a big fine to keep him from going to jail.

Financially adrift, he decided to become an importer, working from the office of Un Maestro Más. I had to tell him this was not appropriate, that he couldn't use the office for his business, so he rented a store, and one night there was a problem. I was never sure exactly what happened, but he was caught breaking the locks, and I had to use my father's influence to get him released from jail.

At home, I continued with the fertility treatments, and after two years of marriage I was ecstatic when the doctor finally confirmed: I was pregnant. My mother was thrilled, too, when I told her the news; but a month later, I miscarried.

As usual, Gonzalo offered no understanding or support. He assumed it was my fault. I fell into a depression at yet another loss, but the doctor told me not to worry: I could get pregnant again. And once more, I simply buried my grief. Another life and the possibility of love had vanished without warning or for any reason I could understand.

Shortly after the miscarriage, I started volunteering in an orphanage in La Paz. I saw so many babies that had been abandoned, and for a while I thought maybe we could just adopt. But Gonzalo wanted no part of it. I don't remember that he gave any thought to what I was feeling. He just said no.

When President Banzer closed Saint Andrew's, the students whose families could afford it transferred to the American School, which was the most expensive private school in the country. Tuition had to be paid in dollars, meaning that the students there were generally even more privileged than their peers at Saint Andrew's. Mostly, they were the children of Americans or of the country's wealthiest families.

In those days, the US State Department encouraged partnerships between American universities and schools in places like Bolivia. The goal was to connect "foreign" teachers with professional-development opportunities in the United States, a relic of the old Alliance for Progress begun during the Kennedy administration.

When I arrived, the American School already had an affiliation with the University of Arkansas. I was tasked with coordinating college courses taught by University of Arkansas professors, and I enrolled in some of them, along with my cousin Cristina Barber, who had studied at Georgetown University. Cristina and I also worked together on developing the American School's Spanish-language curriculum; we recommended adding Bolivian history and government and other courses needed for a Bolivian high school diploma. The American high school diploma was not accepted at Bolivian universities.

Through this affiliation with the University of Arkansas, I also had the opportunity to return to the US, to Fayetteville, and take courses that would count toward a future PhD. Which I did, starting in the summer of 1974. I had to renew my visa anyway, and spending extended periods of time in the United States offered relief from being with Gonzalo.

As the widow of a soldier who died in wartime, I was eligible to become a US citizen. It seemed like a good idea: I would have more opportunities in the United States, and I wouldn't have to come back periodically to renew my green card. It was a very simple process in the 1970s, much different than it is today. So, I took the step.

In the US, I could study, attend conferences, move around freely, meet people—men *and* women—in public places, and be independent. I was inspired by the writings of Gloria Steinem. I read *The Feminine Mystique* by Betty Friedan. I even subscribed to *Ms. Magazine*. I also joined the National Organization for Women (NOW).

In Bolivia, I became known as an advocate for women's rights at a time when most women were controlled by their husbands and when it was acknowledged and even expected that married men— but not married women, of course—would have affairs, just as my father did. I was well known and respected for my work, but I was also considered too radical by many people. My independence was harshly judged. Before I married Gonzalo, the Tuesday group met regularly at my house; most members of the group were married, and their husbands were uneasy about our gatherings. They resented me for hosting these events. In one instance, a newly married member's husband insisted she be home by the time he got home from work in the evening. Eventually he forbade her to come to my house at all. I was even publicly accused once of being *"del otro equipo"* ("from the other team"—in other words, a lesbian) because I had close women friends and went to Georgisimo, a restaurant/bar in La Paz.

Professionally and personally, the more I talked with Bolivian women, the more I became aware of their submissive attitudes and how much they had internalized the culture of control by men. Many were opposed to any form of birth control, which was astounding to me. I also witnessed the discrimination women suffered in public offices, how everyone just accepted the idea that women would be paid less than men for the same work.

I pushed the limits as far as I could. Even though Bolivia was living under President Banzer's repressive government, somehow I never felt personally threatened or at risk because of my views. I did know I had to be careful—and I *was* careful—because of my father's position in the government. But I also felt a calling, to be an agent of change.

A quarter century had passed, but I was still that six-year-old girl in the Plaza Colon, feeling that I had to do something to fight the injustice I was seeing. I was estranged from the church and still angry at God for taking Al away from me, but somewhere inside I was asking once again: Is this what He wants for me?

After I returned from that first summer in Arkansas, I resolved to work on my marriage and the fertility treatments. The relationship with Gonzalo didn't improve, but we managed to conceive a second time. This was 1975, two years after the first miscarriage. I thought, *At last, I'll have a baby and the problems with our marriage will end.*

Two months went by, and one night I noticed blood. I went to the doctor, who informed me that I'd had another miscarriage, and I was devastated. Another loss of life and dreams. Even within the arms of a healthy relationship, a miscarried pregnancy cuts to the bone. It releases a surge of emotions: sorrow, futility, abandonment, loneliness, confusion, exhaustion, and self-doubt. You feel as if somehow *you* have failed.

And ours was far from a healthy marriage.

I became depressed. I couldn't sleep, so the doctor prescribed Valium. Friends told me not to worry, that miscarriages happen and I could still try again. They told me stories about other women who'd had multiple miscarriages before they had their first child, but the stories and the reassurances didn't help.

I was awash in post-traumatic stress and unresolved grief, though I didn't have this language at the time. I didn't understand how grief compounds—that I wasn't just feeling sad because I lost this baby. Al's death—his suicide—and the miscarriage of two babies entwined inside me like venomous snakes. I lost all hope for a happy married life with children.

Gonzalo kept telling me to get hold of myself, to let it go. I was alone even with my own husband, abandoned by him too, in a way. As a counselor, I knew I needed therapy. But I didn't seek it out. I doubted Gonzalo would approve.

Then, in June 1975, I enrolled in training to conduct group counseling with students. It was a hands-on, participatory workshop where I was encouraged and expected to share my feelings and experiences in group exercises. It was designed to tap raw emotions, and that's exactly what happened. During one of the exercises, I started to weep uncontrollably. The trainer talked with me and managed to calm me down, but the next morning I couldn't get out of bed. The trainer came to our home to check on me, concerned about my well-being.

Gonzalo had no idea what was happening, and that night I had a major outburst—what today we might call a meltdown—and he slapped me to get me to stop. I knew then that the marriage was over; and strangely, it didn't matter. I didn't care anymore. I'd been living alone with him for four years anyway. So, I let go, and it was like the floor disappeared from under me. Darkness welled up from below. I went into the bathroom and took all the Valium pills in the bottle. I passed out. All I remember is the feelings of anger, grief, and peace flowing and mixing like colored liquids in a glass.

The next thing I knew, I was waking up in the hospital; the doctors had pumped my stomach to save my life. My mother was there. I told her I didn't want to see Gonzalo. She understood.

When I was released from the hospital, I went to my mother's house instead of "home" to San Miguel. I couldn't sleep, but she stayed with me, she stood by my bed, and little by little, I got better, physically and mentally. It was clear what I needed to do.

The hospital doctor stopped by to check on me. He said I needed to see a psychiatrist or psychologist. That I needed help. My father was also worried; he thought I should take a vacation, go to Yungas. A friend from my Tuesday group agreed to come with me.

When I got back, I told my parents that I didn't want to live with Gonzalo anymore or even see him, and that I would not go back to the house in San Miguel until he left. I asked him to move out, and he did, but when I came back a few days later, my car wasn't there. I guess he thought it should be his car now.

I didn't see a psychiatrist until months later, and I had almost no contact with Gonzalo after that.

He had no boundaries, he had no ethics, and he'd shown himself to be a taker with little or no capacity to give. Many years later, he came to the US, and I saw him once, in Georgetown, and then again at an event sponsored by the World Bank where he was working as an interpreter. We said hello, but the encounters were very brief. I didn't feel anything toward him, positive or negative. He was an episode in my life, I'd accepted its lessons, and when it was over, it was over.

My crumbled marriage wasn't the only site of turmoil in my life. At the American School, some of the students were starting to experiment with cocaine. It was now readily available on the streets of La Paz, and the students could easily afford it. One freshman, a young American woman, was dating a known cocaine dealer and beginning to show signs of addiction. As the school's counselor, it was my job to inform her parents. In another instance, some students and I had raised a substantial sum of money for the local orphanage where I volunteered, and students who were involved with cocaine stole it. A student whose father was head of the UN office in Bolivia was caught with cocaine in class. I had to talk with the family and explain what had happened, and they responded by pulling him out of school and sending him back to the United States.

I talked with the principal and told him I was worried about the way things were going. His response was that I should focus on helping them apply to college, not on counseling for "personal issues." I was angry and discouraged. He seemed more intent on protecting the interests of the school, the institution, and ignored the cocaine problems of the students we supposedly were there to serve.

One crisis followed another in rapid succession. A married English teacher was found to be having an affair with the social studies teacher, who was also married. The English teacher, a woman, was asked to resign, and the students staged a walk-out in protest: How was it fair that the woman had to resign and not the man?

That same year, a male elementary teacher—also married—was caught with a female high school student sitting on his lap. She was supposed to be his student aide. He was reprimanded but not dismissed. This was an American school, but it seemed to embody that same double standard that governed all relations between women and men in Bolivia.

As the school's counselor, I had to deal with all these problems while tackling my own. When word got out that I was separated, married men saw it as an invitation. One night, a friend stopped by, supposedly to see if I was all right. I invited him to come in, and he put his hands on my shoulders. It was clear what he wanted; I told him to leave. Later, the same thing happened in an elevator, when the husband of one of my closest friends tried to kiss me.

I decided to move back to my mother's house, partly to avoid sending the message that I was somehow available and partly because, as a young, separated woman living alone, I would never be fully accepted. But it wasn't enough. I still wasn't free to live and be the person I was becoming.

One day, my father saw me eating lunch with an American male friend at a restaurant, and he came over to tell me not to go out or be seen with men because I wasn't divorced. I felt like I was suffocating.

I spent more time with the American teachers. A group of us, men *and* women, all just friends, went hiking and camping together along the Inca Trail in La Paz. It was a beautiful, transformative experience; but once again, my parents and Bolivian friends did not approve. My mother told me I should stop "running around with American hippies."

Some of the American teachers were also experimenting with cocaine. Maybe it was my upbringing or the residue of my once-deep Catholic faith, but I never succumbed to the temptation. Once, I went to the home of an American friend, and people were sniffing lines of coke from a mirror on the floor. I left quickly in a state of panic and disbelief. Later, that same friend and her husband were caught selling the drug and sent to prison. They were released a year later, and the husband was killed almost immediately by drug dealers.

The whole world seemed to be in chaos, falling apart. I felt shaky on my feet most days and had nowhere to turn. I couldn't talk to my parents about anything I was feeling, so I decided to seek professional help. Which turned out to be the final straw. Almost.

A new psychiatrist had just arrived from Europe. He was a friend of my cousin and came highly recommended. I went to a couple of therapy sessions at his office in the Mental Health Center, and things seemed to be going well—until he asked me to come to his office for an evening session. He said he had to stay at the facility for some kind of vague "administrative" reason.

We started out talking about my problems with Gonzalo, the problems with our sex life, and my depression. He stood up, walked around the desk, and started to kiss me. He pushed himself toward me and told me to relax, that I just needed to relax. Frightened and shaken, I went back to my mother's house. How could he do that to me? And he was married, besides. Then he called, said he needed to talk to me. He came to the house and tried to kiss me again. I guess he saw my vulnerability as an invitation too. I pushed him away and stopped going to counseling, but the damage was done.

My life was spiraling out of control, and there was no one I could talk to about it. I just kept quiet. But there was one more traumatic experience waiting for me in Bolivia: the death of my beloved abuelita.

It was in the morning, the first week of November 1975, when I got a phone call that Abu Julia had fallen from the bed. I went immediately to my aunt's house, where my grandmother lived in a small room. She'd been found on the floor, unconscious. She'd been there alone all night and had developed pneumonia. It's cold in La Paz, even in the spring, and there was no heat in her room.

I rode in the ambulance with her to a clinic on Avda Arce. The doctor came and my father was called. It was unbearable to see her suffering. I loved her so much. She had been my spiritual anchor since I was a very young girl.

My father came that afternoon, and I decided to leave for a few hours, to go home and rest. About two hours later, I got the call saying she had died peacefully. She was ninety-four.

I felt so bad that I wasn't with her when she died. I rushed to the clinic, and when I got to her room, a coffin was already there, in the corner. I watched as my abuelita's body was lifted and placed inside. I remember she was wearing a lilac-colored sweater. The coffin was closed and taken to my dad's apartment, where he lived with his second wife.

When someone dies in Bolivia, it's customary for the body to be kept at home and for people to visit there, before the funeral, to offer condolences to the family and pay their respects. It was the first time my mother, my sisters, and I had ever been to my father's apartment. It felt so strange. My grandmother had to die before I could visit my father in his home. She'd never really accepted his remarriage. I knew she believed in her heart that my mother was still his wife.

I helped plan the funeral Mass. It was in the chapel of the Sacred Heart School, where she had been a student so many years before, the second woman to graduate. She was buried alongside her husband in the Central Cemetery in La Paz.

I loved my grandmother deeply. She taught me how to pray, and I loved hearing her stories about riding on horseback for two or three days to attend boarding school, beginning when she was just six years old. My grandmother didn't have a pension, and in her final years, she'd given away most of her possessions, so she had just a few clothes, a bed, and a chest of drawers when she died. But she never complained. She was always joyous. It was sad that I always had to remind my dad to visit his mother; she was always hoping to see her only son.

My time in Bolivia was almost over. The only joy I had was in my work, and that was fading. It was time to move, to take the next step; but I wasn't quite ready.

By then, my father was the chief of staff to President Banzer. I thought he could help me find work with the Ministry of Education. There was a program of civil service that gave professionals in Bolivia a path to take leave from their regular jobs to serve the government. I thought maybe I could do that.

In retrospect, it was a desperate move. What was I hoping to salvage?

I went to the presidential palace and met with my father in his office. I told him I wanted to serve my country. Wasn't that what he always said? That no, he didn't necessarily agree with the president's politics, but "I can do more for education in Bolivia from the inside, and I want to serve my country"?

Sometimes we look for easy solutions. I thought: *I'm successful. I have a good education. I have the power to change the political situation, to improve the lives of women. I could write articles. I could work in the rural areas.* Besides, my male friends who got their degrees from American universities were all being appointed to important jobs in the Banzer government.

But my father wasn't willing to help me. He wasn't happy that I'd separated from my husband. He told me I had a good-paying job and I should stay there. And so now it seemed that all the men in Bolivia, even my own father, were guarding the glass ceiling and that old double standard. There was nothing to do but to leave.

I was emotionally depleted, surrounded by affairs, drugs, a shattered marriage, the death of loved ones, predatory men. So I went to see the principal of the American School and asked for a leave of absence so I could pursue my doctorate in the United States, at the University of Arkansas. He said yes.

There was nothing to hold me in Bolivia anymore. Once again, a door was closing behind me. I was depressed because I loved Bolivia and because I knew that if things were different, I could do so much more. The needs were obvious: for educating low-income children, serving teachers, counseling students. I could help bring about those necessary changes. If only the glass ceiling and the upheaval everywhere around me weren't making those things impossible; but they were.

I was thirty-one years old, a US citizen. There was only one path forward, and the only way to follow it was to leave my home in Bolivia a second time. Once more, I was searching for a new beginning.

CHAPTER XI
Returning to the United States

In many ways, the decision to leave Bolivia was an easy one. I knew I'd reached an end point, and I told myself: *I want professional growth that's not available to me here, and I want the freedom to be myself, to be an independent woman. I can have that in the United States.*

I decided to rent out the house in San Miguel. I put my new Volkswagen Beetle in storage. I'd been admitted to the doctoral program in education at the University of Arkansas, where I already knew people, and awarded a fellowship that would cover my tuition and fees. The American School gave me sabbatical leave. It was time for change.

I had $5,000 in savings, which seemed like a lot of money in the 1970s; and so I planned to travel to Europe but first to spend time in Alexandria, Virginia, staying with Al's sister, Mary Lou, and visiting my sister Susy in Staunton, a small city in Shenandoah Valley, about three hours southwest of Washington, DC. I would move to Arkansas and start classes in the fall. The future was wide open.

I gave my mother power of attorney, and with a mix of confidence, sadness, hope, and some misgivings—I'd never really lived on my own before—I left Bolivia with two suitcases. It was June 1976.

I don't remember exactly how long I was in the air from La Paz to DC. Twelve hours sounds about right; and if that's true, I think I must have cried for ten. I do remember trying to conceal my tears from the flight attendants and from the people sitting next to me. But whatever

I tried to do, it didn't work; the tears kept coming, and I wonder to this day what they must have thought. The reality of coming back to the United States seemed to tap into an artesian well of emotion. So much pressure had built up below the surface that once we lifted off the runway, I was powerless to hold it in.

It wasn't just the sadness of leaving my family. And I didn't think I was leaving Bolivia for good, so it wasn't even like saying goodbye. I was grieving for my failed marriage to Gonzalo. I knew it had been wrong from the beginning; I had no doubt about that now. But I still felt the way it ended could have been better. Gonzalo and I had never talked about our problems. Was there something else I could have done?

Did I care for Gonzalo? Yes. Did I love him? In a way. Did I want to have children and make a life with him? Yes. Did I want the marriage to work? Yes, especially in the beginning. So, there was that feeling of loss and futility, of time and effort squandered. Divorce is never easy for anyone, and I knew I was leaving damage behind. And carrying some with me, too.

I was also grieving for my beloved abuelita Julia; for the way my hopes of making a difference in the lives of Bolivian women had been dashed; for Nestor Paz; for Father O'Connor; for all the rural teachers I hadn't been able to help because there were too many obstacles in the way.

I was grieving for my own childhood that would never be again; for the two children I'd lost before they were born; for the coldness and hard edges of the world, the world that had split our family and left my father living apart from us and my mother caring for her daughters alone.

And I was grieving for my country—its poverty, its instability, the persistent injustice; and, of course, I was still grieving for Al and the life we *thought* we would have together: the dreams that had vanished eight years before.

I'd been cut deeply by all the pain and disappointment, like an artery sliced open. Flying hundreds of miles an hour into the next phase of my life, alongside the hope, anticipation, and some relief too, I was bleeding tears.

Mary Lou met me at Washington National Airport. She was tall, about five foot ten, slender, perpetually tanned, in shape, and full of energy to the point of being hyperactive. She was working as a special education teacher in Prince George County, Maryland, and she drove a sports car. She'd been a party girl in college, far from what you'd call a good student. Now she was living the life of a single, *liberated* woman, like so many other women our age in the mid-1970s. She welcomed me warmly into her small apartment in Alexandria.

The apartment was in a complex of buildings called Southern Towers. It had a pool and tennis court and was known as a mecca for DC-area singles. Her apartment was tiny, with a foldout couch for sleeping, but she spent most nights with her boyfriend anyway. So, I stayed there by myself, and she took me to singles bars around Eighteenth and K Streets in Washington, which was where I met a man named Jerry Lee.

Jerry was handsome, well dressed, single, thirty-five years old, and also drove a sports car. He lived in a townhouse near Southern Towers and worked as the human resources director for Gallaudet University. He was from Lynchburg. He was financially secure, smart, suave, and charming, and we hit it off immediately. Over the next few weeks, he took me to some of the best restaurants in Washington.

One afternoon, we were having drinks in a bar on I Street overlooking the campus of George Washington University, and he asked me: "Why are you going all the way to Arkansas when you could stay in DC and go to Georgetown or GWU." I didn't take the idea seriously, not right away; but he encouraged me to apply to GW, which I eventually did. Jerry later became the president of Gallaudet and two other universities.

My sister Susy had recently returned from several years in Japan and Thailand. I drove down to spend the weekend with her family in Staunton, and over dinner Susy asked me: "Well, you're single now. What are you going to do?" I told her about Jerry, that I was interested in him but so far it wasn't serious, and then I asked her: "So, who is the most eligible bachelor in Staunton?" and she said, "You should meet my friend Jim Hainer. He lives across the street; I'll call him."

She called and asked him if he wanted to meet her smart and single sister who had just arrived from Bolivia, and he said, "Yes, I'll come right over."

Jim was a bit younger than I was, twenty-eight. He was tall, unlike Gonzalo, and handsome, warm, intelligent, energetic, confident. He was teaching economics at Mary Baldwin College in Staunton and had done his PhD work at the University of Virginia but was still finishing his dissertation.

He was recently divorced and had two children, Jon and Tess, who were almost exactly the same ages as Susy's kids. They lived with their mother near Charlottesville, but when they were in Staunton the children would all play together.

I didn't feel a spark immediately, but I was attracted to Jim Hainer, and he was quick to offer help. I was trying to figure out how to apply for a driver's license, buy a car, create a résumé, and he said, "If I can help you with any of that, just let me know."

The next weekend was July 4. This was 1976, the year of the US Bicentennial, and there were big celebrations—concerts and fireworks—all weekend on the Washington Mall. The city was alive with tourists, and the whole country was in a state of excitement.

Jim and his ex-wife, Alfreda, were still reasonably friendly and planned to take the children to New Wilmington, Pennsylvania, where they'd both grown up and where their extended families still lived. I went back to DC to spend the weekend going to dinners, bars, and concerts with Jerry Lee, who by this time was clearly interested in me, although I knew he also dated other women.

I remember thinking, *My wings are opening up. I have options. I'm meeting lots of interesting men.* The sadness I'd carried with me when I left Bolivia began to slip away. It was then that I decided to take Jerry Lee's advice and apply to other graduate programs before moving to Arkansas, and the first place I applied was GWU.

———

I was interviewed by a professor of Lebanese descent named Martha Rashid. Martha was brilliant, kind, and an exceptional professor. During the interview she asked about my background and my career thus far, and she was clearly impressed by the work I'd done in Bolivia. We bonded almost immediately, and I did very well on a test called the Miller Analogies Test, so well that—with Martha's help and probably some intervention on her part—I was admitted to the EdD program in education right away.

The offer didn't include a fellowship, and the tuition was expensive, but I liked Martha so much and was so excited about the prospect of working with her that I thought maybe I could start out by taking two courses a semester instead of the usual three or four. That way, I could afford the higher cost, and I liked the idea of being close enough to see Susy and her family on weekends. I was also enjoying my still-platonic relationship with Jerry Lee; and being in the DC area for the next two years was beginning to seem a lot more interesting than Fayetteville, Arkansas.

The next time I went to Staunton, I saw Jim Hainer again. I told him I'd been accepted at GWU, that I was thinking about staying in DC—not going to Arkansas after all—and he said, "Why don't you apply to the University of Virginia? They have a very good graduate program in education." I submitted my application, but the professor who interviewed me said I didn't meet their minimum standard because my GRE scores were too low.

From that point on, Jim would periodically remind me that *he* had a perfect score on the GRE. I brushed it off. Then he said that if I was going to stay in Virginia, I'd need a car, so he offered to drive me to Crozet (then a little village near Charlottesville, now a town in its own right) to see a VW Beetle, the same kind of car I'd had in Bolivia. I bought it on the spot.

By this time, Jim was pursuing me actively. There was something growing between us, and the first time we had sex, an entirely new world opened up. It was like nothing I'd ever experienced before. Everything I'd been missing with Gonzalo—the intimacy, the passion—I suddenly found all of it with Jim. It was exciting and deeply satisfying; to put it simply, we were *very* good in bed.

I'd already purchased plane tickets to Europe and sketched out my itinerary by the time Jim and I took that trip to Crozet to buy the car. We were having lunch in a Dairy Queen afterward, and there was a flier on the table that said something like "If you haven't traveled, you haven't really lived."

I told Jim I was going to Europe. He said he'd never even been on an airplane before; and the next day, he told me he'd applied for a passport and was going with me. I thought: *Well, that was fast*, but I agreed. We would go to Europe together.

The week after the Fourth of July, an American friend I'd met in Bolivia and visited when I was in São Paulo for a conference called to say he was living in Pittsburgh now, working for a plate glass company, and he invited me to visit. I did and stayed at the Hilton Hotel. He told me he was planning to travel to Spain and that maybe we could meet there—more evidence that I had many options.

The trip Jim and I had booked was for twenty-one days and included Luxembourg, Paris, Madrid, Rome, Stockholm, and other cities. We traveled mostly by train with a Eurail Pass. When we were on the way to Helsinki, Jim found a towel from the Pittsburgh Hilton in my luggage. He knew I'd gone there to visit a friend, and now he demanded to know if I'd slept with him. More than that, he insisted that I tell him about all the men I'd ever dated before I met him and which ones I'd had sex with.

He was invasive, insistent, and for a moment I was afraid of him. So I told him everything; I was completely honest even though it was none of his business.

When we got to Helsinki, we stayed one night in a hotel together, and then I took a train by myself to Stockholm to visit Carlos, the son of a friend from Bolivia who had wanted me to meet him. I stayed at his apartment, but nothing happened. The next day, Jim was waiting for me at the train station in Helsinki. He asked, and I told him that nothing happened with Carlos. He looked deeply into my eyes and said, "I trust you."

Later that night, Jim told me that he and Alfreda had been high school sweethearts. When they graduated, she went to Swarthmore, he went to Westminster College in their hometown, and they saw each other on weekends. He'd always suspected she was unfaithful to him during that first year, but they decided to get married when they were sophomores and learned she was expecting a baby.

He told me the suspicions about Alfreda had been very hard for him emotionally. I understood a lot about feeling abandoned, and because of that I also understood then why he'd pressed me the way he did, with so much intensity. So I let it go.

We flew back home to Washington. We were tired when we got in and went straight to Mary Lou's apartment in Alexandria, thinking we would spend the night there. Jim would drive back to Staunton the next day. Almost as soon as we walked in the door, Jerry called to say he had a "welcome home" cake for me with a Bolivian flag on it, and he wanted to bring it over, to see me and hear about the trip. I'd told him about going to Europe but not that I'd be traveling with Jim.

I put him off, said I was too tired and made an excuse; but Jim overheard the conversation. He was clearly upset and said we couldn't stay there, that we had to go to a Ramada Inn nearby. When we got to the hotel room, he became insanely jealous, so angry that he shook me and told me he couldn't stand the idea that I would be with another man. Once again, I was frightened by his rage, only this time I felt threatened physically. It worried me; but just like before, I let it go.

It didn't take long for me to make the decision: I would stay in Northern Virginia, enter the EdD program at George Washington, study with Martha Rashid, and forgo the fellowship in Arkansas. I was also falling in love with Jim Hainer, so I decided to break off the relationship with Jerry Lee. I wrote to the principal at the American School in La Paz to say I wouldn't be coming back. I rented an efficiency apartment of my own in Southern Towers, and I was ready to start classes in the fall.

Jim and I saw each other on weekends, alternating between his place in Staunton and mine in Alexandria. We had a honeymoon every weekend. It seemed like a perfect arrangement.

But when the tuition bill came from GW, I realized I'd made a serious mistake. What I *thought* was the cost of a full year's tuition was really for just one semester. Buying a car, going to Europe, and renting an apartment, I'd burned through most of my savings. How was I going to support myself? I started looking for jobs right away.

I thought the search would be quick and easy, but it wasn't. There was an active Latino community with a cluster of nonprofit organizations in DC, many of them in the Adams Morgan neighborhood off Eighteenth Street, so I started knocking on doors. None of them opened. I looked for work in Alexandria, in Washington; I looked in Staunton, at Mary Baldwin. Everywhere, the results were the same. I couldn't even find a receptionist job.

I was running out of money, getting desperate, so I searched for temp jobs as a last resort, and I found one doing clerical work—typing, filing papers, helping to organize events—at the American Psychological Association (APA). It didn't pay well, and there was nothing glamorous or particularly challenging about the work, but I was grateful to have it. At least I could pay my rent, put gas in the car.

Although on the surface the job seemed like a dead end, it wasn't. It might have been blind luck, or it might have been the hand of destiny, but one day I was working at an APA conference and met a woman named Sharon Steindam. This chance meeting opened the door to the rest of my professional life.

Sharon was a principal with Arlington Public Schools, and we struck up a casual conversation. I told her I was a graduate student at GW, about my work in Bolivia, and that I was looking for a job. She said APS would soon be advertising for a director of bilingual education and that I should contact Todd Endo, the man who had written the grant to support this new position.

Todd, who was working as an assistant to the superintendent, Larry Cuban, explained that the grant was supporting several positions and urged me to apply.

I was already falling in love with Arlington. It was unlike anywhere else I'd been in the United States. The waves of migration that would transform the county—and eventually all of Northern Virginia—were just beginning to build in 1976. There were war refugees arriving from Vietnam and later from Laos, Cambodia, Thailand; and there were small but growing communities of Bolivians and people from Central America.

In Arlington, I could get salteñas. I could attend Mass in Spanish. Sometimes I'd hear my native language on the street. I saw people who looked like me. The public schools were reflecting these changes. I was interested, to say the least.

The impulse behind Arlington's push to create bilingual education programs in the schools was not idealism; it was the threat of losing federal funds. The county was out of compliance with the Office of Civil Rights following a US Supreme Court ruling issued two years earlier, in January 1974, in the case of *Lau v. Nichols*.

In *Lau* the court ruled unanimously in favor of a group of Chinese and Latino students and their families in San Francisco. The justices argued that by not providing supplemental language instruction for students with limited English proficiency, the San Francisco public schools were violating these students' rights under Title VI of the Civil Rights Act of 1964.

English-only instruction was not sufficient, and the *Lau* decision required the schools to provide these non-English-speaking students with accommodation and "appropriate relief," which meant instruction in their native languages. Any public school system in the United States that received federal funding henceforth had to provide bilingual options for children in such situations.

In the aftermath of the court's decision, the federal Office for Civil Rights developed a set of guidelines that became known as the *Lau* Remedies. Among other things, these guidelines stipulated that bilingual programs and remedial instruction in English were required whenever there were twenty or more students from a non-English-speaking background in a single grade.

In 1976, Arlington had enough Spanish- and Korean-speaking students to trigger the *Lau* mandate, and everyone knew that it was only a matter of time before those same requirements would apply to students speaking Vietnamese, Khmer, and other non-English languages—eventually ninety or more different languages, including Arabic, Amharic, even Mongolian. Arlington officials also recognized that this presented a staffing challenge: They needed to create an office of bilingual programs right away.

The prospect of implementing such a program in a place like Arlington dovetailed perfectly with the work I was doing with Dr.

Rashid. Martha brought a strong cross-cultural awareness into the heart of her course on human development. My other course was on intelligence testing, and there too the focus was on cross-cultural differences.

My experience in Bolivia was turning out to be a major asset in my graduate work. Back home, teachers who spoke Quechua as their first language hadn't done well on tests written in Spanish. The same was true of Bolivian children forced to take tests that were developed in the US and then translated. I had seen that the approach wasn't working; it was obvious, but I hadn't yet framed in my mind exactly why. Then, one day in Martha's class, the light came on. We'd been using invalid instruments developed in different cultural contexts; and *it didn't work*.

I researched *Lau* and the grant. I started visiting the schools (Key Elementary and Patrick Henry High School) where Latino students in the county were concentrated. I met with APS staff and teachers. I knew I wanted to do this work, and when the director's job was advertised, I applied. I was late to the interview because I couldn't initially find the school administrative offices, but I did well. Several of the staff members I'd already met were on the selection committee. I felt confident.

In the end, I didn't get the director's position. I was disappointed, naturally, but soon learned about another job with APS: a bilingual resource teacher and community engagement specialist. I applied, and this time I was interviewed by a panel and had a follow-up interview directly with Superintendent Larry Cuban.

Dr. Cuban was a progressive educator and champion of civil rights in what was then still a very conservative county. The son of working-class Jewish immigrants from Russia, he'd attended public schools and then studied education, first at the University of Pittsburgh and later at Stanford.

Before coming to Arlington as superintendent, he was a high school social studies teacher in Ohio and Washington, DC. He was a protégé of Michael Timpane, the president of Columbia University, who at the time was also chair of the DC school board. He knew and understood the field of public education from many angles.

Larry was very personable and caring and known for hiring excellent staff. From the first, he was a strong supporter of bilingual education; and when the Office of Civil Rights filed a complaint against APS, he moved quickly to address it. He would be a strong ally and supporter of mine later on—a mentor, confidant, and friend.

I was offered the position in Arlington, as well as another one teaching fifth-grade Spanish at the Oyster Bilingual School in DC. They were both good opportunities, but I saw more creative potential with Arlington Public Schools. I'd be involved in starting a new program "from the ground up." And besides, the Arlington job paid $4,000 more.

I started work in the first week of November 1976. I met stiff resistance right away, and it came from multiple directions. Understandably, some teachers and administrators saw the *Lau* requirements as an extra burden. Also, the county was still adjusting to the school desegregation mandates of the *Brown v. Board* decision, and some African American parents, seeing that their children weren't getting all the attention and resources *they* needed, wondered—again, understandably—why so much new money and instructional attention was being given to these "foreign" students.

One island in this sea of resistance (or at least skepticism) was Brenda Hadiji, a Montessori teacher at Key Elementary. Brenda welcomed me and the first bilingual assistant into her classroom.

As a bilingual resource teacher, I was supposed to start teaching in Spanish on the very first day. Since I was not trained in Montessori methods, I observed what Brenda did and tried to support her Spanish-speaking students with vocabulary development, using the techniques I'd observed.

Brenda also asked me to teach Spanish to the entire class. As in my student-teaching days, I fell back on the songs and stories I'd learned from Tía Mecha, introducing the Spanish language to pre-K students using a cultural, expressive lens. The children loved it, and the Latino parents were thrilled to see their children speaking Spanish in a US school. For many of them, it was a pleasant and welcome surprise.

But the other teachers, including English as second language teachers, didn't want me to work with Spanish-speaking children who needed first-language support. Somehow, I think they felt threatened. The principal at Key was relieved that at least one teacher welcomed me into her classroom.

It was a new way of being in the classroom, a challenge for both of us, but Brenda was supportive and encouraging, and she and I eventually became good friends, taking classes at GWU together. Brenda was a gifted teacher.

My graduate studies were off to a promising, inspiring start, and I'd found stimulating professional work that paid reasonably well. There were challenges, but I was confident I could meet them. I had strong, supportive mentors in Martha Rashid and Larry Cuban, colleagues I liked and respected, and a growing network of Spanish-speaking families who welcomed and valued the influence my work was having on their children.

I felt part of a larger movement that was bringing changes to the way people thought about education. I began to see that the work I'd done in Bolivia really was important and valuable, not just for its own sake but also in setting the stage for what was to come.

I was also happy in my relationship with Jim. He was attentive and loving, and he seemed devoted to me and to nurturing our relationship. I'd put aside any worries about his jealousy.

As the months went by, I thought less about the past and more about the present and the future. I was also moving deeper into the fourth stage of an acculturation process that had started back at Mount Vernon High School, fourteen years before. This is a process and experience shared by many—perhaps most—migrants, whether they come here as immigrants or refugees, with or without "documents," looking for opportunity or fleeing war, famine, or persecution.

Stage one of the process is like a honeymoon, full of hope and expectation. Stage two is the adjustment phase, sometimes complicated by the "sting" of assimilation. Stage three is where many migrants begin to feel the culture shock, the loss of something, or of many things, and in some cases start to lose hope, becoming resigned. And stage four is integration: becoming a citizen and part of the community, growing comfortable in a new identity, finding ways to contribute, learning how to navigate the "system," gaining facility and respect, feeling stable, making friends.

Sometimes, the integration stage also means having adult children, going to college, owning property, starting a business or an organization, taking risks, taking control. In my case, these pieces of the integration process were all still to come in the winter of 1976 to '77. By then, I also wasn't thinking much about the grief I'd left unresolved. I was looking ahead, drawing energy from my surroundings, and becoming the woman, the educator, the person I wanted to be.

CHAPTER XII
Welcome to Arlington

In November 1976, there were more than 2,400 non-English-speaking students in Arlington's public schools: 1,235 at the elementary level and 538 at the secondary level. It was just the beginning of a migration tsunami that would continue to transform Arlington County and the entire Northern Virginia region.

Spanish- and Korean-speaking families were already present in large numbers by the time the *Lau* decision was handed down, but the end of the war in Vietnam caused demand for bilingual education in Arlington County to soar. In the face of exploding opposition at home and the failure of the US military strategy on the battlefield, most American ground forces had been withdrawn from South Vietnam by the fall of 1972. The Paris Peace Accords were signed in January 1973, and from then on, it was a matter of time before the South Vietnamese army succumbed to the forces of the North.

The winding down of the war left all of Indochina in turmoil. Phnom Penh, the capital of Cambodia, fell to the communist Khmer Rouge on April 17, 1975, and less than two weeks later, on April 30, tanks from the People's Republic of Vietnam breached the last remaining defenses around Saigon, and vanguards of the North Vietnamese Army entered the city, killing as they went.

In Cambodia, a genocide resulting in the deaths of up to three million people at the hands of notorious dictator and butcher Pol Pot began almost immediately. Anyone suspected of ideological impurity or who had been among the ruling classes—meaning doctors, lawyers, teachers, anyone with even modest wealth or education—was either imprisoned in a gulag of "reeducation camps" out in the countryside, where death from starvation or summary execution was rampant, or killed outright.

In the months and weeks prior to its final, chaotic withdrawal from Saigon, the United States helped with the evacuation of some South Vietnamese: diplomats, people with connections or close ties to the US military effort, and so on. But their number was relatively small. Fear verging on terror gripped those who remained behind, especially people living in and around the capital, and most especially those who could be accused of collaborating with the Americans or the South Vietnamese government. Images of desperate men and women, even children, clinging to the struts of US helicopters, begging for a way out, are burned into the memory of anyone who lived through that time.

Most of those first arrivals were resettled in the Washington, DC, area. Refugees fleeing deprivation, persecution, and violence at the hands of the new communist government in a unified Vietnam would arrive over the next half dozen years, many of them carrying trauma that was seared into their DNA: personal loss, separation from their families, witnessing the death of loved ones, wounds to their bodies and minds.

The second wave of refugees were the so-called "boat people" who took extreme personal risks at sea, leaving behind everything they'd known in search of freedom and safety for themselves, their children, their elderly parents. In those early years, many of them came to Arlington, in numbers so great that the Clarendon neighborhood where they first resettled, established businesses, spoke their language, and began to reassemble pieces of their lives and cultures soon became known as Little Saigon.

I was stepping into this tidal wave, but I didn't see how powerful it was at first. I just knew I'd come to a place where my skills and experience could be put to use in ways that seemed to fit my ambitions and dreams. My first task was to establish bilingual programs in Spanish at the two elementary schools—Key and Patrick Henry—where the bulk of Spanish-speaking students were concentrated.

There were two federally funded positions, one serving Spanish-speaking students and the other for Korean speakers. John Park directed the Korean program, and we became close colleagues and friends almost immediately. Our struggles were similar as we sought to build innovative bilingual programs from the ground up, with no precedent, in a politically conservative county where the school board was still appointed by the board of supervisors.

Fortunately, Superintendent Larry Cuban was supportive, and John and I both leaned heavily on his support. When I was appointed, one of the members of the school board asked Larry, "Does she speak English?" To which he answered, "As well as you do." My first office was in a locker room adjacent to the gym at Patrick Henry, and when Larry saw it for the first time, he wrote me a funny but encouraging note—something about great work coming out of small spaces. Without him, I don't know that I could have made it through those first few years. Because resistance came from other places too.

Ahead of the surge in migration, Arlington had been losing population in the early to mid-'70s, and some schools were forced to close due to lack of enrollment. At the same time, more than twenty years after *Brown v. Board*, desegregation in the public schools of Arlington remained relatively new. The county and its White leadership were still adjusting to the idea when I arrived, and like other localities around the country, they turned to the busing of African American students as a strategy for complying with mandates they did not always warmly embrace. Five years earlier, the Supreme Court had affirmed in the case of *Swann v. Charlotte-Mecklenburg Board of Education* that federal courts (and therefore local school systems) could use busing as a tool to achieve racial balance in the public schools.

In Arlington, the school board's plan was that schools in the African American neighborhoods of Nauck, Halls Hill, and Arlington Heights would close; the students there would be enrolled in other (formerly all-White) schools; and the school buildings in these Black neighborhoods would be turned into community centers or would house "choice programs" like the ones established at Drew Elementary and H. B. Woodlawn High School. These programs tended to serve wealthier families.

Other features of the plan included a limit of no more than twenty African American students in any grade in any single school. Not surprisingly, many members of Arlington's Black community were less than thrilled with this arrangement.

Prior to desegregation, African American schools with African American teachers had been keystones of the Black community. This was true in many places, not just in Arlington. The teachers were familiar figures, neighbors who enjoyed wide respect. They shopped at stores in their neighborhoods and were members of local church congregations and part of the glue that held their communities together. As such, they were invested in their students' success on multiple levels, personal as well as professional. In many cases, they knew their students' parents and grandparents by their first names.

And so, for many Black families, Arlington's desegregation plan represented a loss. As community schools disappeared, relationships between teachers and the families of their students also disappeared. Among a host of other irritants, Arlington's desegregation plan also made it harder for some Black parents to attend school functions, simply because of the distances involved.

In this charged environment, I was not always warmly welcomed by my African American colleagues, especially at Patrick Henry. And I could well understand their question: "We've been in Arlington as long as many of the White families. So how is it that when *our* children still aren't getting what they need, Arlington is now providing *extra* resources for the Spanish-speaking kids?"

At the same time, the school board didn't want—and in fact actively discouraged hiring—teachers whose first language was not English. Some members expressed their "concerns" openly, seeing no need to hide the bias they held against "foreigners." We had "accents," and they feared these accents would be an impediment to teaching "all students"—which could be fairly understood as code for "White students."

The United States had seen this pattern before: the xenophobia, the prejudice against people coming here from other places. Why should Arlington be immune? But I was seeing it for myself now, both first- *and* secondhand. I was seeing it in the way that Arlington County took steps—shrewd, manipulative steps in some cases—to rid itself of perceived threats posed by the foreign-born.

An example: In the mid-'70s, Arlington's Korean children attended Fort Myer and Abington Elementary Schools. Shortly after John Park and I started working in the county, the Fairlington apartment buildings where many of these families lived were rezoned and then sold for "redevelopment" for condominiums, all of them at practically the same time. The older, less expensive residential apartments were upgraded to higher-priced residences; in response, most of the Korean families, priced out of the Arlington housing market, moved west into Fairfax County, and the Fort Myer school was closed.

This was not the first and it would not be the last time Arlington County took a step like this, to remove a target group of people using legal but morally questionable means. In this case, the victims were Koreans. Watching it happen took me back to my years in Bolivia, reawakening that old feeling of injustice and my empathy with those in need.

It also triggered a commitment to resist injustice with activism—an activism that became one of the most important threads in my life journey, although, once again, I had no idea where this impulse was leading. I just knew it was something I couldn't deny.

I started systematically convening groups of Latino parents. This was partly to support what was happening in the classrooms—to make sure these parents fully understood the work we were doing and endorsed it—and partly to demonstrate that we saw their roles as crucial in their children's education. In many cases, this represented a drastic change from their home countries, where parents were expected *not* to be involved directly in their children's schools.

In those years, Cubans dominated Latino politics in Arlington, working through an organization called El Comité Hispano. I learned about this organization from one of the Teacher Corps staff members at Key Elementary, Dama Vasquez, who was then serving on the Comité's board of directors. Dama suggested that I start attending their meetings and learning about their work.

I took her advice and was welcomed by the group's president, Luis Vidaña, who had been a senator in Cuba before he and his family fled to avoid persecution (or worse) by the Castro regime. Remember that many—perhaps most—of the Cubans who came to this country, especially in the early years, were from the wealthiest, best-educated classes. They favored policies that supported business interests, entrepreneurship in particular, and most of them were fervently anticommunist, meaning that they tended to align with more conservative political interests in the US and were suspicious of "the Left."

Luis encouraged me to volunteer. His wife, Marta, was the head of the Comprehensive Employment and Training Act's (CETA) Arlington office, and she was curious about me, perhaps a little suspicious, although I didn't understand her reasons at the time. I just knew that the Comité had experienced great success in mobilizing Hispanic voters—Luis would load scores of people on a truck and bring them to the polls—and that he and Marta had close connections to the county board and staff. I was eager to be involved.

It's a testament to the political skills of the Comité's leadership that Arlington County at the time was providing it with funding *and* an office, where Spanish-speaking people could go to get translation and interpretation services and apply for jobs. The office also provided English classes and job training, and at first the Comité seemed to be natural allies in the work I was doing—and wanted to do.

But there were murmurings. Some of the Latino parents complained to me that the Vidañas had their favorites, preferring to address the needs of the Cuban community over others'. Still, after several months working as a volunteer and getting to know people in the organization, I was invited to join the Comité's board.

About the same time, I met a man named Andres Tobar, who became a close friend and supporter and who, decades later, served as my campaign manager when I ran for the Arlington County School Board. Andres was born in California, the son of first-generation Mexican immigrants, and in the late '70s, he was a federal employee administering multiple programs within the US Department of Education's Office of Postsecondary Education.

When I met him, Andres was also serving as a regional vice president of the League of United Latin American Citizens (LULAC), which was then--and is still--the largest Latin American civil rights organization in the country. In the early 1990s he went on to become national vice president as well as chairman of LULAC's National Education Committee.

Andres understood the complexity of the Latino community, the particular challenges faced by migrant families, and the value of bilingual education in and for the public schools. With his help, I founded a LULAC council in Arlington, but that was a bit later. In the shorter term, it didn't take long for tensions to emerge within El Comité Hispano. I was self-assured and a little outspoken, and the Vidañas began to resist my influence.

I don't question their commitment to Latino causes, but they were strongly invested in seeing that new arrivals joined their programs.

They understood, rightly, that learning English is a key ingredient of success for immigrants, and while the bilingual programs we were pioneering at APS were in no way antithetical to this goal, I think they saw my work as a threat.

It took me a while to realize what was happening inside the Comité. I was still politically naive, believing that most people—especially those involved in the work of supporting immigrants—were acting from a place of idealism and service, not self-interest. I would go to meetings of the Comité and open my heart, only to have the Vidañas or their supporters report what I was saying to my supervisors at APS.

It's true that I was pushing hard, and at one point I got into hot water by bringing a group of Latino parents to a county board meeting to advocate for the funding of our bilingual programs. Larry Cuban wasn't happy; neither was my immediate supervisor, Marie Djouadi. And I understand the reasons now. I'd gone directly to the county board when I should have worked through the superintendent's office and the board of education; but I was impatient. I wanted results. I wanted to do whatever was required to help these students and their families.

The final break occurred over the issue of creating a bilingual GED program. As part of the course work I was doing with Martha Rashid at GWU, I designed a project to interview Latino mothers about their educational and job-training needs. The message coming out of the interviews was undeniable: these parents, most of whom had not graduated from high school in their home countries, desperately wanted to continue their own education alongside their children's. And to me, the need was obvious.

I saw how bright they were, how much they wanted to continue learning. But the only place to take GED-preparation classes in Spanish was in DC. Transportation and other factors made this difficult for many parents living in Arlington. Few had cars of their own, and many were working two or more jobs anyway. But if they could find a way to get the GED, their job prospects—and thus their economic situations and the lives of their families—would improve.

The Vidañas were opposed. Therefore, the Comité was opposed. I was in trouble with Marie Djouadi over reports that I'd been complaining about APS in Comité board meetings. It was clear that trust had broken down between the Vidañas and me; and so Dama Vasquez and I resigned from El Comité Hispano together. We wrote our separate resignation letters, brought them to the meeting, and promptly left.

The Vidañas immediately set about working to discredit us. I shared my resignation letter with Marie Djouadi and with Superintendent Cuban, who told me not to worry about it. Seeing that my position with the public schools was secure and they weren't going to fire me, Marta Vidaña began reaching out to the Latino parents in what can only be described as a campaign of disinformation. She told them that if they enrolled in a bilingual GED program, they could not continue to receive job-placement benefits through the CETA office, which wasn't true; but as often happens in these situations, the parents were afraid of losing what they had, and that fear made them cautious about standing up—whether to question, disagree, or advocate for something more.

We offered to help prepare them to take the test. The seed had been planted, and I wasn't about to be defeated. The need was too strong. I would find a way to create a bilingual GED program; and the momentum of this effort was boosted by two factors, one organizational, one very close to home.

I worked with a new coalition of Hispanic Americans employed in the federal government called IMAGE of Virginia. The purpose was to recruit more Latinos into government service, and education was crucial to success in this effort, at all levels. For me, it was the dawning of what became a lifelong commitment to social activism and political advocacy—of refusing to accept defeat in the face of a pressing need for change.

I then recruited the members of IMAGE to help make the case for the bilingual GED.

At the same time, my sister Anneliese moved to Virginia from Bolivia. She was twenty years old, her English was limited, and she started English classes right away. She hadn't graduated from high school back home, but she was hungry for education and saw its value in practical as well as personal terms. She enrolled in the DC program and passed the GED.

Now the issue had planted its feet firmly in the soil of my own family. The logistical challenges my younger sister faced in attending GED-prep classes in DC were formidable, but we could manage them. Not all families could. The question I kept asking was "Why isn't this an option in Virginia?"

I doubled down on my efforts. I had the stories from my graduate school research. I had support from some Arlington colleagues and from inside the federal government, through IMAGE. And now I had the example of my own sister. I could make the case powerfully, and I did.

Efforts by the leaders of El Comité Hispano to undermine the idea hadn't worked; in fact, they backfired, especially with the parents who knew and trusted me. And by this time, the Vidañas were losing influence anyway, preparing to leave Arlington for Miami. The hour had come; the time was right. Superintendent Cuban gave his blessing, the board of education agreed, and just like that, Arlington County created the first bilingual GED program in Virginia.

I still see the creation of this program as one of the most important and far-reaching accomplishments of my life.

During most of the Carter presidency, federal funding for new initiatives in public education was relatively abundant, and this included funds for bilingual education. The CETA program provided jobs and job training. There were also reading-intervention programs like Right to Read and a Teacher Corps program funded under the Higher Education Act, designed to prepare bilingual education teachers.

This program was just starting up when I arrived at Arlington Public Schools. Trinity College (now Trinity University) and the public schools collaborated in the preparation and placement of teachers. MA-degree students were interning at Key Elementary and Wakefield High Schools, and we had bilingual interns in Spanish and Vietnamese. The program was so successful that several of its interns became long-term members of the APS faculty.

Federal funding was obviously no guarantee of success in these or any other programs, but we relied on it.

As I settled into the work, I felt that I was moving away from the years of disappointment and personal loss. This feeling was driven largely by the joy of the work I was doing with Martha Rashid—work that spoke to many of the deepest impulses I'd carried with me, some since early childhood, and that also challenged me in ways I found exhilarating. I was working during the day and taking classes at night, and the two meshed perfectly. They reinforced one another.

I was also happy in my relationship with Jim. We'd been carrying on our long-distance relationship for months when I found myself in the emergency room. I'd been bleeding, and the examination found I had a tubular pregnancy. I recovered, but this experience forced the issue: Were we going to get married?

The weekend relationship was wearing thin for both of us. Jim still hadn't finished his dissertation, but he got a two-year contract for a nontenured position teaching economics at George Mason University in Fairfax, which had one of the hottest young economics departments in the country. It seemed like time to take the next step as a couple.

We both knew we wanted a child. I'd had two miscarriages with Gonzalo, now a tubular pregnancy, and my periods had been irregular all my life. We decided to see a fertility specialist at Johns Hopkins, who told me to come back after my next period—which never arrived. Three months after the visit, in late March, I discovered I was already four months pregnant.

It was a Sunday. Jim and I were on our way to afternoon Mass, and I turned around to get something out of the back seat. I felt a strong pull from deep inside, and in that moment, I remembered something my mother had told me many years before: that this kind of pulling sensation could be an indication.

I wasn't thinking about getting pregnant since I'd had so much trouble conceiving in the past, but the next day we went to the drugstore, got an over-the-counter pregnancy test, went back to the apartment at Southern Towers, took the test, and it was positive.

I was overjoyed. Jim was too. I called my mother in Bolivia and told her I might be pregnant and that Jim and I were planning to get married in the summer anyway. We agreed she would not come to the wedding but would be there soon after the baby arrived, to help out.

I called an obstetrician. I had to wait several weeks to get an appointment, and I went alone; Jim was in Staunton for the end of the spring semester. The doctor showed me the sonogram. I saw the baby's heart beating. I wept—tears of joy this time, not grief. The dream I'd had for so many years, of bearing children, being a mother, building and nourishing a family, it looked like it was all coming true. All of it was within reach now.

Jim finished his classes at Mary Baldwin and moved with me into a larger, two-bedroom apartment at Southern Towers. He was loving and thoughtful. We bought a house on Military Road using a preferred interest loan I qualified for as Al's widow, so the deed was in my name. We got married in August, and our son, James, was born on October 25.

In the late 1970s, the Arlington County School Board was extremely conservative, and so were many members of the staff, Larry Cuban being one notable exception. There were only a few bilingual staff outside the dedicated programs and only a few colleagues who could fairly be described as progressive. It was still a rock-hard system in some ways. But there was room for movement too, and the needs and opportunities were about to increase exponentially with the arrival of refugees from Indochina and, a few years later, the waves of migration from Guatemala, Honduras, Nicaragua, El Salvador, and eventually all parts of the world.

By the spring of 1978, Vietnamese were arriving in Arlington in much larger numbers. Similar waves of Lao and Cambodian refugees followed soon after. Todd Endo had secured another grant, this time to support the position of secondary coordinator of bilingual education, and I applied. My being pregnant was not supposed to make a difference in the hiring process, since it had nothing to do with my qualifications; but I think it probably did.

I was one of seven finalists, but I didn't get the job. The stated reason was that I was "Spanish" (actually, I was Bolivian) and would therefore be "too focused on Latino students." The office secretary showed me the memo to that effect. I was angry; that old hatred of injustice reared its head like a cobra. So I went to the personnel department, talked to the director, and told him that I intended to file a grievance against APS and the county if the decision was not reversed.

He reviewed the case, reconsidered, and decided that I would be hired.

Marie Djouadi wasn't happy. A former nun who had earned a PhD in linguistics from Georgetown, she was a skilled organizer and excellent at supervising classes, but she was known to have unrealistically high expectations of her staff, and she was never wholeheartedly in support of bilingual education anyway. The truth is, I think she was still holding on to some resentment about the ways I'd chosen to involve the community, the parents, in our bilingual education work. She was a by-the-book educator unprepared for the changes happening around us. I respected her but never considered her a friend.

One of the first actions I took in my new position was to hire Nguyen Bich—himself a refugee who had experienced severe trauma—as a secondary resource specialist for bilingual education in Vietnamese. I also hired my old friend John Park as the Korean resource teacher; he spoke Korean *and* Spanish. Together, we created a new "intake center" at Wakefield High School to register all non-English-speaking students at the secondary level.

We had a staff of just five people, including Bich and myself, and the work ahead of us would have been overwhelming under any circumstances. But Marie told us we couldn't even begin registering these students until *after* I returned from maternity leave. I had barely five weeks of leave under APS guidelines, which put us into the holidays, and therefore, practically speaking, into the spring semester of 1979. There was no paid maternity leave; I had to use sick leave and unpaid absence.

The stipulation was a not-too-subtle way of applying pressure. You could also say that it was not-so-passively aggressive. Either way, it added huge weight to the challenge of balancing graduate studies, new motherhood, a marital relationship, and the demands of a thriving career. But I was up to the challenge, and I loved the work, even though—with the exception of Larry Cuban—the school administration was not welcoming to a Latina administrator. I was helping my fellow immigrants. I could apply the lessons I was learning in the real world of public education to my graduate studies, and vice versa.

That first semester, we had 300 Spanish-speaking students coming through the intake center, along with many students speaking Vietnamese, Farsi, Korean, and other languages. Arlington Public Schools was on the verge of creating, then adopting, a pair of new and exciting approaches to bilingual education that would define much of my work over the next fifteen years: English for speakers of other languages (ESOL) and high-intensity language training (HILT).

We were about to embark on a journey that would create a national model, and the timing was impeccable. The work that lay ahead wouldn't have succeeded if we'd started ten years earlier or later; and I don't think it could have been done anywhere else in Virginia *except* Arlington County at that time.

All the pieces were in place. When the door swung wide open, I rushed through it, eager to create—without having the words for it at the time—a "community of learners," one that included teachers, parents, and students. It was the beginning of my life's work. I was swimming in the tsunami.

CHAPTER XIII
The Shifting Landscape

The idea of teaching English as a second language wasn't new in Arlington in the late '70s. The county had a program in the 1960s at Washington-Lee (now Washington-Liberty) High School, but the number of students was small. In July 1975, there were ESOL classes at the newly opened Career Center, and APS had two half-time positions devoted to teaching English-language learners: one for the elementary grades, the other for secondary. A high-intensity language program was offered at Wakefield High School for all high school students who needed an intensive English as a second language program.

But the landscape was changing fast.

The first wave of refugee students, primarily from Vietnam, were mostly educated to grade level but were not English-proficient. The second wave, including the Vietnamese "boat people," as well as refugees from Cambodia and Laos, were often *not* educated to grade level and did not speak English; and some of them had grown up in camps or in hiding and had never been to school at all.

It's important to be clear about the words we use. Being an immigrant is not the same as being a refugee, at least as far as US government policy is concerned. Refugees, according to the 1951 Refugee Convention and US law, are migrants seeking entry to another country who can demonstrate that they've been persecuted or have reason to fear persecution based on their race, religion, nationality, political opinion/affiliation, or membership in a particular social group. The United States has a well-developed pipeline for receiving and resettling people who enter the country as refugees. There are resettlement services available to them that are not available to most other migrants.

"Immigrant" is a term used broadly to describe people who leave their homes and cross international borders seeking economic opportunity or to escape some form of hardship. Those who come without formal refugee status generally must rely on friends, family members, or the community to help them get established.

After World War II, the US passed its first legislation governing refugees, accepting approximately 650,000 Europeans who had been displaced by the war. Thirty-five years later, the US Refugee Admissions Program was created through the Refugee Act of 1980; in those intervening years, the acceptance of refugees occurred on a more or less *ad hoc* basis, often in response to mass migrations, such as the flight of large numbers of people from Indochina following the end of the Vietnam conflict.

The 1980 law established procedures for vetting, admitting, and resettling refugees. The number of refugees admitted each year has fluctuated widely since then—from 200,000 in 1980 to 25,465 in 2022—and at times the program has been suspended altogether, as in the months following the September 11 attacks.

But it's more complicated than that. For example, many of the people who came to this country from Central America in the 1980s were refugees in the sense that they were escaping war and political violence in their home countries, seeking refuge in the United States. They had been the targets of persecution, even death, but they didn't enter through the established refugee channels, they were not part of whatever quotas were in effect when they arrived, and their status has been ambiguous since then as a result.

Regardless of formal immigration status, and with or without "documents," the Supreme Court's *Plyer vs. Doe* decision clearly established that immigrant children have a right to education in America's public schools and that it's the responsibility of states and localities to provide it.

That was the broader challenge Arlington Public Schools was facing when I arrived in 1976. The special challenge was how to provide a strong educational foundation to children who arrived speaking little or no English.

Shortly after Ronald Reagan became president in January 1981, the US Department of Education suspended the *Lau* mandates for bilingual education, but the other requirements outlined in the Supreme Court's decision remained in effect. Strong voices at every level—federal, state, local—were arguing for English-only instruction. Bilingual education faded and ESOL took its place, using HILT as the instructional framework.

Larry Cuban was still the superintendent, but he soon resigned under pressure from the conservative school board, taking a teaching position at Stanford. His successor, Charles Nunley, wanted the word "bilingual" removed from my job title immediately; and the chair of the school board at the time, Claude Hilton, said publicly, "I don't want to see that B-word anyplace."

In Richmond, state legislators and the state board of education went on record as supporting English-only instruction, and the school board in neighboring Fairfax County agreed.

Elsewhere in the state, it was not as much of an issue in the early '80s because the number of non-English-speaking students was much smaller. But in Arlington, we were no longer allowed to teach, for example, US history in Spanish or Vietnamese.

Context is important, and what was taking place in Arlington wasn't happening in isolation. Public education has been—and still is today—a key battleground in the so-called "culture wars." Another battleground is immigration policy, and the two have been closely linked ever since the *Lau* decision.

E pluribus unum is our national motto, prominent on the Great Seal of the United States. It means "From many, one." This might seem like a benign, even idealistic concept in the abstract; but the question of who we are as a people and how the history of the country is represented and transmitted to younger generations often acts as a wedge, dividing the country along ideological lines. People want and expect different things from our educational system; they want and expect different outcomes.

Two years after President Reagan took office and suspended the *Lau* mandates, the US National Commission on Excellence in Education chaired by Secretary of Education Terrell Bell issued its landmark report titled *A Nation at Risk: The Imperative for Educational Reform*. The most widely quoted passage from that report reads as follows: "The educational foundations of our society are presently being eroded by a rising tide of mediocrity that threatens our very future as a Nation and a people. . . . If an unfriendly power had attempted to impose on America the mediocre educational performance that exists today, we might well have viewed it as an act of war."

The report said American public schools were "failing" and called for "rigorous and measurable standards"; and in so doing, it ignited a push for educational reform at the local, state, and national levels. After that, it was hard to identify a campaign for elective office anywhere in the country where the alleged failings of America's public schools were *not* an issue.

Two books, both published in 1987, seized on this fear of national decline. One was *Cultural Literacy: What Every American Needs to*

Know by University of Virginia English professor E. D. Hirsch; the other, *The Closing of the American Mind* by philosopher Allan Bloom of the University of Chicago. Both advocated strongly for a return to "basics" in education and against the threat they said was posed by multiculturalism.

Then, in 1993, former state delegate George Allen was elected governor of Virginia. He immediately declared his intention to create Standards of Learning (SOL) that would hold teachers and local school systems throughout Virginia accountable by testing their students' achievement at regular, established intervals.

The first iteration of the Virginia SOL was adopted by the state board of education in 1997. Its effect was to disempower classroom teachers and to short-circuit their autonomy and creativity by forcing them to "teach to the test." Thousands of dedicated and experienced teachers across the state left the profession in the years following adoption of the SOL. Meanwhile, Allen's political stock soared, and for a while he looked to have a credible shot at the Republican nomination for president in 2000.

His critique of public education in Virginia added fuel to a nationally growing fire. Everywhere, it seemed, public school teachers were accused of promoting not just mediocrity but a liberal agenda; and the mania for testing and "accountability" was firmly entrenched.

Still to come was the passage of the No Child Left Behind Act in January 2002, a signature piece of legislation in the first term of George W. Bush's presidency. No Child Left Behind expanded the federal role in education. Like Virginia's Standards of Learning, it emphasized accountability, testing, and outcome-based evaluation. It also mandated a national standardized test to be administered annually to all students in every jurisdiction receiving federal funds.

The legislation left each state free to develop its own set of standards. But overall, the result was the same as in Virginia. In many cases, teachers simply no longer had the time to follow the trail of an exciting classroom discussion or to introduce material and concepts that were not directly related to the standards.

It was in this shifting environment that we began the work of creating a "community of learners," pushing the boundaries of what seemed possible. We did it with a cadre of some of the best and most dedicated teachers in the profession, with help from a supportive administration, and in a brief window of time when we were granted the freedom to innovate.

And this is also true: No teachers or administrators, however gifted and committed to the task of bilingual education, could have done what we did without the active engagement of the students' parents and families—or without first imagining the child.

CHAPTER XIV
Imagine a Child

I magine a child. A boy or a girl, it could be either. When I close my eyes, I see a girl of nine or ten. I'll call her Thao, which in Vietnamese means "grass" or "herbs."

Imagine that Thao has spent four days in the ocean in a small, leaky boat filled with strangers. She's thirsty and her face and lips ache from the sunburn, but she thanks God that her mother, her grandmother, and her younger brother are with her. She knows that many other children just like her have made this same journey, sometimes alone, or maybe carrying an infant brother or sister, and that many who began this journey did not survive it.

Thao hasn't seen her father since he went into hiding when the soldiers from the North rolled into Saigon three years before. She doesn't know if he's alive. After she and her family fled their home in the city, they lived for a while in the forest, then in a detention camp near the coast. They drank water from a ditch and ate rats cooked in kettles over an open fire. Then, one night, word came: There was a boat waiting. And they ran while the guards were sleeping. The only light was the stars, and Thao and her grandmother both fell many times.

Her grandmother has an ugly purple bruise on her cheekbone and can barely move her arm. But they're alive. They made it to the sea. They've heard that somewhere out there is an American ship that will take them to the Philippines.

Only one man in the boat knows how to swim. The ocean is

rough, but they've been lucky; there hasn't been a storm. The first day, they ate the pieces of dried fruit they brought with them, and the next night a raw fish that someone caught in a net and gave to them. Since then, they've eaten nothing. Thao is hungry, but she's not worried about that; she's worried about her grandmother, who is pale and listless. Their clothes are all soaking wet.

Thao has seen her little brother beaten by the camp guards. She watched a woman in their boat be raped by pirates and thrown into the sea. She's seen people die, many people, back in the camp. One of them a boy she knew well.

But now there it is—an enormous gray ship, with flags, and guns, and a small boat with a motor and a towline coming out to meet them.

And now, her eyes focus. Thao is sitting at a desk, in an elementary school in Arlington, Virginia, surrounded by other children laughing and speaking a language she hears but doesn't understand.

Now imagine a high school just a few miles away from where Thao is sitting. Imagine another child, a boy of fifteen; call him Fernando. Fernando is from a small town called Las Marias in the north of El Salvador, in the Cabanas Department near the border with Honduras. Like Thao, he has also been a refugee.

Two years ago, soldiers from the notorious Atl*a*catl Battalion, trained in the School of the Americas and funded by the United States, conducted what they called a "sweep" in that part of Cabanas, an area that had already been the target of death squads and paramilitary units of the Salvadoran government.

Fernando's family were peasants who grew coffee on land they didn't own. When he was ten years old, 77 percent of the arable land in El Salvador was owned by .01 percent of the population. It was the Cold War era, fear of communism was rampant, and all across Central America there were struggles between those seeking land reform and greater economic equality and those who wanted to protect the status quo.

Beginning in the late 1970s and continuing throughout the

1980s, the government of El Salvador and its paramilitary units, some of them sponsored by the CIA, murdered union leaders, students, teachers, journalists, priests—anyone suspected of sympathizing with the Left. In March 1980, they killed an archbishop, Oscar Romero, after he wrote an open letter to President Jimmy Carter, urging him to suspend aid to the Salvadoran regime; and then government-sponsored snipers shot forty-two mourners at his funeral. Eight months later, members of the El Salvador National Guard raped and murdered four Catholic women, three of whom were nuns, part of the Maryknoll Sisters and Ursuline Sisters orders.

The government's broader strategy was to "drain the sea" by displacing or killing peasants in the countryside, even innocent people like Fernando and his family, thereby emptying out the land and squelching support for leftist guerrillas. Fernando's father fled to the United States just before the El Mozote massacre, another "sweep" in the nearby department of Morazán in which more than a thousand men, women, and children were murdered. The soldiers were given orders to "kill everyone." Some of the dead were decapitated with a homemade guillotine.

In one respect, Fernando, his mother, and his four younger brothers and sisters were the lucky ones. They survived. But they couldn't go back home, so they entered a makeshift refugee camp on the Honduran border, a place where starvation and disease were facts of daily life. One day, Fernando decided he would leave and join his father in the United States.

Like Thao, he left at night, walking, not running down a dirt road where eventually he caught a bus. He crossed the border somewhere near Laredo, Texas—crossing was easier then; and even though he spoke no English, he somehow made his way to Virginia, where he found his father, whom he hadn't seen in four years, living in Arlington with a new wife and a new baby.

Fernando hasn't been to school, anywhere, since he was ten years old. At fifteen, he's ready to enter high school, but he's reading at the fourth-grade level—in Spanish. He knows about a dozen words of English, he has no money, his father's new wife doesn't want him, and he still wakes up at night in a cold sweat, gasping for breath, remembering.

A friend told me once, "Emma, education is your DNA," and I think he was probably right. But at the heart of my passion for education lies the question: What can I do? How can I change the rules to shift the balance toward equality of opportunity, toward removing every obstacle to a student's success, regardless of whether the obstacle lies on the outside or within?

The DNA molecule is made up of two linked strands that wind around each other like twisting ladders, which is a pretty good image of the way my professional life developed after I came to Arlington. One "ladder" was the work with K12 students and their families at Arlington Public Schools; the other was my graduate work and everything that flowed from it, culminating in a dissertation that focused on different cognitive and learning styles and their impact on limited English proficiency (LEP) students, immigrants and refugees in particular.

The intersection of these two strands and the interplay between them pointed the way forward in my journey as an educator. It started in the fall of 1978 when I became the secondary coordinator of bilingual education for Arlington Public Schools and continued through my more than twenty years as supervisor for K12 ESOL and HILT programs, system-wide.

The *Lau* Remedies required localities to provide programs that would help non-English-speaking students become proficient in English. They also required bilingual instruction in the students' native languages; ESL programs with bilingual assistance; and procedures for following and measuring student progress. Beyond these general requirements, there was little guidance on *how* to accomplish what the mandates required, so we had to create our own system.

Oversight was to be provided by the US Office of Civil Rights, and Arlington Public Schools was one of two school systems in the country selected for "intense scrutiny." The other was Dade County, Florida.

When a student arrives as most of the Indochinese and Central American students did in those years, fleeing war and violence, safety is the first priority. Learning comes second; but in my experience, many parents placed a very high priority on their children's education. We quickly came to see the parents as vitally important participants in a community of learners.

We needed to first create an environment that was welcoming to the parents as well as to the students, and then to think holistically about ways to keep these parents engaged. One of the first steps we took was to begin forming parent associations.

Fundamental to our early success was Nguyen Bich. Bich was a journalist and poet, a gifted organizer with strong empathetic qualities, and a leader within the wider Vietnamese community. He was also a survivor, which gave him a deep understanding of what many of the Vietnamese families had lived through and the wounds they were carrying, as well as a level of "street cred" in the community.

My experience with newcomers to this country is that most of them are grateful to be here. They want to contribute when and however they can—to be part of the larger community, not separate from it. Bich understood this too. He also understood the breadth of their need and how difficult it can be for someone in the early stages of acculturation and assimilation. And he knew, firsthand, what experiencing violence and trauma can do to a person's psyche and how the residues of trauma seep into every aspect of daily life. Bich later wrote: "We helped [the] parents when some got into trouble with the police. We went to court, to jails. We had to worry about everything—shelter, food, eyeglasses."

I felt a personal connection to the Vietnamese and immense respect for them. They were victims of war, but most of them bore no hard feelings. They were gentle, humble, eager to help. They were grateful that their children's schools were safe. Most were Buddhist, and they were respectful of the teachers. They accepted their situation and, for the most part, adapted easily to change. But in general they were not as keen on the idea of bilingual education: They wanted their kids to learn English as quickly as possible.

Working with the Lao and Cambodian parents and students was more complicated. Many had spent months or years in squalid and dangerous refugee camps. And not surprisingly, some of them had been damaged by what they'd seen amid the genocidal actions of Pol Pot and the Khmer Rouge.

Again speaking generally (there were exceptions), the Lao-speaking parents were harder to reach than the Vietnamese. They stuck together. They were more tribal. The leader of the Lao community was a former general named Sananikone. He was highly respected in the Lao community; fortunately, he was receptive to what we were proposing.

From the beginning, our goal was 100 percent parent involvement. Working with the parent associations, we hosted back-to-school nights; we created bilingual guides to community services; we produced orientation handbooks in Spanish, Vietnamese, Lao, and Khmer and "cultural capsules" designed to help teachers and administrators understand, for example, differences in the way names are used within a culture to express and signal identity.

We also organized and hosted sessions on how to get help, on resources available through the county and how to access them. We created "memory quilts" to keep the memories of family and home alive and hosted multicultural conferences with exhibits, food, and performances. The pride these communities felt in coming together to express their identities and showcase their cultures was a gift to everyone who experienced it, including the teachers. It energized all of us.

Forming the Latino parent association was in some ways easier because, regardless of their country of origin, they all spoke Spanish. There were different dialects and accents, and the community networks were separate, obviously, but we didn't have to create an association for each country the way we did for the Vietnamese, Cambodian, and Lao families.

Looking back, I see the creation of these parent groups as a signature achievement and an essential step in building our community of learners. My way of creating change was to bring people together and in so doing identify and develop leaders who could advocate for themselves.

Emerging research demonstrated the importance of native language in cognitive development, which would eventually be a focus of my dissertation. But as educators, our hands were tied: We had to teach in English.

What could we do about a student who had never learned to read or write in his native language, much less in English? How did we begin to build that student's content knowledge while helping him or her to learn English through English-only instruction? It was a challenge without precedent in the experience of most educators. It required a shift in philosophy—a shift that would unleash tremendous creative energy and empower the community of learners we were hoping to build.

What we wanted to prove was that it's possible to teach, for example, relatively advanced third- and fourth-grade concepts using materials developed for grade one. To put this a different way, if you're trying to teach Virginia history to a fourth-grade student who is reading at a first-grade level, how many vocabulary words might be needed to accomplish this?

What we found, eventually, is that using simplified vocabulary and sentence structure helps to ground students who are reading at lower levels, but it doesn't have to compromise or forestall the presentation of more advanced content. This was a radical concept at the time, one born out of necessity and which presented a host of challenges, not the least of which was how to make sure that, in the process, older students weren't bored or insulted.

It was a challenge that Arlington's ESOL teachers savored and wholeheartedly embraced.

In the beginning, ESOL was targeted toward elementary students, while HILT started as a high-school-level program that eventually made its way to the middle and elementary grades. The simplest way to describe it is that HILT is an English-immersion program with content knowledge embedded in it.

Initially, the program focused on social studies, with the instruction organized around content "themes." One of these themes was Arlington as a community. Students learned that Arlington is a county within the state of Virginia within the United States of America and that it is governed by an elected board of supervisors with agencies or departments whose purposes are to address a wide range of community needs.

The goals of the HILT program were twofold: first, that each student would succeed academically, becoming proficient in English; and second, that each student would become a contributing member of the community. Learning about Arlington while learning English accomplished both.

We also recognized the need to adopt what later became known as a "whole child" approach. No other option made sense. The whole-child approach meant that we could not limit our involvement solely to instruction. We also had to consider each student's family situation, his nutritional needs, his fears, the trauma he had suffered, and his psyche, along with a host of practical concerns, including finances, navigating the legal system in some cases, and the myriad challenges that come with being in a new and unfamiliar place.

To do the work we were charged with doing, we had to uncover the uniqueness of each family's—and each student's—situation; and we had to teach with that unique situation in mind.

We faced some difficult decisions at the outset, such as whether to award high school credit for HILT classes and how to determine teacher qualifications. Remember that this was an entirely new approach, and *no one* had been formally trained in its methods. We also had to determine the best ways to oversee the program and evaluate its success.

Success came quickly on several fronts. Within a relatively short period, the program had its own supervisor, intake center, and planning framework. We were also free to develop and provide curricula, resource materials, strategies, assessments, and exit criteria, as well as workshops and classes for staff.

None of this was easy or instantaneous, and there were unexpected challenges. For example, the HILT and non-HILT students tended to self-segregate; there was an "us" and "them" mentality ("them" usually meant the HILT students). Sadly, even some of the teachers and administrators who were not affiliated with the program would speak dismissively about "those HILT kids."

But the program flourished and became recognized nationally, in part because we emphasized essential content concepts and because it was broad-based, offering English instruction in science and mathematics as well as language arts, reading, and social studies. It was an integrated style and method of instruction, and one that asked a great deal of the teachers.

The zenith of Arlington's ESOL/HILT program was in the early to mid-1990s, a time when the state SOL and related testing requirements did not yet exist. After that, the increased focus on testing lowered the morale of many educators. Students with limited English proficiency rarely did well on these tests and were thus considered "failures" by the system. As far as the state was concerned, it was the test scores that mattered, not the deeper values of education or our effectiveness at bridging cultures.

Eventually, we included SOL objectives in our HILT instruction. We had to. But testing in English when the student doesn't have the English-language skills to do well is misguided and self-defeating. I had seen this inherent testing bias before, in Bolivia. In the early years, in Arlington, we had our own assessments and rubrics and portfolio assessments demonstrating that our students were learning and making solid progress. But the SOL framework didn't differentiate between or account for varying levels of second-language acquisition. It is in some ways the antithesis of the whole-child approach.

We were fortunate that there were no existing guidelines or models for what we were attempting to do at the outset. A flood of creative energy was released to fill the void, and innovation and collaboration quickly became hallmarks of the program. Teachers thrive when they are involved in curriculum development—when they are free (and freed) to respond to the needs of their students.

Teachers were empowered. They were cutting a trail through the unknown. They could see a problem, devise a solution, and implement it. The superintendent, Larry Cuban, saw to it that the program was fully integrated within the division of instruction and that we had the funds we needed. Motivation soared. Working together, often on the weekends and in the summer months, teachers produced scores of program guides, curriculum units, activity books, and, later, integrated lesson plans based on the recognition of different learning styles, multiple intelligences, movement-based learning, and connecting with student families and communities.

Likewise, there were no ESOL certification requirements in Virginia at the time, so we developed our own hiring procedures and guidelines. Eventually, these served as the basis for the state guidelines for ESOL certification. But that was in the future.

I discovered I was very good at hiring people; it was my gift. At the start of the program, I hired Peace Corps veterans and teachers who already knew how to develop materials. All of them had prior ESOL teaching experience, and I was looking for people who had an intuitive grasp of what we were trying to do.

Teachers also needed to understand the cultural background of our students. We had bilingual resource educators who understood the cultures and languages of the students and who served as bridges between parents and teachers, but we also had to learn the personal background and previous schooling of each student.

This collaboration between and among teachers and with the students and their families was the realization of our dream to create a community of learners. The work became more than a vocation. It was a calling. Years later, many of the teachers still said it was the best job they'd ever had, the highlight of their careers.

The work with immigrant and refugee families uplifted me too. I was helping the children. I was helping the parents. And I identified with both. I could feel what the children felt because I remembered what it was like, being in a strange country, not knowing the language. I empathized with the parents and the relief they felt in being able to drop their child or children off at school, knowing they'd have books and caring teachers and that they would be safe that day.

As the supervisor, I was always in and out of the classrooms. I was seeing the students. I was observing the teachers, talking with the parents, building relationships. Things are different now. The supervisors are no longer in touch with the community, the parents. It's not their job to be in touch with them, and they don't have the time to build these relationships, even if they were inclined to do so. The administrative burden is too great. The focus has shifted from relationship-building and collaboration to a more transactional way of thinking.

The intake center started in a small room at Wakefield High School. As it grew, we recruited people who could speak the various languages, people who could conduct interviews with parents and ask the right questions about the sociocultural background of the student—such as "Has your son (or daughter) been separated from you? If so, for how long? How did he or she arrive in the US? What is the educational background of your child? Has your family spent time in a refugee camp? Are there family issues we should know about that might affect the student's outlook or performance?"

Students were tested in their native language and English. Center staff also explained to the parents how the educational system in Arlington worked.

Another strand in the braid of the community of learners was our university-level higher-education partners. At places like the Center for Applied Linguistics in DC, the University of Maryland, George Mason University, Trinity College, and Georgetown University, Arlington teachers worked directly with faculty to research, develop curricula, and take university courses on-site. There was reciprocity in these partnerships. Teachers played a role in shaping the kind of training they themselves and their future colleagues would receive, gaining valuable experience in the process. Universities knew that with K12 teacher input, local teachers were more likely to take the courses they were developing. It was a win-win arrangement.

On a personal level, I later began teaching courses at these institutions: Language Development at GW, Family Engagement at Trinity (in the Teacher Corps program), and Bilingualism and Foundations of Education at Georgetown, where I was helping to prepare teachers from all parts of the metro DC area. It was another way to serve the larger cause of uplifting public education and building strength within the teaching profession.

When the Central American students began arriving in large numbers, many came as so-called "unaccompanied minors." Like Fernando in the introduction to this chapter, some of them were older, in their late teens. Many hadn't been to school for years due to war, violence, or other circumstances.

When they arrived, these students had no choice but to start looking for work immediately; they had no other way to support themselves. The high schools often didn't want them because they were too far behind, so they would end up assigned to middle school or nowhere at all.

Imagine an eighteen-year-old in the fifth grade; and if they were older than eighteen, the principals and administrators would sometimes say, "They're adults. We don't have to educate them now." I would tell my colleagues, "These are our students. Picture what they had to go through just to be here, sitting in our classrooms. They are resilient people, and they bring a different kind of knowledge with them. We should see them as resources, not as burdens."

For those who had to work during the day but wanted to go to school—and there were many of these students—night school was the obvious choice. A high school continuation program was offered in the evenings at Arlington Mill, but the director of the program refused to accept anyone who wasn't comfortable speaking English.

There was an obvious need. I knew that if we could staff a program, the students would come, but we would have to pay the teachers comparable salaries and benefits and provide textbooks and other resources.

There was resistance at first, but eventually I convinced the school board to allocate the funds, and the county's first formal night-school program was established at Arlington Community High School.

These students would come to class at night after working all day. They would go home, shower, change clothes if they had extra clothes (some didn't), and show up for school. They were working as adults during the day, but when they came to class in the evening, it was like they were young people again. It would be hard to overstate how rewarding this was; it was yet another strand in our growing community of learners.

If I were to sum up the years we spent building one of the best, most innovative instructional programs in the country, riding the waves of migration, the changes in public policy and attitudes, and the impact of these changes on the ways our communities receive and welcome immigrants and refugees—if I were to boil it all down into one word, that word would be "service."

Service is an overused word with a complicated set of meanings, as I found out when I was in that Radford "helicopter," delivering books to Black children in the local community; but I do know that true service never flows just one way. The principle of reciprocity, of *ayni* in the Quechua language, is and must be at work, always, and it works through strong relationships like the ones we built.

While we had it, this community of learners united teachers, parents, administrators, academic experts, public officials, and the students themselves in a common cause, which was to "imagine" a child, the *whole* child; to understand her needs and the needs of her family; to imagine what that child could become, what she could dream of becoming, and then work to make it happen.

CHAPTER XV
"That's It!"—How Do Children Learn?

It's 1978, and I'm three semesters into my coursework at George Washington University. It's a spring night, warm outside and inviting, but I'm cloistered in the apartment in Southern Towers, facing down a stack of books, thinking about where to begin.

I've already chosen a major—human development—within the broader field of education, and I'm deeply interested in it, but tonight, I'm having trouble getting started. Instead of jumping into the reading, I'm sipping tea with the windows open, wondering as I have for weeks how this is all going to play out.

The courses are challenging. They're giving me a solid background, mapping out the landscape, so to speak. But soon I'll have to decide on a focus. You can't write a dissertation on human development; it's a vast field, and every PhD student eventually has to narrow it down.

One of the courses I'm taking is on cognitive development: How and when and in what ways do people learn? How does the architecture of the human brain develop? What are the stages? What are the forces at play? How does cognitive development differ between individuals? What are the well-traveled roads in understanding human cognition? And how much of it really is individual, a reflection of family circumstances, of the community and cultural environment in which the child is growing up?

These questions have all been researched by others. The ones I'm facing tonight are more personal. Where will I plant my dissertation work so it can take root and flower? And beyond just meeting an academic requirement, how will it make a difference in the lives of real people, especially the refugee and migrant children I'm working with at APS?

One of the books in the stack is called *Cultural Democracy, Bicognitive Development, and Education* by Manuel Ramírez and Alfredo Casteñada. The title is interesting, and for no particular reason—maybe I'm just drawn to the title—I pick it up.

The book is the end product of a study the authors undertook a year or two before, focusing on Mexican Americans. I start reading, and by the time I get to the end of the first chapter, I'm pacing the apartment, repeating out loud, "That's it, that's it."

The book links cognition and associated learning styles to cultural values and identity. It discusses how people who migrate are often leaving behind one set of cultural values while striving to adopt another in an effort to fit in. This blows the lid off the "melting pot" analogy that has long been the touchstone of the American myth and our collective thinking about immigration. For many people in power, it still colors how they think about immigrants.

Casteñada and Ramírez pose a new option: What if the immigrant doesn't have to choose between cultures after all? Can we conceive a new paradigm for "assimilation"—one that supports and affirms bicultural identity? And what if the public schools could actively work to acknowledge, honor, and reinforce this option?

I know immediately that I am looking at the future. And the beautiful thing is that what I'm reading isn't theoretical; it touches me personally because I already know I have two cultures; and how fortunate I am to be able to affirm and not be forced to suppress or deny it.

In the storm that was happening in my head that night, I saw clearly that a person can be bicultural and still be a United States citizen. I could also see—because I recognized it in the memory of my own childhood experience—that *how* a student learns is a product of home and community. That's what the authors were saying.

Their book was the spark, the beginning. It was also where I first encountered the terms that would move quickly into the center of my work, both in the dissertation and at Arlington Public Schools: "field dependent," which refers to working from a more expansive, global perspective; and "field independent," which is more analytical, more focused on individual experience and motivation.

I'd seen this dichotomy at work when I was testing rural teachers back in Bolivia. And I had seen it in myself: I was and am a strong "global" learner, less strong in situations that require analysis.

I realized that we have to teach both ways, not just one. We must understand, for example, that some students don't do as well as others on multiple-choice tests. Often, it's because these students tend to see global or bigger-picture relationships; they see how in different situations, more than one of the answers can be "right."

I knew intuitively, although I wasn't yet able to summon research proving it, that Latino children tend to be more global in their thinking; they absorb information directly and need to establish personal relationships with the teacher and their classmates. Which means that in a typical US classroom setting, they respond in ways that are different from many of their peers.

That night at Southern Towers, I felt like I'd discovered the key to a locked door. I saw how to weave the second strand of my DNA with the first. Both as a student and an educator, I'd entered a new phase.

When the time came to focus my graduate research, I was already immersed in working with LEP students, most of them recent immigrants and refugees. I knew how important family was to these students' progress, and I knew how crucial a person's first language is when he or she is trying to assimilate into another culture.

I also knew that most people coming to this country from abroad, regardless of their personal circumstances, *want* to learn English and are strongly motivated in that direction. But there are impediments in this process, as well as disparities in how children succeed in school. Some of these impediments and disparities, I now came to believe, were the result of differences in cognitive and learning styles.

In the United States, individualism, individual initiative, and individual achievement are part of our national mythology. The story of an individual overcoming formidable obstacles and achieving success through his own grit and determination takes many forms, but it permeates American culture in a way that few other stories do.

Not surprisingly, the design of the American educational system has long reflected these individualistic values, and that was also my experience. Students were encouraged to work independently. In this environment, the highest-achieving students received the best grades and were therefore judged to be more successful and more intelligent ("gifted") than their peers. Competition was deployed as a stiff tonic, rewarding individual achievement and punishing anything perceived as laziness or a lack of motivation, thus—or so the theory went—encouraging every student to reach his or her highest potential.

But it was a brutal system for many. Students with intrinsic motivation were rewarded at every stage. Those without it tended to fall behind. The presumption was that school offered everyone a level "playing field," but that was never true. Structural biases favored certain kinds of students over others. It wasn't an overt racial or ethnic bias, although those surely existed; it was a bias toward one way of perceiving and interacting with the world.

In most high school curricula in Arlington, teaching methods emphasized an analytical approach over others that were less analytical. Separate classes for higher- and lower-level students exacerbated the challenge many students faced, especially immigrant students. Even the brightest of them often struggled more than their peers. To top it off, there was a motivation-and-reward system in place that assigned extra "quality points" for grades received in advanced classes, pushing the wedge between high achievers and lower achievers more deeply into the fabric of every school.

What was *really* causing many obviously bright young people from Indochina and Latin America to fall behind and struggle to catch up? It wasn't *just* a lack of English-language proficiency. Were there other factors at play? Other differences that we, as educators, weren't accounting for? And if so, what could we do about it?

Most binaries are suspect. Human beings don't fit easily into categories. There are gradations in human nature and experience, and when it comes to things like cognitive or learning styles, people tend to fall somewhere on a continuum instead of neatly into catch-all baskets at either end.

Knowing this, I still came to see the value in a framework that projects two basic styles of cognition. The terms "field dependent" (or "field sensitive") and "field independent" describe a more integrated vs. a more highly differentiated way of perceiving when it comes to the relationship between the self and its environment. To sum this up briefly, people (students in this case) who are field dependent get their cues and motivation from the world around them; field *independent* students tend to locate these cues and motivations internally.

Field-dependent people have more acute sensitivity to social context. They look for acceptance and guidance from the world around them, from authorities of all kinds—laws, customs, elders in the family and the community, religious leaders, teachers. They are sensitive to the views and opinions of others. They also tend to give more attention to the global characteristics of a situation as opposed to the individual elements of a task. They thrive in warm, structured environments. They value personal ties and a group spirit. They benefit from opportunities to ask questions and to work with others. They seek external reference points and concrete representation in learning (classroom) situations, meaning they perform better with clear, explicit instructions and perceive the world and their place in it through personal experience (apprehending) instead of through abstract concepts (comprehending).

Related to this, the two groups generally process printed matter differently as well. Field independent students are more comfortable with printed instructions and with learning through texts as opposed to direct experience. They tend to outperform their field-dependent peers in situations where individual research is required.

It needs to be said: The two groups are not different in learning ability or innate capacity; they just favor different learning approaches. And these differences are not inherently good or bad. They can be judged only in reference to the individual's (the student's) life circumstances.

Likewise, it's a mistake to use this or any other cognitive-style framework to characterize a particular group of people or to assume that cultural values *cause* differences in learning style or achievement. I knew—because I'd seen—that cognitive differences result from a combination of biological, sociological, ecological, and cultural factors. It's complicated, in other words. But it's also true that an individual's cognitive or learning style is, in part, the product of socialization, and this includes child-rearing practices that are culturally based.

When I began my dissertation, there was already a body of research that focused specifically on Mexican American elementary-age children and on the ways cognitive development is shaped by a culture that encourages obedience and conformity to parental and religious authority. Other studies found that Latin American children, including Mexican Americans, from more traditional land-based communities tend to be more field dependent than those who grew up in urban or nonagricultural areas.

The effects of different learning styles have real-world implications, especially when it comes to classroom learning. They also have an impact on how teachers teach, how teachers and students interact, and how educational and vocational choices are made.

I was observing these effects daily, so when I first learned about the field-dependent/independent framework, it was a revelation but not a surprise. But once I had the vocabulary and began to view the landscapes of our classrooms with this framework in mind, I knew what I wanted to learn. I could see where I wanted my research to go.

My dissertation work would be different from what came before. It would focus on LEP immigrant students from Indochina (Cambodia, Laos, and Vietnam) and from Central and South America. And it would focus on high school, not elementary students. I wouldn't be looking for simple answers; I wanted to ask harder questions and find a new way forward.

The more fundamental question: How can schools create learning conditions and develop teaching strategies that meet the needs of *all* students, not just those who experience the world and their relationship to it in one predetermined way? This was simply another way of asking how to consider and meet the needs of the *whole child*, acknowledging their uniqueness while removing structural impediments and giving them every possible chance to succeed on their own terms.

Asian cultures are diverse, but most reflect the influence of Confucian thought as well as other cultural influences emphasizing obedience; veneration of/respect for authority figures, including parents, elders, and teachers; harmony and nonconfrontation; formality; and deference. Likewise, most of the Hispanic students were raised within the bounds of Catholicism, which also values obedience and deference to religious teaching and authority.

My research involved administering several tests, each one designed to assess the student's performance, cognitive style, and learning preferences from a different angle. Without getting deep into the weeds of how these tests were administered, I will say the conclusions were striking in the ways they reinforced what I had observed.

First and foremost, it was clear that learning improves when the student is exposed to materials and teaching methods that match his or her preferred cognitive style. English-proficient students score higher on the measures of abstract conceptualization and active experimentation and are more analytical than their peers whose English-language skills are more limited. Students with limited English proficiency generally prefer to learn through concrete experience and reflective observation. They sense and feel their way toward grasping concepts.

We also found that cognitive style largely determines students' placement in high school English classes; and this is true regardless of a student's proficiency in English. In the 1970s and '80s, Arlington Public Schools was assigning students to classes in one of three tracks: basic, regular (intermediate), and advanced. The highest percentage of minority students were enrolled in the basic classes, the lowest percentage in advanced.

Field independent students tend to be placed in advanced classes largely because they perform better on standardized tests—which tend to favor these students because of their analytical strengths. It becomes a self-perpetuating cycle. Likewise, grouping students in these "tracks" creates a clustering of cognitive styles and therefore of students from different racial/ethnic backgrounds. And valuing high achievement in advanced classes over high achievement within the other two tracks has the insidious effect of a self-fulfilling prophecy.

In the United States, formal education opens the door to more abstract thinking. The longer students stay in school, the more the educational system's preference for abstract, analytical thinking and field independence matters. In Arlington, the bias wasn't hard to see—and it wasn't unique to Arlington: concrete, direct experience was devalued.

To me, the challenge was clear. We needed to create an educational environment that valued *both* styles of cognition. For field-dependent students especially, the industrial model of education—geared toward consistent, measurable outcomes for all students—doesn't work.

It wasn't just the dissertation research that was informing and transforming my professional work. I also had expert guidance and unflagging support from Martha Rashid. Through her, I was introduced to the work of other scholars and thinkers—people like Lilly Fong, Joshua Fishman, and Luis Alberto Machado—who were also probing into the role of the first language, the power of bilingualism, and what Machado called "the right to be intelligent." I was working among these thinkers. Eventually, I met and knew them personally.

For me and many of my colleagues, the critiques of public education—and of educators—that were coming out of DC, Richmond, and the conservative think tanks, the false accusations of liberal bias, the scapegoating, the cheap shots against teachers and school systems taken solely for political gain, stung like scorpions. But this was also a time of immense creativity, passion, collegiality, and a sense of shared purpose. I was inspired every day by the students and their parents, and by the dedication of colleagues like Nguyen Bich, Larry Cuban, and Etta Johnson, who documented the work we were doing in her book *A New American Community of Learners in Arlington, Virginia*. Etta would become a spiritual ally, dear friend, and confidant years later.

In short, we knew we were on a life-affirming journey together. There was a feeling of excitement and uplift all around us, despite the setbacks; and I was in the middle of it all, caught up in the surge. Education was not just *in* my DNA; it *was* my DNA.

I knew in my heart that I was in the best place, at the right time, with the right colleagues, doing the work I was born to do.

Once I finished the dissertation, I told myself, *I have to share what I've learned. I have to put it into practice. It can't be left sitting on a shelf somewhere. I have to "bring it home."*

The research confirmed my intuition that Latinos tend to be more feeling-oriented and less analytical. But I was also interested in the experience of other students and in the roots of the "achievement gap," in which Asian and White students often did better in school than their Latino and African American peers. At least according to the test results.

Of course, this was not true of every student; it never has been. But at the group level, the "gap" was measurable, glaring, and impossible to deny. I knew it had nothing to do with innate intelligence or the ability to learn. I suspected it was due instead to the failure of our educational system to take account of differences in cognitive style and work with them.

My conclusions were in direct opposition to the thinking behind the push to measure every student's progress—along with the performance of a single school or school system—based *solely* on test results. The question wasn't whether there was an achievement gap, and it wasn't whether one group of students was more or less motivated. The question was, how do we introduce teaching strategies that can motivate *all students* while breaking the loop of bias that created the gap in the first place?

I would tell teachers: "When a new student comes into your classroom, he or she will quickly observe what's in there. Does he see himself reflected? Does she feel like she has a place there?" A teacher might ask: "How do I indicate social acceptance through nonverbal means?" My answer: "This doesn't have to be a complicated problem with a difficult or expensive solution. Simply displaying the flag of his or her home country could be enough."

If Latino children tend to be more field dependent, then—even more than many of their peers—these students need to understand *why* they are being asked to learn something, and it also helps them to know, or have some relation to, their teachers as human beings. In Bolivian culture, we personalize relationships, but in the United States, relationships are largely grounded in preestablished roles. It's as if the roles have the relationship (teacher and student, for example), not the people who inhabit these roles. And the effects of this can be pernicious, especially when the relationship is between the student and a teacher who has no understanding of that student's background, family, or personal life.

This understanding made me think about the loss that many Black communities experienced with school desegregation. This is *not* to argue for a return to the days when African American schools were housed in inferior facilities, made do with hand-me-down textbooks, and otherwise had to live within a system that was not equitable in any sense. But the relationships fostered in those schools *supported* the goals of education.

Not surprisingly, my research also showed that Black students tend to be more field dependent, like their Latino peers. Thus, their cognitive and learning styles are similar, and so are their needs, which were not being fully met in a system weighted heavily toward more analytical styles of learning.

I started giving presentations on this concept, in Arlington and throughout the country. My work eventually came to the attention of the Fulbright Foundation, leading to a six-month fellowship in Bolivia to provide training and support for educational reforms emphasizing bilingual instruction and the importance of a student's (or teacher's) first language.

The good news was that the fellowship was a rare opportunity to go deeper and stoke the fires of educational reform in both of my cultural homes. The bad news was that while I developed strong relationships with the teachers I was working with in Bolivia, I wasn't exactly welcomed by the bureaucrats in the Ministry of Education, as we'll see. They weren't keen on the idea of an American expert—which was what I'd become in their eyes—"telling us what to do."

Back in Virginia, the implications of what I was discovering and the impact of this new way of thinking spread into every aspect of our teaching. It forced us to rethink everything.

For example, teaching English with a grammatical focus on the ways sentences are built may work fine for more field independent children, but to reach many of our ESOL students, we needed a different approach. We needed to select books, regardless of reading level, that would speak to them directly. This approach fits hand in glove with the focus on themes and concepts I described earlier.

Our teachers started developing lesson plans with this in mind. With no models or guidelines at the state level, we had the freedom to choose the books that *we* thought were best suited for use in this new context. But we weren't doing this work in isolation. We were finding allies and using materials produced elsewhere. Excellent curricula were being developed by the National Clearinghouse for Bilingual Education; by George Mason's Center for the Study of Education and National Development; and by the Center for Applied Linguistics in Washington, DC.

I also organized workshops for parents using this framework. Parents understood and quickly embraced the idea that when their children's learning styles differed from what had once been perceived as the norm, new approaches were required; and this *did not mean* their children were not as bright or as motivated as their peers. The parents could see the results for themselves, in their children's school performance and their renewed thirst for learning.

So, my work was having an impact. A chapter I wrote in a book titled *Learning Styles in the ESL/EFL Classroom*, edited by Joy Reid, circulated widely, and a similar publication emerged in Bolivia. The messages were clear. First, we needed to change the ways we understood and taught ESOL students. And second, we needed to take steps that would make learning meaningful to *all* our students, system-wide. *This* was how we could begin to close the insidious achievement gap that was pushing so many bright children toward the margins.

In Arlington, I had the good fortune not to do business as usual. Luck of timing? Accident? Coincidence? Destiny? Fate? Whatever it was, the opportunity I was given in my years with Arlington Public Schools played to the strengths of my own cognitive and learning styles. I perceive the world primarily through feeling, but I process information through action. Thus, the two questions that best summarize or encapsulate my style of learning and cognitions are "What if?" and "What can I do?" The same questions I was asking at the Plaza Colon.

I don't want to give the impression that this all happened in a straightforward, linear way. I had the active, enthusiastic support of two open-minded superintendents who understood the need and gave us the latitude required to meet it: Larry Cuban in the early years, from 1978 to 1982; and Robert Smith from 1996 until the time I retired in 2007. In between, I had to push harder, but I also had the help of parents and colleagues; a record of success that became hard—impossible—to deny; and, for a while, the blessing of that vacuum at the state level, which gave us the freedom to innovate.

There were times when I thought I might not finish the dissertation after all, with two small children and the excruciatingly slow pace of progress, first through the coursework and then through the writing of the dissertation itself. I recall being eight months pregnant with my daughter, Julia, taking courses during the summer, and asking myself, *Why am I doing this?* I had a good job that didn't require a doctorate, so what was the point?

Now I know the answer. But I was headed toward a crisis in my personal life, one that sent me back into a dark place of anger, feelings of abandonment, and self-doubt. What had seemed in the beginning like the fulfillment of a beautiful dream soon revealed itself to be a costly and damaging mistake.

CHAPTER XVI
Love Is Blind

Love is blind, so the saying goes. But on that August day in 1978 when I married Jim Hainer, light filled every corner of the Covenant Church on Military Road, and it seemed to be coming from a thousand directions at once. It came through the stained-glass windows and down from the vaulted ceilings, from inside the flowers at the foot of the altar and through the folds and buttons of the blue dress I was wearing, setting it on fire.

Light flowed in rivers across time and space, wedding gifts from the peach trees inside our magic garden in Cochabamba, the jacaranda in the Plaza Colon. It entered the church like travelers at the end of a long journey, from the heart of my beloved abuelita Julia, her whispered prayers; from the voices, the love of my mother and father, unstoppable over mountains, rain forests, oceans, deserts, city streets, through layers of grief, hope and promise, and unbounded joy; arriving in the here and now, bringing with them the greatest of gifts—gratitude.

Most of all, the light was coming from the face of the man I loved and was about to marry, his eyes, his smile, and from inside my pregnant belly.

The power was immense. I felt like I was standing in the morning of creation, in the fulfillment of a beautiful but long-abandoned dream. I felt the earth move. I felt—I knew—that in this moment I was part of everything that ever was or ever would be. There was no past, no future, no distance, no more sorrow; the world had been drained of sorrow, and I felt no fear.

As the ceremony began, walking to the altar, I wept.

It was a simple wedding, a brief service. Jim's parents, brother, sister, and grandmother were there; so were his children, Jon and Tessie; three of my sisters; and one or two friends. After the ceremony, we went back to the house on Military Road for champagne and a reception. That night, we stayed at a hotel in DC, and the next day we went with Jim's family to Rehoboth Beach where we'd rented a house. Our honeymoon was a family vacation.

James was born eleven weeks later. I was already feeling pressure because there was no paid maternity leave at APS and the intake center couldn't open and begin its work in earnest until I returned. Adding to this stress, James was jaundiced when he was born, and I had to leave him in the intensive care unit, where he was given several days of ultraviolet light treatments. He came home, and we had a precious five weeks together before I had to go back to work; there was no choice.

I loved the work, but it was excruciating being away from my new son. I'd breastfed him in those first few weeks, forging that beautiful bond between us, but I couldn't see a way to continue breastfeeding once I returned to work. It was a different time; there were no rooms set aside and no provisions made for nursing mothers to pump breast milk, much less breastfeed their children at work.

Jim was teaching at Mason, and we hired a nanny to be with James during weekdays. Our pediatrician recommended a soy-milk formula as the best alternative to breast milk, but on my second day back, the nanny called to say that James had been throwing up constantly. I called the doctor, who said that soy allergies were common (so why did he recommend the soy formula to start with?) and that we needed to take him to Fairfax Hospital right away. By the time we got there, James was already dehydrated, and at barely five weeks old, he needed intravenous fluids. The doctor couldn't find an artery in his arm or leg, so the needle drip was placed in his head.

Once he'd been partially rehydrated, the nurses suggested I try breastfeeding him. When I did, I was told abruptly and with obvious disdain to "please cover yourself up." It was a horrible experience—one that I know has been shared by many women in this country and is still commonplace today.

I sat by the side of James's bed almost nonstop for three days, feeding him as best I could until he was released. What could I do? I had to take care of my son. I took leave without pay. Marie Djouadi wasn't happy about it, and I felt guilty not being there to help launch the intake center, but to this day I've never regretted the decision. I just felt angry that things were the way they were.

We tried different formulas, but none was a good substitute. I continued to breastfeed James morning and night but still couldn't pump milk working in a high school setting. There was no accommodation whatsoever. It's also true that in those days, many—maybe even most—people in this country, women included, thought breastfeeding in public, "covered up" or not, was obscene.

It wasn't easy balancing the demands of professional life, graduate studies, marriage, and family; it never is. We weren't wealthy, but with two reasonably good incomes, at least we weren't struggling financially. Every day I was reminded that other families weren't so fortunate.

Having a nanny to take care of James while I was working helped, and within a few months, my mother came to live with us, which also eased the pressure. She and Jim got along well; he could be exceedingly gracious and charming. And little James adored his grandmother.

Her voice and her presence calmed him when he was upset, and when she sang to him in Spanish, it felt like a golden cord, full of love and healing energy, connecting the heart of the wife, the mother, and the professional woman I'd become to the little girl I'd been back in Cochabamba, to the smells of my mother's kitchen and the soil of my native land.

In so many ways, I was living the life I'd dreamed of having with Al. I loved Jim, and in those days I rarely thought about Al or about what had happened since his death. Jim was supportive of my work, and although he wasn't the kind of husband who would change diapers or wake up in the middle of the night to soothe a crying child, I wasn't expecting that. My father had been the same way, a man who embodied the ironclad separation between gender roles in Bolivian society, the strict delineation between what was expected of men and women. But I knew—or thought I knew—that I would never be abandoned again.

I was wrong.

In Bolivia, people drink. My father had his scotch in the evening. When they reach a certain age, Bolivian children have wine at dinner. It's just a part of life, familiar and unthreatening. But Jim and I hadn't been married for long, less than a year, when I became aware that his drinking might become a problem.

He seemed happy teaching, but he wasn't working on his dissertation. He'd come home and start drinking bourbon at 5 p.m. He grew increasingly remote and hard to reach. I was aware of what was happening, fearful when I let myself think about it, but I kept the worry to myself; I covered it over. The demands of my professional and academic work, and of raising James, made that easier. Months passed, and I told myself everything was normal.

Two years after James was born, I was pregnant again. At thirty-seven, there were heightened risks of complications for the baby, and the doctor advised amniocentesis to make sure there were no issues or causes for concern. Amniocentesis also reveals the sex of the fetus, and when the test results came back, I was in my office at APS. I screamed at the top of my lungs: "It's a girl." And she was healthy. I'd dreamed this too, of having a daughter. I was overjoyed, but the joy was clouded over because by then I knew that Jim had been unfaithful—not just once but several times.

It was toward the end of the spring semester. I'd known, or sensed, that something wasn't right. I knew that Jim was in the middle of "finals," and that morning I noticed that he was getting dressed up, more so than usual. I felt a shiver when he left, and when he didn't come home at the normal time that afternoon, I went to look for him. His car was in the parking lot at Mason, but he wasn't in his office, and he wasn't in class.

Following my instincts, I went to the Lamplighter, a restaurant and bar just off campus, and found him there, drinking with one of his students. I knew as soon as I walked in the door and saw them that this was not a platonic meeting. There was no mistaking that.

I confronted him, hot with rage. Here it was again. I was abandoned. It was like seeing them there together jabbed a needle into a balloon filled with toxic ditchwater, and it just exploded. I picked up a drink from the table, threw it in his face, and walked out.

The next few days passed in a blur. I held myself together for James and for my work, but the fuel I was burning was pure anger—anger and all the pent-up grief and feelings of failure and unworthiness that go along with abandonment. Abandoned by my father, by Al Giddings, Gonzalo Ponce, the unnamed children I'd lost before they were ever born; by God himself. It was like being caught inside a howling cyclone. I just kept asking, pleading over and over again: *Why?*

My friends and sisters gave us a baby shower. Within the joy of that gathering and celebration of new life and family, the knowledge of Jim's infidelity was a dark blotch. On the other hand, the pain of his infidelity was mitigated by the joys of pregnancy and birth. It was like a fluid, ever-shifting version of the yin-yang symbol. Light and darkness intertwined, each contained within the other.

My mother had gone back home to Bolivia by the time Julia (Julie) was born. I hadn't told her about the problems Jim and I were having, but she must have known in her heart something was wrong. We were strongly connected in that way; there were things that didn't need to be said. It was the kind of mother-daughter relationship I hoped Julie and I would have one day.

I persuaded Jim to go to counseling, but it didn't turn out well. The counselor said his infidelity was not the problem; it was a symptom, and the root cause was alcohol. He advised Jim to join Alcoholics Anonymous and me to enroll in Al-Anon, an organization for the families and loved ones of people with addiction problems. Jim refused to go, but I joined enthusiastically, and in the end the work with Al-Anon opened other doors along the path of my own spiritual development. But for the moment, I wasn't giving up; I wanted to heal the relationship. So we tried another approach.

The Catholic Church was sponsoring a "marriage encounter" program, popular in the 1970s and '80s. At these sessions, couples would be given prompts for private, one-on-one conversations with each other; and in one of these, the question was "Is there anything you haven't told your spouse that he or she should know?"

It was like a mountain collapsed on top of us. Jim told me that a year earlier, when he'd gone to New York for an event, he slept with a woman named Monica, who was also his student. Worse, they'd been together a second time.

Now I knew that my husband had had affairs with at least two of his students. But what was I supposed to do? I had a son. I was having another baby. The last thing I wanted was a divorce. I decided to keep trying, keep hoping things would change.

But people don't change, not really, and not in fundamental ways absent some kind of religious or conversion experience, and many of those don't last.

By this time, Jim had lost his position at George Mason because he failed to complete his dissertation in the time allowed. He bought a print shop in Manassas; he was drinking heavily now, and we began to struggle financially. Then Jim discovered something called the Universal Life Church, and one night he proposed a scheme to me: He'd become a minister in the church, and then we wouldn't have to pay taxes, or so he said. He would use our home address as the address of the church.

I was uneasy about it, but we met with an attorney who assured me that this was legal, so I reluctantly agreed. When the time came, I signed the tax return, and within a few months the IRS was bearing down on us. Our financial situation became even more precarious. Dire wouldn't be too strong a word.

Jim went to our safe deposit box at the bank, took the engagement ring Al had given me all those years ago, and sold it without telling me. When I eventually found out, it was devastating—first, to have lost the ring; and second, to know and be unable to deny that I was married to someone who could do this, who had so little regard for my feelings, who had grown so out of touch with the difference between right and wrong.

I was bereft. I started going to therapy. I was still trying to manage the situation, still believing it was something I could control. Jim's drinking got worse, and he started gambling, hoping, I suppose, for a quick fix to our rapidly deteriorating financial state. He sold some of my other jewelry to pay for his bets.

Miraculously, I was able to keep up and do what was needed—even thrive—at APS. By then I'd also assumed almost total responsibility for raising James and Julie. My children were my happiness. I was so proud of them both and wanted them to have every opportunity and not be pulled into the emotional vortex our marriage had become. I enrolled them in after-school programs—soccer, swimming—but the burden of getting them from place to place fell entirely on my shoulders. Jim didn't participate in any of their activities; his excuse was that he was working in Manassas.

Our problems came to a head at Christmastime. I was sitting in the living room at home, writing cards. One was to a male friend I'd met when I was taking classes at the University of Arkansas. By now he was happily married with four children of his own. I was writing to him about James and Julie and about the work on my doctorate.

When Jim saw the card, he became angry and verbally abusive. Then he hit me, disconnected the phone, and knocked me down again; then tried to lift me by my legs, upside down. Fortunately, both kids were asleep, so they didn't see it happen. But I knew then that there was no hope left for our marriage. It was doomed. It was over.

I woke up early the next morning and went to see my niece Angie Kelley, my sister Julia's daughter. Angie is an attorney, and she told me, "You need to think about your safety and the children's safety." The friends I'd made at Al-Anon told me the same thing, and so did my friend Dama, now a counselor in Arlington County, who said, "You have to leave, but when you do, take most of the money from your bank account. Don't leave it there."

I reached out to a lawyer who could represent me (Angie's expertise is in immigration law), and his advice was to leave Jim a note saying that his drinking had to stop immediately and that I was taking the children to Charlottesville to stay with Julia while he thought it over.

Which was what I did.

I can't explain how I was so blind for so long. It was like I had a veil covering my eyes. The veil of love initially; of stubborn devotion later; and maybe also fear of the unknown, of being single again, or acknowledging that another marriage had failed.

My old digestive problems returned, a consequence of stress and anxiety. I was still thriving in my profession, giving everyone the impression that I was doing well. But I was being torn apart inside.

The final unraveling began when Jim went to Pennsylvania for Christmas and then announced he was going to Brazil with his daughter, Tess. He said he wanted me to go with them, but I refused. The attorney was pressing me to get more clarity about our finances, and it was then I discovered that Jim had emptied several of our joint bank accounts. I had to call the superintendent's office from Charlottesville to get the authorization to have my paychecks redirected from our joint bank account.

I came back to Arlington while Jim was away in Brazil, and I learned that he'd also depleted our home equity line of credit. He'd given me another diamond to replace the one from Al that he had sold, but he took money from the line of credit to buy it. We were in the middle of a financial collapse. The IRS placed a lien on our house. I went to court to ask for a protective order and to a priest I knew, Father Ambrose, to ask for his advice.

Father Ambrose knew Jim, he knew our family, and he knew the judge who had granted the protective order. His gentle, caring way of urging me to take the actions I knew I needed to take reassured me, and he did it without pushing or judging either me *or* Jim.

It was the beginning of my turn back toward the Catholic faith after years of estrangement. At last, here was a priest who showed me what love in action looks like and how much solace comes from believing, knowing, there's a higher purpose at work, even in times of darkness like the one I was experiencing. I'll be forever grateful to this man for showing me the way out of darkness by letting me find the path on my own.

Meanwhile, my attorney told me, "When Jim comes back, inform him of the protective order, but don't be there with the kids when he arrives." I took James and Julie to a hotel in Fredericksburg for a week. It was hard for them. They still loved their father, but they were also afraid.

School came back in session in January. There was a protective order in effect, but the weight of the anxiety and uncertainty was with me from the time I woke up in the morning until I drifted off to sleep at night. How could I manage? How could I construct a fence around the anger, the fear, the resentment, the confusion, and still raise my children and do my work?

In the end, my work was my sanity. I remember touching the walls of my office one day and thinking, *I'm safe here*. My secretary knew what was happening at home, though at first the rest of my colleagues didn't. I maintained pieces of the routine, picking the kids up after school, trying to keep things as normal—and normal-looking—as possible.

But Jim would appear at the house unannounced. He wrote me threatening notes, accusing me of being schizophrenic. At one point, he wrote me a long letter, and there's nothing else to say about it: It was sick. I showed it to my therapist, who agreed, and she told me, "I don't think it's safe for you and the children to have *any* contact with him now."

So I had no choice but to let friends and colleagues at work know the situation. The personnel office, the superintendent, the children's teachers: I had to tell them all that there was a protective order and they should not release James or Julie to Jim's care, no matter what he said. It was humiliating.

On one of my visits to Charlottesville, Jim showed up and threatened me—said he was going to take the kids and it didn't matter what the judge said or what I thought about it. My sister Julia called the police.

Back home, I had all the debts. Jim hired an expensive lawyer. I still have no idea how he paid for it. Over the next two years of our formal separation, he made many promises and broke them all. He said he was sorry, that he would go to therapy on the condition that I sign for some loans he'd applied for in both our names. I refused and eventually had to pay an expert from the FBI to clear my name when the loans went bad.

Finally, it was over. After two grueling years of separation, tens of thousands of dollars in legal fees, a string of threats and broken promises, no child support, and living in constant fear, the divorce was final. I signed the agreement on March 27, 1991. My attorney asked me, "Emma, what are your priorities in this?" and I told him: "I want full custody of my children," which was granted.

In the last year of our separation, Jim had a girlfriend, a woman in her early twenties, the same age as his daughter. They got married a few weeks after the divorce, but the marriage didn't last, and he soon began dating another young preschool teacher, Susan. I liked her, and she was kind to James and Julie.

Through the children, I learned that Susan did an "intervention" with Jim, and he agreed to enter a six-week rehab program. He stopped drinking for a while, and a measure of stability seemed to return. I'd held on to some hope that James and Julie would have a different and better relationship with their dad now that we were divorced, and if it took a younger woman like Susan to make that possible, so be it.

I didn't want him back, but I did want our children to be whole, which in my mind meant knowing and loving *both* their parents.

Years later, when I was awarded a Fulbright Fellowship to spend six months in Bolivia working again with teachers in the rural areas, I wanted to take the children with me. But James was a senior in high school by then, and he asked to stay in Virginia with his dad. So Julie and I went to Bolivia without James. I gave my sister power of attorney and rented out the house on Military Road.

About a month after we arrived in Bolivia, James called and told me, "I don't have anything to eat."

"What do you mean you have nothing to eat?" I asked him; and he said: "Dad's drinking again and Susan has left him. I think it's for good this time."

I booked James a flight to Bolivia, and he stayed with us through the remainder of the fellowship. A sad coda to the dissolution of our marriage and a difficult passage for my son.

I learned many lessons through the ordeal of my marriage to Jim—lessons about dealing with addiction and the insidious effects that alcohol addiction can have on a person, a marriage, a family. It was also a lesson, a web of lessons, about my role and responsibility as a mother.

It's natural. You want to stay with the father of your children. You'll sacrifice; you'll believe, even when it's foolish to believe anymore; and you'll keep trying, even after the last of the reasons to keep trying have disappeared.

But when the person you once loved is an alcoholic who refuses to take responsibility for his addiction, when the marriage has devolved into abuse and financial chaos and it's not safe to stay in the home you've made together, you have no choice: You have to separate.

I wouldn't be who I am today if I'd stayed married to Jim Hainer, and James and Julie wouldn't be who they are. The whole episode had immense financial and emotional consequences. My will to survive strengthened because it had to. For the kids' sake, I couldn't buckle. I had to keep going. I had to rise above. The good news is that James and Julie have grown and persevered through their own pain and confusion over what happened. They've become strong, responsible, compassionate adults, and I'm grateful for that.

I'm also grateful that despite everything that was happening with the marriage, my career soared: Its high point lasted from 1988, when I separated from Jim, to 2007, when I retired from Arlington Public Schools.

Jim was intelligent, charming, and gracious at times, with an exceptional gift for language, but I think he was also narcissistic. He could spin webs and create appearances that fooled the people closest to him, me included. Probably even himself. It's true that I loved him in the early years of our time together, and the joy I felt when I stood up to marry him that afternoon in August 1978 was real. The beginning of the end was when he stopped taking responsibility for finishing his dissertation and for our finances.

Financial problems are a consequence of alcoholism, and alcoholics are often very good at covering things up. Jim was a master at this, and at justifying what can't be justified—like selling the diamond Al gave me all those years ago or refusing to pay child support. I spent many thousands of dollars in attorney's fees trying to obtain at least *some* child support, but it never came, and it took me years to resolve the

IRS debt and put the financial mess Jim created behind me.

Anger is corrosive, like battery acid. I had to put it to rest. After his separation from Susan, Jim married a woman from Saudi Arabia, someone he met when he was selling Lexus cars. He brought her to the house on Military Road one day; I never understood why, but I didn't invite them in. We stood outside for a while, and I offered her my condolences. This must have surprised her, but it seemed like the natural and right thing to do at the time.

They moved to Texas shortly after that, and he permanently laid aside his responsibilities to our children. For all practical purposes, he stopped being their father.

How do you transform and heal a devastated heart and spirit? What is the work that makes this possible?

Time helps. So does spiritual practice, which in my case would be a blending of Catholicism and the Buddhism of Thich Nhat Hanh. And so does mature love.

Twelve years after the end of my marriage to Jim Hainer and the desolation that followed it, I met someone who would show me what a good man *really* is: a man of faith who accomplished much but lived simply, who was modest, humble, a friend and lover who was healthy at the core of his being. A man named Jim Weber.

I was twenty-one years old when I married Al Giddings, forty-four when I divorced Jim Hainer. In between, there was the marriage to Gonzalo Ponce. These are the years that our society earmarks for partnership, relationship, marriage, family, having and caring for children. The golden years of life. For me, they were filled with pain and disillusionment, the ghosts of abandonment. But thankfully, that wasn't the end of the story.

If I could speak to myself as a young woman, I would tell her this: Before you decide to get married, take a closer look. If you notice excessive alcohol or if your partner exhibits anything that *looks* like the desire to control you, be cautious.

Not everything that shines in this world is gold; and real gold may not shine in *this* world very much at all. At least not in the way you expected or were led to believe.

CHAPTER XVII
Moving On, Starting Over

W hat now?
That's the question newly divorced mothers ask ourselves as we struggle to find balance while keeping our heads above water, day to day. Whatever else happens, we have to care for the needs of our children. We have to manage a job or career to see that the bills are paid. We have to do what it takes to recover from the loss of a relationship that was once a pillar of our lives before it became toxic and destructive. And at the bottom of things, we somehow have to find renewed meaning and purpose as we gaze out at the years ahead of us and ask, *What now?*

In many ways, I was fortunate. I had a doctorate and a thriving career. I knew that education was my path. I had friends, supportive colleagues, and a loving family. But it was hard; some days it was brutally hard. On bad days, I felt like I was slipping away. On the worst days, I felt I couldn't do it anymore—that my reservoirs of energy were bone-dry.

This feeling wasn't completely new. There were times during the years of my marriage to Jim Hainer when I thought I might not finish the dissertation. I had two small children with an alcoholic father who had been unfaithful to me. I was working full-time. For a while I could only manage one course per term, which is far from ideal. And toward the end, I was trying to hold the marriage together—it felt like single-handedly—while knowing in my heart that it was dissolving out from under me. By the time Jim and I finally split, I'd already had years of experience feeling alone.

James and Julie were my salvation. I loved them and would do anything to keep them safe. Julie was seven years old at the time of the divorce; James was ten. I was solely responsible for them as I struggled to repair our family's shattered finances and rebuild our emotional lives.

Jim would tell the kids that lawyers were costing us a lot of money, so it wasn't surprising that they were anxious and worried about that, far more than children ever should be. At church, during a community affirmation ceremony, Julie was asked to state a need during "prayers of the faithful." She prayed for money.

They still wanted to be with their dad, and it wasn't easy for them that he remarried so quickly, and to a much younger woman who, it turned out, had mental health issues. Plus, James was struggling in school. He was restless and had trouble concentrating. He was diagnosed as having attention deficit disorder (ADD), but part of the problem was that the environment at Taylor Elementary, where he was first enrolled, just wasn't a good one for him.

Taylor was a neighborhood school with open classrooms, and James needed more structure. He was highly creative, with an agile mind and unusual ways of seeing the world. At Taylor, reading was taught using an analytical approach. He didn't always understand (or care) what answer was "correct." In kindergarten, he was identified as needing special help and placed with the group of students receiving ESOL instruction. Not surprisingly, he disliked being separated out, and he became rebellious: He would tell the assistant who was administering a test, "Let's just get this over with."

Naturally, I was distraught. I even wrote an article for the PTA newsletter titled "Lessons in Humility: Attending a ParentTeacher Conference." I realized something had to change; and the answer turned out to be Key Elementary, where Julie was already enrolled in an immersion program, with half the classes taught in Spanish and half in English.

I had wanted my children to attend a school that was diverse, which Taylor wasn't. It was a majority-White school with mostly higher-income families from North Arlington. Key was different. At that time, the student population there was 70 percent Latino. Teachers and school administrators were welcoming and supportive. Lori Maes, the first Latino PTA president in Arlington, had just been elected. I enrolled James at Key for third grade, and he began to thrive almost immediately.

I felt comfortable and welcomed by Latino families, and Julie and James became friends with kids from many different income levels. As a result, they became more sensitive, less judgmental, and more aware and accepting of differences between people than they would have been otherwise. We all felt at home, socially and culturally. The school was responsive to the needs of individual students and their families.

By fifth grade, James was on the honor roll. At one school, he was a problem; at another he was an outstanding student. For me, the experience of what happened with James was another tributary of understanding, another piece of evidence, that each student is different, and each family situation is also different. That public education *must* be designed (or rebuilt) to serve the needs of individual students, individual families, and not to treat every child and family the same.

Julie excelled academically wherever she was; she was that kind of kid. But James was different, and to have that difference acknowledged not in a negative way but with love and caring was a blessing and a relief for me. When things were difficult at home, a counselor at Key would take both James *and* Julie out of class to read them a book about children who were living—or had lived—through their parents' divorce.

I tried to get them the help they needed while maintaining as much normalcy as possible in our lives. It helped that Key had an excellent after-school program. Finding childcare was a major challenge in those early years post-divorce, and one of the teachers at Key took me aside and said I could feel free to drop Julie off early, before classes started, which was a godsend. I needed a place that understood and responded to the needs of working parents, single parents, and my children's school met that need.

The work we were doing at Arlington Public Schools was gaining notice throughout the country, even abroad; and my influence grew quickly as a result.

By the time I was awarded the doctorate in 1987, I'd already acquired an educational philosophy based on the intersection of my academic study and direct personal experience. I was in the right place at the right time, doors were open that would later close, and I'd formed in my mind and heart a commitment to service through education and advocacy that would be the foundation of my life's work. Finishing the dissertation, I'd told myself: *I have to share this; I have to share what I've learned.*

I wanted to bring the knowledge I was rapidly gaining into the fertile environment of Arlington Public Schools. But I also wanted to bring it into the realm of professional development for teachers, to help them see the validity and the benefits of different cognitive and learning styles. I wanted to create new models for family/school collaboration; to help give teachers and aspiring teachers both the tools and the motivation to see cultural differences as assets, not liabilities. I wanted to break down the achievement gap.

I knew how fortunate I was to have two cultures, and I despised the "melting pot" analogy and the stark choice it imposes between setting aside one's native language and culture for the sake of "assimilation" or remaining perpetually a "foreigner" in a new and unforgiving land. Public schools could be an ideal place in which to foster and encourage bicultural identity instead of being hostile to it. I wanted to be a midwife for this change.

I accepted adjunct and visiting-faculty positions at several universities: Georgetown, George Washington, George Mason, and, years later, the University of Virginia. The affiliation with GWU was especially meaningful, in part because I was teaching the same courses I had taken there in graduate school; and because I was teaching teachers in a master's program that drew educators from across the United States.

I was preparing them to become ESOL or bilingual teachers, developing strength and capacity within the broader field of education, having a national impact. The work we were doing was valuable, not just to the students and teachers involved, or in their classrooms back home, but also to the vitality and health of their communities.

At Mason, the courses I taught had been designed for local teachers, with their input. I also taught a course there designed for immigrants who had been teachers in their home countries but were working here as teaching assistants.

It was immensely gratifying, but also difficult at times. These classes were mostly taught in the evenings, and the students were often tired after a long day in the classroom. Still, the excitement and dedication they brought to the work was palpable, a sign that the field of education was changing for the better, even if the change was coming slowly, and it was thrilling to be part of that change.

The Georgetown Linguistics Department had received a Title VII grant from the US Department of Education to offer courses specifically for ESOL and bilingual teachers. The grant also provided fellowship stipends to graduate students. The dean established a partnership with Arlington Public Schools and with the public schools in Washington, DC, to offer internship opportunities as an enhancement to these students' classroom work. He asked me to teach courses on bilingualism, teacher practicum, foundations of education, and other courses needed for certification.

I accepted the offer gladly—only partly because the salary was double what I'd been receiving at GWU. The graduate students did their teaching in Arlington and DC, and I also supervised some of their student teaching. Arlington ended up hiring many of them at the conclusion of their coursework; once again, it was pure synergy: Everyone involved benefited.

Sadly, once the Title VII funds were exhausted and the fellowship stipends disappeared, the cost of tuition at Georgetown was so high that the MA for teaching program had to be suspended. There wasn't enough demand. It was hard to see this program shuttered because the economics of the market didn't work. But I continued to teach an undergraduate course called Foundations of Multicultural Education, and a fair number of these students eventually entered the Teach for America Program.

I even supervised the thesis work of a sociology graduate student studying the barriers to higher education that undocumented students and their families face. And when the Dream Project was launched in 2010, one of the sociology students at Georgetown organized its first mentoring program. I taught for twenty years at Georgetown, from 1998 to 2018.

The year was 1995. As a US citizen and a professional educator with a doctorate and more than ten years of teaching and administrative experience in US public schools, I had the opportunity to apply for a Fulbright Fellowship, to teach in another country of my choosing. Naturally, I chose Bolivia. I wanted to return to the work I'd started: empowering rural teachers. The application process was rigorous, the competition stiff, and one stipulation was that I had to have the support of the Fulbright committee in Bolivia.

I knew the head of the committee, Dr. Manuel Arellano, who had been appointed by the minister of education to reform Bolivian higher education. My proposal was to assist in the broader educational-reform effort by creating frameworks for including bilingual education so that children from the rural areas could learn in their Indigenous languages—Quechua, Aymara, or Guarani.

My background in bilingual education and teacher training was a major asset. The Ministry of Education's goal was to begin requiring teachers to graduate from a university, not just from normal schools that only required three years of postsecondary education. (Normal schools were still training teachers in the United States well into the twentieth century, and many of these later became accredited colleges. My alma mater, Radford University, had been founded as a normal school in 1910.)

My proposal was accepted. I applied for and was granted a professional leave of absence from APS, and I arranged for one of the resource specialists to act as supervisor while I was away. I had the option of a one-year fellowship but chose to apply for a six-month term instead, mainly because James was a senior in high school.

Julie would come with me. She wasn't particularly happy about the decision, but she was admitted to study for one semester at the American School, where I'd been a teacher and counselor twenty years before. The Fulbright award covered her tuition.

It was barely a month into the fellowship when I got that terrifying call from James, telling me he had nothing to eat, and I soon had both children with me in La Paz. It was a dream come true but also challenging. James's senior year had been thrown into chaos—another way his father's alcoholism affected all of us—and he arrived in La Paz anxious and traumatized. He'd found his dad passed out at the country club and had to drive him to the hospital. It hurt to imagine what those last days with his father had been like, but at least both children were now safe, and James was also enrolled in the American School.

The prospect of the work ahead was thrilling to me; it was like coming full circle. In La Paz, I connected with Dr. Arellano, who introduced me to the minister of education, Enrique Ipina, and to the educational-reform team, directed by one of my former university students, Amalia Pacheco, and a woman named Sonia Comboni. They were not welcoming, to say the least.

I was blindsided. I thought my American credentials and experience would be welcome assets. They weren't. Being Bolivian, I thought I would have instant access and credibility. After all, I'd built a solid reputation as a teacher and a teacher of teachers in Bolivia decades earlier. Besides that, my father was well known and respected, having worked at the highest levels of government. My roots in my home country were deep. Back in the US, I was on the leading edge of a revolution in public education; I felt I was in a strong position to help.

But Amalia and Sonia and many of their colleagues at the Ministry of Education saw me as an outsider, an interloper; and most surprisingly, they saw me as an American—not a Bolivian—who was coming to tell *them* what they should do. I wanted to scream, "You're wrong! I'm Bolivian like you."

It was a painful lesson but one for which I've since learned to be grateful. We aren't always seen by others in the way we think we should be seen. Good intentions have little power to dispel mistrust. Sonia and Amalia hadn't asked for my support: I just showed up, a foreigner in their eyes. My expertise—my American credentials, the stamp of approval from Fulbright, all of it—was taken as an insult, not a gift.

When the educational-reform team told me point-blank that my American expertise was "not helpful" to them, it was like an electric shock. Now I understand where it came from; and the experience left me wiser and much better prepared for my work back in the United States.

The fellowship ended up being a success despite this apparent setback. I had a computer and started working in a house I'd rented from my aunt Cira. Dr. Arellano was an ally, and I soon learned he was one of the owners of a new private university, Universidad de Aquino Bolivia, that was offering training courses for normal-school teachers, helping them qualify for a university degree and, with it, a licentiate equivalent to a bachelor's degree in the US.

The woman overseeing this training program was a friend from the American School days, Liz Kiyonari. She welcomed me warmly and immediately asked me to teach a course on the learning process. A stipend was paid by the Fulbright funds, and so I asked if I could use this course as an opportunity to conduct my own research on teachers' learning styles. She happily agreed; her only request was that I make copies of all my teaching materials in Spanish, since the teachers had no textbooks and neither did the university library.

I started teaching with a class of approximately thirty normal-school teachers, all from La Paz. They loved the instruction, loved taking the learning-styles inventory, analyzing their results, and exploring the ways this information could be helpful in their teaching. They also appreciated the handouts I gave them, the help with preparing lesson plans, and the whole process of curriculum development.

Again, the help didn't flow in only one direction. The principle of reciprocity, of ayni, was at work here too. Teachers from my courses connected me with the rector of the Normal School in La Paz, and through this connection I was able to offer workshops for teachers free of charge. Liz asked me to teach a course in the city of Oruro, and in the process I was introduced to the heads of normal schools in other Bolivian departments: Potosi, Sucre, Santa Cruz, and Cochabamba.

One high point of the fellowship was the training I was able to offer to teachers in the rural areas. I bonded with an Aymara teacher who traveled with me to the rural *normales*. In all, I was able to give the learning-styles inventory test to 2,600 Bolivian teachers and offer training to them. Almost without exception, they were responsive, enthusiastic, and grateful for the opportunities this afforded them.

For me, the satisfaction came from giving back to my country, despite the resistance inside the Ministry of Education. But the experience brought change there too. The minister later invited me to come back to do more training; and they also published a monograph I wrote about the learning process.

I'd gone back to Bolivia with what I thought was the advantage of being a US citizen, bringing a rich body of knowledge and experience with me. The education bureaucracy threw down barriers, but

I surmounted them and in the end was free to do the work I had come there to do—work that had started all those years ago with Un Maestro Más.

The lessons gained from this experience were many, and I know the impact of the work we accomplished didn't stop with the teachers themselves. It continues even now, almost thirty years later, in classrooms across Bolivia, which is for me the most profound gift of being an educator: knowing that even small changes ripple out across time in ways that can't be measured or calculated. I remain forever grateful for the opportunity I was given through this fellowship—to serve, to make a difference, and to broaden my *own* education in ways that would not have been possible otherwise.

I flew back to my life in Arlington feeling fulfilled.

After Al's death in Vietnam, I moved away from the Catholic Church. I didn't go to Mass for a decade or more. I just couldn't shake the questions: Why did this happen to Al? What did his death—and the *way* he died—mean, if it meant anything at all? Does God even care what happens to us here on earth?

I lost faith because I couldn't see hope. I moved in and out of depression. At one confession, a priest tried to kiss me. I was thoroughly disillusioned with the church.

What drew me back to faith was my children, the desire to see them brought up in the church and to give them a strong spiritual foundation, even if mine felt shaky. And the truth is, I don't think I ever *really* doubted the realms of spirit. I don't even think I doubted that, somehow, God was there with me.

I think I was just angry at Him—for showing me the pure love I had for Al Giddings, that such a love was possible, and then snatching it away. For not somehow rescuing Al from whatever demons were surrounding him on that awful day in Long Binh, the despair that was pressing down and blinding him so he couldn't see that I was there, that I would be there soon and would always be there to hold and comfort him and to shield him from the evil wind whispering that there was nothing I or anyone else could do—that he was alone and would somehow be better off leaving the world and my love behind.

Even now, I have no answer to the question "why?" I've merely come to a place of peace with mystery. There are things I'll never know or fully understand, at least in this life.

Back in Arlington, Father Ambrose, who had been so helpful during the divorce, was working closely with the Latino community at the same time I was forming support networks and other organizations within the Latino communities at Arlington Public Schools. An organization he founded, Hogar Hispano, still exists as a nonprofit whose mission is service to Latinos.

To me, this man was a saint. He lived and breathed compassion. He loved the church but saw its flaws and limitations. He was a superb counselor who supported me during the most difficult periods of my marriage to Jim Hainer and its aftermath.

For instance, at Jim's insistence—and his family's—James had been baptized in the Presbyterian Church. I was never comfortable with this decision, but I went along with it. Father Ambrose sensed my struggle long before I verbalized it to him. Sometime later, he made a visit to the Holy Land and returned with consecrated water—I believe it was from the Sea of Galilee. He came to visit Jim and me, and without any fanfare, in just a very low-key kind of way, he told us: "If it's okay, I'd like to use this water to baptize Julie"; and so Julie was baptized Catholic. That's the kind of man he was. And while his simple gesture wasn't the sole cause, it was the beginning of my return to the Catholic faith.

When James was about six years old and Julie three, I started taking them to Mass and then Sunday school at St. Agnes Catholic Church. One day, I got a note from his Sunday school teacher saying that James "isn't taking this seriously." They didn't understand, accept, or seem to care that his hyperactivity, his ADHD, might be the cause. They were more concerned about their rules, and with punishment when the rules were broken. It was clear that this was not the place for James, or for any of us. It seemed like I'd reached a dead end in my search for reconnection with the church. But it wasn't.

I'd heard from a friend about a group called the NOVA Catholic Community—that it was rooted in Catholicism but was not a church in the conventional sense. It was, in fact, a community, and the values of community, service, acceptance of difference, compassion, and "love in action" were its foundation. I attended a Sunday service and instantly felt, *This is the place for me and my family.* I loved the joy I saw and experienced there, the dancing, the children playing, the atmosphere free of dogma or judgment. The community included several former priests and nuns who had left their orders and were now happily married.

The Arlington Diocese at the time placed far less emphasis on community and more on adherence to church dogma. Their focus was narrow and their outlook on the world divisive in the sense that people were either saved or not saved, and the only road to salvation was through the Church of Rome. I didn't believe it.

By contrast, the NOVA Catholic Community placed a high value on service to humanity, on justice and social action. They supported progressive work in El Salvador, Nicaragua, Haiti, Sudan, and Uganda, as well as here in the United States. The outlook of its members was progressive. At my urging, the community started sending financial support to Solomon Klein, an orphanage in Cochabamba.

I'd first visited this orphanage for newborn children in 1974 and was deeply affected by what I saw there. The conditions were horrible. The babies were being taken care of in two small, poorly lit rooms. There was no running water. When I returned to Cochabamba in 1980, I learned that the orphanage had since moved to a more modern building and was no longer just for newborns. My family and I began donating.

The generosity of the NOVA Catholic Community toward this cause touched me deeply. It was an affirmation of what I've always believed the church should be in the world: a place not of judgment but of openness and generosity. And then later, when my father was in the US for cancer surgery, he came to Mass with me at NOVA Catholic, and one of the priests there readily agreed to serve him Communion when none of the mainstream Arlington churches would consider it because he'd been divorced.

Finding NOVA Catholic changed my spiritual outlook. It also brought healing to my life in other ways.

My marriages to Gonzalo and Jim Hainer had been disastrous, as had my experience with priests and therapists. As a result, I'd become deeply cynical about men in general. But a man named Jim Weber changed that. Not right away, but gradually, over time, he would show me the path to a mature love rooted in friendship, becoming a beloved role model to my children—to Julie in particular—of what a father should be. He would also inspire and humble me at times with his grace, steadfastness, and commitment to living fully in the present.

I met Jim Weber, his wife, Marjorie, and their two children soon after I joined NOVA Catholic in 1985. The leaders of the community were elected by consensus, and Marjorie was the co-chair. When she was diagnosed with cancer, the entire community organized to support the family, and I was part of that effort. After she died, Jim continued to attend Mass. He was admired and respected by all, but I knew little about him, and we were more like acquaintances than friends.

It was 2000 when my sister Paty said to me one day, "Emmy, you know that Jim Weber is available. Invite him to dinner."

I wasn't really looking for a partner. After my experience with Gonzalo and then Jim Hainer, my attitude was that it just wasn't worth it. Still, I liked what I knew about Jim Weber. He was handsome, quiet, and capable, so one day at Mass I asked him if he could help me with some kitchen repairs. He said yes, and when the work was finished, he stayed for dinner. Two weeks later, he called and asked me out. I was surprised at how happy I felt. I said yes.

Jim was from Perrysville, a small town in Ohio where his parents were dairy farmers. As a boy, he'd worked with his father making milk deliveries and building barns. He excelled in school, but the local schools weren't good, and opportunities were limited. One day, his older sister, who had been a nun but left the convent, told their father she thought Jim should go to the St. Thomas Military Academy. And he did.

Pretty quickly, he learned that his fellow students were much better prepared academically than he was and he'd have to catch up. He went on to become one of the school's top-performing students. He developed an interest in engineering and was accepted at both MIT and Notre Dame. Coming from a devout Catholic family, he chose Notre Dame. After graduating with a degree in mechanical engineering, he was drafted into the Army and stationed at Fort Myer, which was how he and his family came to live in Arlington.

Jim was devoted to his family. He would say, "Family always comes first." He was also exceptionally intelligent, skillful in his work, but modest and unpretentious. For as long as I knew him, he never tried to impress me. He was frugal, responsible, and down-to-earth. It was so different from my two previous relationships, and refreshing. Jim was loving and generous and valued his independence—and mine.

As our relationship developed and we became intimate partners, we traveled together, first to New Orleans, then Oregon, Exuma in the Bahamas, Paris, Canada, and eventually, years later, to Bolivia. We enjoyed each other's company. Jim never demanded attention; he was not possessive in any way. He would often tell me: "Love is trust."

I think I fell in love with Jim Weber watching him babysit his granddaughter. He was so gentle, playful, attentive without hovering. We would babysit together some nights, and being with him in those situations was so easy. He felt like family but without complications.

I began to develop close friendships with his two adult children, Matthew and Jennifer; and Julie liked Jim from the first. They accepted "us" completely as a couple. We would all go to church together. Matthew even joined us on the trip to Bolivia. I took them to Cochabamba, La Paz, and to the Solomon Klein orphanage, and they were both moved by the experience.

But the truth was, Jim wasn't much of a traveler, especially as he got older. When he was a child, his family never went on vacations or other trips together because the cows had to be milked and cared for. For him to go with me all the way to Bolivia was a major show of love and support.

Jim was there the night I made the decision to retire. And he was supportive a few months later when I decided to run for office and during my years on the school board. He didn't understand why I was willing to suffer as much as I did when the work was frustrating or depleting, as it often was; but he never complained that I was taking time away from him, or from us. He accepted that it was important to me, and that was enough.

When my mother came to live with me full-time, Jim would often join us for dinner, and he and my mother grew very close. He'd bring her peaches, which she loved, and on her hundredth birthday, he gave her a gift of 100 one-dollar bills. Once, he gave me a garage-door opener and said, "This is so every time you open the garage, you'll be reminded that I love you."

That's the kind of man he was, and slowly, my cynicism fell away. We had twenty-one years together, and his death in 2021 taught me not just to believe but to *know* the ways that love survives and even grows after loss.

All of this lay in the future when I joined NOVA Catholic Community. I was beginning to rebuild my life and spirit in the difficult aftermath of my second, even more painful divorce. In the meantime, I was still looking to make a difference in the lives of immigrant students and their families, and to change the ways we think about schools and learning and discover other paths of service in the community. I was inspired and beckoned forth by the work ahead. I had started over before; I would start over again. I was moving on.

CHAPTER XVIII
Advocacy and Change: The Question of Identity

April 2023

It boils down to the question of identity.

Today is the day. I spent most of last night wondering why I agreed to do this, thinking about how to prepare. I'm at the main branch of the Arlington County Public Library (ACPL). It's a warm Saturday morning. Sunlight spills through the window behind me. The staff is moving around frantically, setting up chairs, getting ready for the Human Library to open.

As for me, I'm sitting at a table with the other books, waiting to be read.

The Human Library identifies itself as a "worldwide movement for social change." The organization was founded in 2000 and has been hosting conversations "designed to challenge stigma and stereotypes" across the country. One of its taglines is "Unjudge someone."

ACPL is the host site for today's program, and I was asked by the director to be here, to share my story with whoever shows up and is interested, anyone who wants to ask me questions. The idea is to create a safe space for dialogue where sometimes difficult topics are discussed openly "between human books and their readers," the brochure says.

Today, I am a human book, and I'm not feeling particularly safe or open, only unsure of what I really have to offer.

According to the Human Library's website, every "book" on its bookshelf for these programs represents a group in society "that is often subjected to prejudice, stigmatization, or discrimination." I'm leery of the idea that any person represents a group. People represent themselves, and maybe that will be the saving grace of this experience: I've been invited here to talk about myself.

But how can I explain who I am to perfect strangers? What am I supposed to say? I'm an immigrant. I've been through the acculturation and assimilation process and have helped others in their journeys, their own wrestling matches with the question of identity. I'm also a lifelong educator, but I don't know how helpful that will be in a setting like this.

As the front door swings open and the first patrons of the day stream through, some of them heading for our table, I wonder: *Did I make a mistake? How is this going to go?* I feel more like a reader than a book, like I'm the one who should be asking the questions—which is exactly what happens when a young woman from El Salvador approaches, holding a sheaf of papers.

The woman introduces herself. She tells me she was adopted by a US State Department family when she was very young. She doesn't say what happened to her birth parents, but she's the same age as many children who were orphaned by the war that consumed El Salvador in the late 1980s—a civil war in which the United States, both overtly and covertly, played a major role.

She starts the conversation by telling me she attended Washington-Lee High School in Arlington. She's a citizen of the United States raised within an envelope of privilege, fully assimilated almost from the start; but she says, "I still have within me the feeling of connection to immigrants, especially from Latin America."

She's currently working with unhoused people, and she spent time in the Peace Corps in Peru, where she learned to speak fluent Spanish. "I have," she tells me, "a deep connection to people whose culture is different from my parents'." She wants to connect with her ancestors, her blood lineage, to gain a better understanding of who she truly is.

"Am I a Latina or not?" she asks me, and I'm not sure what to say.

"It's possible to have two identities," I tell her. "We tried to foster this idea of bicultural identity when I was working with Arlington Public Schools." She seems bolstered by this, but I wonder if I've said anything helpful. The sheath of protection I was carrying with me when I sat down at the table with my fellow "books" this morning is beginning to crack.

A young man approaches next. He's from Korea. His mother was from a poor family, and she left the boy's father to marry a man from the US Army who was stationed in Korea. In the years since they came to this country, his mother has kept her connection to the Korean church, and to a handful of rituals and other touchstones from her past; but he asks me the same question the Salvadoran woman asked: "Am I really Korean? Or am I an American from Korea?"

I shudder as the weight of his question hits home.

He tells me he's working in the technology field now but wants to be an advocate for justice and for the preservation of all traditional cultures. But he doesn't know how to go about doing this. He wants to actively oppose efforts to redevelop the Eden Center site in Falls Church, where scores of Vietnamese grocery stores, restaurants, music emporia, and other businesses now thrive.

Most of all, he wants to know about himself. "Do I need to go back to Korea?" he asks me.

"Maybe so," I tell him. "It depends."

The words ring hollow, but I'm beginning to feel the power of these two exchanges moving inside me; and there is more to come.

I speak next with a young woman from Iran, and with another from Tunisia, and these two conversations are almost identical to the ones I've just had. I sense the strength of these young people's desire, their need to understand themselves; and most of all, I feel their suffering at being in a place where their identity feels precarious, shaky at times, and complicated.

The young man from Korea is a follower of Thich Nhat Hanh, as

I am. The woman from Iran talks about her grief. Her mother died when she was sixteen, and her father is an American engineer who doesn't talk with her at all about Iran.

The woman from Tunisia came to this country to be married to a permanent resident, and now she wants to go to Tunisia to see her ailing father. But if she goes, will she be able to return? If not, what will life be like for her, living in a traditional Sunni Muslim culture, in a country where the official religion is Islam and the constitution states explicitly that the government is the "guardian of religion" and the president by law must be a Muslim? She's applied for a permanent resident visa, but since her husband is not a citizen yet, she's in limbo, with no idea when or even if her visa will be granted. I suggest that she contact her elected officials to see about getting help with their applications. She says she hired a lawyer, but he wasn't helpful.

And so, the "book" is becoming the reader after all. I feel their suffering. Because suffering is something all migrants go through, even those who arrive here in privileged positions, with wealth and access. It's a painful and difficult search we all must begin at some point—to find out who we really are. To make that decision.

In school, we aren't taught about our backgrounds, about the countries we come from, even if these markers of our true selves are acknowledged at all, which they mostly aren't. The truth of this part of the migrant experience is brought home to me again this spring morning, when and where I least expected it.

Because the truth is, we don't know. And most of the time there isn't anyone to tell us. We have to make this portion of an already difficult migration journey alone.

Driving home from the event, I realize I've learned much more from this experience than I dreamed I would. These young people, and tens of thousands of others like them, are searching for answers just as I did long ago—and am still doing. They crave ways to voice the questions they have in themselves, about themselves; they crave someone who will listen.

The young man from Korea framed it in a single question, as stark and pointed as any question can be: "I'm Korean, but I'm really not Korean. So, who am I?"

It boils down to a question of identity.

The United States is a developed country, fabulously wealthy and rich in opportunity, even with its entrenched reservoirs of poverty and hopelessness. People come here with a hunger—yes, for freedom and safety for themselves and their loved ones, but for that opportunity above all else, especially for their children. And for many who migrate here, the most important opportunity is access to education that was not available to them or to their children "back home." This is one reason why I don't take our public schools for granted and why public education has been the focus of my life's work.

In Bolivia, even today, public K12 education needs improvement, and there is still a marked disparity between those who have the money for their children to attend private school and those who don't. This is especially true in the rural areas, where the Bolivian version of the achievement gap is greatest.

I've seen thousands of talented and highly motivated young people who ask only for an unobstructed pathway to succeed. And I've also known thousands of their parents, who come to this country filled with gratitude, dreaming not of what they can take away but of what they (and their children) can give back.

The search for opportunity and the tangled web of questions surrounding identity, language, culture, and assimilation are part of the migration journey, regardless of where people come from or the circumstances of their leaving. This is true for those who come here, as I did, planning to return home someday, the same as it is for those who arrive and don't look back.

For many, migration is marked by a blending of two impulses—the longing to be back in a familiar place, surrounded by their language and traditions, where the bones and the spirits of their ancestors reside; *and* a desire to build a new life, to do what it takes to become part of this country. And this process almost always includes some kind of forgetting, some letting go.

Family has been my anchor. So has education. So has creating for myself a bicultural identity. And so has the ideal of service, of reciprocity, and the necessity of giving back. I'm an educator—at heart and by training. But the scope of the need I see in families and communities of immigrants, human beings whose roads are at times exceedingly difficult, is one reason why my work could never be confined solely within a classroom setting, or even within the mission of the public schools.

The more I succeeded in my profession, the more I saw the need and felt compelled to work in other ways to advocate for bicultural identity, remove obstacles, and create opportunity for my fellow immigrants—to be an agent of positive change.

There's a lesson I had to learn as someone who came to the United States never thinking I was going to stay. At Radford, I was known—and I thought of myself—as a "foreign student." Until I met Al Giddings, my strongest allegiance was to Bolivia, and I never thought I'd end up living here for most of my adult life. When Al died, my mother told me, "Come home"; and I did, returning to the US only to finish graduate school, partly because I thought it was what Al would have wanted.

But I went back home when it was over, home to Bolivia; and what I found there is that once you leave, a piece of your identity is altered permanently. Even if you *can* go back to your home country (and many immigrants can't), you can never go back all the way. It won't be the same.

Because I'd changed. Bolivia had changed too, but not necessarily in the same direction. I wanted something more now. My expectations and my dreams were different. I was still in my early twenties at the time, and I'd only been away a few years, but my identity had become bicultural without my realizing it. This same lesson was hammered home two decades later, at the beginning of the Fulbright Fellowship, when people in the Ministry of Education made it clear that in their eyes, I was more American than Bolivian.

I'd returned to a place I recognized, that was still inside me, and in that sense, I've been back to Bolivia many times since. But I will never come back all the way. It's a harder lesson for some than for others, but it's one that every migrant has to learn.

There are people who do make the decision to go back after many years living in this country. Life is stressful here, especially for people who don't have the documents that make their lives easier. And even among those who do, there are many who were professionals in their home country—doctors, teachers, engineers, college professors—but have no choice but to work at lower-level, lower-paying jobs because of obstacles like stricter licensing requirements: an architect working as a construction laborer or an experienced teacher working as an aide.

In addition, people who come here as adults might never become fluent in English, even after decades, maybe because they've been working two or three jobs and don't have the time or the money to take classes. They might still have family back home, an aged parent, a sister or beloved aunt they have seen only twice in thirty years. The cost of living in their home country is probably lower. They might have saved a little money, enough to buy a small place in the countryside for far less than they're paying to rent a house or an apartment in the DC suburbs. And so, once their children are grown and have received an education and made lives for themselves in this country, the parents go back.

But it's always complicated, whether they go or stay. "Home" has changed. So has their identity.

At Arlington Public Schools, my work with immigrant families was always uplifting. I helped the children and supported the parents. My way of advocating for all of them was to create a community and develop leaders who could advocate alongside me. We had to find a way to create a bilingual GED program in Arlington; and we did. We had to make sure there were enough teachers to handle the number of new students who were arriving from other countries and that the county would find the funds to hire them; and we did.

Successful advocacy often requires looking for alternatives and thinking outside the box. If there's not enough classroom space to handle the arriving students, and if we know it takes years to build a new building, what about a "mobile classroom," a trailer in the parking lot?

Most of all, successful advocacy depends on building and maintaining strong relationships with allies in the community and within the institutions where the power to make changes resides: in the superintendent's office, among the various supervisors and administrative personnel, and on the school board. It also helps to have relationships with policy and other experts *outside* the bureaucracy—people whose voices will be taken seriously.

In many cases, as we'll see, it's also vitally important to have support within the local and state governing bodies: from county supervisors, state delegates, and senators with the power to initiate change, to fight for it, and who have both wide-reaching networks and a close-up knowledge of how the "system" works.

At every stage, I was fortunate to receive strong support from many of Northern Virginia's elected representatives in Richmond, and of one state delegate in particular, Alfonso Lopez. Alfonso's passion and commitment to improving the lives of immigrants and refugees and their families, especially children, in Virginia have inspired and nourished my own.

Looking back, I can draw a straight line from that six-year-old girl standing in the Plaza Colon in Cochabamba and asking herself, *What can I do?* to the middle-aged woman standing with one foot on the cutting edge of change in American public education and the other in a surging tide of migration from Latin America, Southeast Asia, and eventually the whole world, asking the same question.

There would be many answers. Project Family and Escuela Bolivia are two examples of how to answer it by bringing a community together to address a shared and urgent need.

One very important person in this chapter of my own story and in the broader story of service to immigrants in Northern Virginia is a Venezuelan author and scholar named Luis Alberto Machado.

Working as the minister for the development of intelligence in Caracas in the late '70s and early '80s, Machado brought some of the best minds in the field of education together in his home country to explore the relationship between language and cognitive development, poverty, and class. He wrote a seminal book in 1980 called *La Revolución de la Inteligencia: El Derecho a Ser Inteligente* (*The Intelligence Revolution: The Right to Be Intelligent*) that spoke to the heart of my dissertation work. Its central thesis is that we already understand a great deal about the process of language and cognitive development, so why is this knowledge not being applied to the poor as well as to the privileged?

Among Machado's other books is *The Democratization of Intelligence*, which was also revolutionary in its two basic arguments: that intelligence can't just belong to people with money, and that "if it can be done, it must be done," meaning that educators and politicians must take action to address the stark disparities in language and cognitive development between groups of children who are different *solely* in their socioeconomic status.

I met Dr. Machado at a conference. Hearing him speak and reading his works was like listening to a great piece of music. It spoke not just to the intellect but to the soul. With support from the superintendent's office, I brought him to Arlington to meet with teachers, administrators, elected leaders, and families. I hosted a dinner for him at the house on Military Road and invited various leaders, including the budget director and the human services director of Arlington County.

They were enthralled by his ideas, and Machado was asked to be the keynote speaker at a Multiple Intelligence Conference at George Mason University. My colleague Etta Johnson was at the conference, as was Isabel Hoyt from LULAC; the three of us would later cofound an organization for mutual support and spiritual exploration called the Joy Group.

This conference was the inspiration for Proyecto Familia, initiated by Dr. Beatriz Manrique in Venezuela. She agreed to allow Proyecto Familia materials to be reproduced by LULAC; and these, in turn, provided the impulse to create a similar program in Arlington, Project Family.

Project Family's mission was to offer services to parents and other early-childhood caregivers, focusing on the initial stages of child development, including information on prenatal and postpartum nutrition as well as development of the brain and nervous system. Booklets for each stage of development were available to be taught by a Spanish-speaking facilitator who worked with Latino families.

For me, the motivating principle, the guiding spirit of Project Family, was that if I or my child can go to college, so can the children of poor and less privileged families. But these parents who are working so hard just to make ends meet need support. They need information and resources. They need to understand the milestones of infancy and early childhood, of cognitive and language development, and of the ways that physical and intellectual development are related.

Most of all, these children need the same advantages, the same access that wealthier children from more educated families have as a matter of course. There should be no difference, because there *are no* inherent differences, between rich and poor children, except those differences that are embedded in (or created by) what we call class.

The principle of *ayni,* or reciprocity, is paramount to this way of thinking. Within the spirit of ayni live the ideals of cooperation, sharing, and mutual support—the exact opposite of the values of competition, zero-sum, and inherent difference that predominate in Western, capitalist cultures.

We were, in fact, imagining a revolution in intelligence, affirming every child's right to be intelligent, and striking at the class- and income-based differences in opportunity that haunt all of society. Because every child whose cognitive and language development is limited by outside impediments that can and should be removed—every child who is categorized and labeled as being less intelligent and therefore less deserving of encouragement to excel—represents a loss to the common wealth.

I still consider the conception and birth of Project Family to be one of the most important milestones of my personal advocacy for and on behalf of immigrants. Convincing Arlington County to support this effort in its early years was a political success that was in some respects a trial run for other battles on the political front yet to come.

I think every immigrant has this experience at some point: of feeling pieces of their culture dissolving and slipping away. It's worse for people and families living in places where there is no one else from their home countries. But others feel it too. Even in a community as culturally rich, accepting, and diverse as Arlington. Even where you can hear your language spoken on the street or at Mass on Sunday. Even where there are festivals and other events that honor and affirm the traditions of your homeland: dance, music, dress, food and drink. Something is still missing.

What's missing is your history—not the history of events, necessarily, but more the way your history weaves through and within your native language and its idioms; the festivals; the ways people eat together, celebrate together. And here too the issue hearkens back to the question of identity.

You might experience this loss yourself and take steps to address it, but what about when you see this slippage in your own children, watching how much more quickly and easily they assimilate and take on the ways and the mannerisms of their adopted culture and forget or lay aside their native language? What can you do when it seems like every day, they're looking and acting more and more like all the other kids, in their dress, the way they talk and carry themselves, the things they want? When there's less and less they remember about their life back in Vietnam, or Bolivia, or Sudan?

Or maybe they were brought here as infants or toddlers; maybe they weren't even born yet when their mothers arrived. Maybe they don't remember anything at all about the place and the people they come from. So, what do you do? How do you stop the hemorrhaging of their identity, *your* identity?

These questions lingered in the minds and hearts of so many people I knew in those years at Arlington Public Schools—years when, despite our best intentions, there was only so much we could teach immigrant children about the countries they came from. Bilingual education had been eliminated in APS, except for the immersion programs. A void cried out to be filled.

In those years, too, I was being pulled closer and closer toward the center of the rapidly growing Bolivian community that was settling in Arlington. For natural reasons, I felt a special bond with them. I'd experienced the disconnection many of them were feeling myself, seen it in my own children, and I felt I had to do something; *we* had to do something. We had to create our own *Bolivian* school, not as an alternative to mainstream public education but as a vital complement to it.

It was sometime in the fall of 1997 when the idea for Escuela Bolivia was born. A similar school, Escuela Argentina, had been established in Montgomery County, Maryland, a few years earlier and was thriving there. Could it serve as a model?

Through my father, I'd become acquainted with Marcelo Perez, who was then the Bolivian ambassador to the United States. My sister Paty was his secretary. We arranged for a group of parents to meet with the ambassador and the Arlington Public Schools superintendent, Robert Smith, to talk about the founding of a Bolivian school and about whether the Bolivian government could offer some support and perhaps even official recognition. Perez was open to the idea and offered to help. More than 200 people attended this meeting. I also arranged for the superintendent to meet separately with Ambassador Perez.

The parents spoke forcefully and with passion, telling the ambassador: "Yes, we want our children to learn English; we know how important this is. But we also want them to understand Bolivian culture—to *continue* speaking Spanish as well as English, to be proud of their heritage."

The Afro-Latina principal at Patrick Henry Elementary, Cynthia Johnson, offered space for the parents to use. Almost immediately, Escuela Bolivia was a success, beloved by parents and embraced by the community. It became the model for several other "Saturday schools" established over the next few years in Arlington, most notably the Mongolian School.

Much of this early success was due to the goodwill of Ambassador Perez, who served as the first president of Escuela Bolivia's board. But because of the fluidity of Bolivian politics, I knew we couldn't depend on his goodwill and personal engagement for the long term. The government could change; a new ambassador might be appointed at any time.

We decided early on that the school's teachers should be paid;

that we needed a head administrator, a principal; and that the school would need materials printed in Spanish. These did not yet exist, so we had to create them. We also needed to purchase books from Bolivia, everything from history to works of fiction, and to do this, we needed money.

Above all, we needed to keep the tuition affordable, so we incorporated as a 501(c)(3) organization in order to raise and accept tax-deductible donations. We hired Julia Garcia, a native Quechua speaker and Spanish teacher from Cochabamba, to serve as principal. Julia was later recognized by the Virginia Foundation for the Humanities as a "tradition bearer" for the ceremonies of the Andes region. Several other Bolivian teachers joined the faculty.

The school received official recognition from the Bolivian government, which meant that students who attended could also receive credit for these courses back in Bolivia. Otherwise, American credentials were not generally accepted there. This accreditation made the path easier for children who spent their early years in this country and wanted to go back to Bolivia to attend high school or even college.

To my great joy and delight, Escuela Bolivia became a community in its own right, and I was glad that we'd thought to establish it as a nonprofit organization, not dependent on the embassy. After Ambassador Perez returned to Bolivia, the new ambassador was not nearly as supportive; she said that being involved with a school, even a Bolivian school, in the United States was not her role.

Escuela Bolivia thrived for more than a decade. Things began to change soon after I resigned from the board in 2007. I had to take this step once I made the decision to run for a seat on the Arlington County School Board. After I withdrew, the organization became more corporate in its outlook and its policies.

This happens often when organizations reach a certain size and stage of maturity: They become more focused on advancement of the "institution," which was what Escuela Bolivia was becoming. Its stated mission was still to provide the children of Bolivian parents living in this country with immersion in Bolivian history, culture, and language; but as the years went on, the focus—increasingly reflected in its culture and policy decisions—was on the growth of the organization itself.

Eventually, the name was changed to Edu-Futuro, a change I'd opposed when I was still on the board. Elementary-level programs were eliminated, and teachers were no longer required or even necessarily expected to be native Spanish speakers. The mission shifted to providing educational opportunities for Latino students generally, and within two years of my departure, there were no longer any Bolivians on Edu-Futuro's board. The organization still offers leadership training for parents, along with other highly visible programs such as the television program *Línea Directa*. But from my perspective at least, the fire is gone.

Everything has a lifespan; some lives are long, some are short, and this is true of organizations as well as people. I regret the disappearance of the spirit that gave life to Escuela Bolivia and was nurtured by it in return. But in its time, the school served a vital purpose. It enriched the lives of many Bolivian families and played an important role in keeping Bolivian culture alive when so many forces were working against it.

Those forces pushing young Bolivians toward full assimilation and away from their cultural roots have only become stronger since 2007, and public schools are doing even less now to honor and lift up the heritage that immigrant children and the US-born children of immigrants carry with them when they step off the school bus and into their classrooms—fragile connections that stay with them for at least a little while before dropping toward the horizon, slowly at first, like a sunset, until they disappear.

Careers have lifespans too. By the mid-2000s, I was thinking about retirement, wondering if the time had come to step down—not to withdraw from the essential work of education and of advocating for the needs of migrant families but to turn my attention and my energy in new directions, to look for other ways to serve.

I'd been lucky. For the better part of two decades, I was in the right place at the right time, and I knew I'd accomplished a great deal in my role as supervisor. I'd reached a pinnacle, made my mark on public education in Virginia; and I'd done it within one of the most creative and forward-thinking school jurisdictions in the state—and in the country, for that matter.

I'd been an agent for change. My colleagues and I had found ways to do what seemed impossible—to take the unprecedented tsunami of migration and channel that force so it would irrigate the landscape of public education in Arlington County rather than inundate it. And we'd done this while never losing sight of the human needs we were there to address. It was never perfect, but we made an impact.

Now I heard other voices calling. I grew more frustrated and discouraged by the movement toward standardized testing that stood at odds with everything I knew about the way children learn. It was like a mania, a virus that infected the minds of elected officials, both in Richmond and in Washington; and local school boards throughout the country were contracting it too. In Virginia, Governors Allen and then Gilmore lit up the culture wars with incendiary attacks on teachers and public schools, blaming them—blaming us—for a host of ills, real and imagined. The same thing was happening at the federal level under President George W. Bush, who rode to office partly on his indictment of the country's public education systems and teachers.

To be fair, the national movement toward standards-based education reforms began in 1993, during Bill Clinton's first term as president. The idea that setting high standards and measurable goals would lead to improved educational outcomes wasn't new when the No Child Left Behind Act was signed on January 8, 2002. But it *had* grown longer, sharper teeth, you might say; and the fact that this legislation was enacted less than four months after the attacks on

September 11, 2001, was a toxic coincidence, in which surging anti-immigrant feelings across the country mixed with public anger over the lingering impact of *A Nation at Risk* and its progeny.

The fear and the anger were both being stoked by politicians. The schools were an easy target for demagogues then; they still are. And sadly, some sectors of the press who should have known better went along for the ride.

I was still an educator in my heart and bones. I still believed in public education. The needs that had inspired me along this twenty-year winding road had not diminished. There was much work still to be done, as much as ever and maybe more. But I'd reached a turning point.

Some of the currents swirling around me at the time were personal. Some were the product of exhaustion, the kind that comes from fighting the same battles over and over again. Others came from reading the wind as it was changing, as APS was changing. And still others came from the sounds of new voices calling, even if I was unsure whose voices they were. I became convinced that I'd done what I could in my current position, that the system was being slowly locked and bolted against the kind of meaningful change we'd achieved early on. I needed to break free.

Public schools are unique in some important ways, but they're also just like other institutions. They're driven by internal and external politics; they reflect the society they represent; and they hold power that is often far greater than most individuals can have by themselves.

For many years, I was in a position to mobilize the power of my institution (APS). But this was becoming more difficult, sometimes impossible. The institution created its own obstacles and hurdles in response to the ones being imposed from outside, to shifts in the political environment, and to the growing influence of the education bureaucracies in Richmond and Washington. I was losing hope that the system could change.

The insidious effects of what was happening around me were brought home in a piece of information I discovered almost by accident. It was 2006, and I was serving on the board of Northern Virginia Community College (NVCC) at the same time I was chair of the scholarship committee for LULAC's Northern Virginia branch. This positioning gave me access to data showing that an extremely high percentage of Arlington's public school graduates were being placed in remedial classes when they enrolled at NVCC. Many of these students had come through the ESOL program, the same students we'd been working so hard to lift up. The scholarship money LULAC was awarding went to those who'd graduated with nearly perfect GPAs, but in many cases these funds were paying for remedial courses that *did not count* toward college credit. Forty percent of the APS graduates enrolled in NVCC were in this leaky boat.

I was stunned. It was not just possible but common for a student to pass the SOL and still end up in remedial college classes when he or she was tested prior to enrollment. Another grim statistic I uncovered was that depending on the year, between 40 and 60 percent of the students who dropped out of high school in Arlington were Latinos. What were the glaring lack of preparedness and high dropout rate telling us?

What they told us was that there were unseen barriers embedded within the testing system. Despite all we had done to try to remove these barriers *before* the SOL and No Child Left Behind came on the scene, they were still there.

I was not and am not opposed to testing. What I'm opposed to is using test results as the sole determinant of a student's future, and to the perverse negative effects of testing and measurement on the system as a whole.

During this time, I met a young Latino student who graduated with a 3.7 GPA. She'd arrived in Arlington as a seventeen-year-old, not knowing English. She met all the graduation requirements while learning English as a second language. Imagine the strength and determination that takes! But when she took the admission test at

NVCC, her reading and comprehension were not at the college level.

This student was obviously very bright, and she was highly motivated. What she needed was support and for the "system" to take account of her unique situation, not expensive remedial courses that did nothing to advance her progress while they squandered precious scholarship funds.

As I was trying to make sense of what I was seeing, two things happened. First, Jim Weber invited me to go with him to the funeral of his daughter's father-in-law. The man had died of a heart attack barely a week after he retired. I'd just been to a No Child Left Behind conference two weeks before and came home feeling disillusioned and depressed.

I was also bone-tired. I'd been burning my candle at both ends for a long time, and when I heard about the father-in-law, I said to myself, and to Jim that night at dinner, "I don't want that to happen to me, and it could. I can teach in college. There are other ways I can work in this field of education without constantly fighting my way uphill against a mindset that is so deeply ingrained, not just in the rhetoric of politics but in the ways the school system is operating now, day to day. It isn't worth it."

I gave my notice the week we got back.

The second thing that happened was I went to a meeting with my old friend Walter Tejada, who had just been elected to the Arlington County Board of Supervisors—the first Latino to hold a seat. The meeting was at the home of another friend, Rosa Briceno, who was then working as a family-engagement specialist with APS.

Rosa and her husband were active in the Arlington Democratic party, and they'd invited Walter, Andres Tobar from LULAC, and Alfonso Lopez, who was then a rising young star in the county's Democratic political circle. The meeting started out as a kind of freewheeling strategy session for bringing more Latino voices into the center of local political life.

A seat was opening on the Arlington County School Board, and someone—it might have been Alfonso—said, "We need a Latina to run for school board."

Walter turned to me. "Emma, you've announced your retirement. I think you should run."

I was stunned, at first. Running for office was the last thing I'd imagined myself doing in whatever this next chapter, post-APS, was going to be.

But the ball was already rolling. I said I'd think about it. Walter said, "Don't." I said I don't know anything about campaigning. They said: "We'll help you."

Alfonso suggested I immediately apply for a space in the next class of the University of Virginia's Sorensen Institute for Political Leadership, a nonpartisan organization that trains prospective candidates and campaign managers for local and statewide races in Virginia.

Was this what I'd been preparing for all these years? As a member of the school board, I'd have a voice and a platform to *really* make a substantive difference. I thought about Luis Machado: Could I be that voice saying, here in Arlington, "If it can be done, it must be done"? Could I be the one fighting for the "democratization of intelligence" from the inside? Could I be that ally in a powerful place, taking what I'd learned and making that knowledge part of our decision-making at the highest level?

Announcing my intention to step down after so many years as part of the APS staff created a void within me. And now, within a matter of days, a new and unforeseen (and unimagined) opportunity was rushing in to fill it. I was intimidated. I was flattered. I was intrigued. I was inspired and humbled; and I was about to step into a whirlwind. I felt its pull in my heart.

I said yes.

CHAPTER XIX
Service in Politics: Working in a New Arena

It wasn't a decision I took lightly. I was unprepared in many ways, but I understood politics at the most basic human level, I knew how to work with people, and I knew the field of education as well as anyone. What's more, I had strong convictions, a solid grounding in the values of ayni, and I knew the community I was looking to serve.

Of course, although I'd proved I could be an effective public speaker, I'd be stepping into the spotlight in a way I never had before, presenting myself in competition with other candidates. As much as my campaign would be about the issues facing Arlington and its public schools, it would also be about me, about my fitness and my readiness to serve.

Throughout my career, I'd sought and gained the experience to influence outcomes—to shape the views of my colleagues and coworkers as well as the policies and decisions that determined how Arlington Public Schools would fulfill its mandate. That mandate was to create learning environments that effectively served the needs of *all* our students and their families, not just those with wealth and privilege and citizenship, and to prepare these students to rise to their highest potential.

In one respect, that would still be the mandate if I were elected, but now I was actively seeking political office for myself; no matter how pure my intentions, I was asking to be lifted up to a place of authority and invested with a different kind of power. I was asking for the buck to stop with me, with Emma. *Was* she ready? Could she handle what was coming?

I was about to find out.

I applied for admission to the training program offered by the Sorensen Institute and was accepted. Walter, who enjoyed wide respect at all levels of the Arlington community, would serve as my chief advisor. Andres Tobar would be my campaign manager.

Andres had retired from the Department of Education and was the former national vice president of LULAC. His mother, a first-generation immigrant from Mexico, had limited literacy, and he understood the struggles many people in our community were facing. He was smart, wise, experienced, and extremely articulate, but also down-to-earth and far from being part of any elite.

Andres had run for a seat in the Virginia House of Delegates. He lost the race, but he was savvy now and knew what to expect. He was also the executive director of the Shirlington Employment Center, working to forge and strengthen connections between local employers and many of the people who would be part of our core constituency, our "base." He was keenly aware of the barriers ingrained in the system of modern public education and their crippling effects. It also helped that he and Walter were longtime friends. They had cofounded the Virginia Coalition of Latino Organizations years earlier. We made a very effective team.

Six candidates were running for two open seats on the board. One of those seats was being vacated by Frank Wilson, who had served seven terms and was the only African American serving on the board at the time. Of the six candidates, two were African American, and I was the first Latina ever to run.

One of the three White candidates, Libby Garvey, was running for reelection. Another, Karla Hagan, was a leader and an influential voice in the Arlington Democratic Committee who had already been endorsed by three of the current school board members.

By 2008, Arlington was a solid blue dot on Virginia's political map, and the Democratic establishment dominated local politics. They had at least one clear favorite in this election, and it wasn't me. The challenge was, I had to win the school board Democratic caucus to be endorsed by the Democratic Party in Arlington. I went to the Arlington County Democratic Committee meetings and felt like a fly in a glass of milk. People wouldn't even acknowledge my presence. It was like being back at Mount Vernon High School again, all these years later. But Walter had broken through the political ice, so to speak, years before, and he took responsibility for introducing me to the people I needed to meet.

Did the election have a racial charge? Not overtly. But at least among the old guard, my Latino background wasn't exactly seen as a strength, and the committee was still far from reflecting a commitment to diversity or to choosing candidates who represented the school population. Previous volunteer work on other people's campaigns, paying one's dues with the party—these were the more important qualifications; and from their perspective, I hadn't paid.

Besides, the Democratic Committee in those days was mostly White. I remember that some of the older committee members kept confusing the names of the two Black Democratic Committee members at meetings, even though they looked nothing alike. Frank Wilson was not James Lander or vice versa. It was not a laughing matter.

We started raising money. It was slow going at first, but eventually we raised more than $48,000 for my campaign war chest, which was a lot of money for a local school board race at the time. (It would be several more years before national political parties started getting involved in local elections like this one.)

I also had to prepare for the debates, which were organized and hosted by local neighborhood associations and the Democratic Party. I was far from being a natural debater or stump speaker, at least at first. Libby Garvey went so far as to tell me I needed a speech coach. I was hurt and didn't understand why I needed one, but I hired a coach anyway; and it helped.

In the debates, and in the campaign generally, the main challenges were, first, to nail down a few key talking points; and second, to distinguish myself from the other candidates in ways that voters could easily understand and appreciate. I found this difficult, the second part especially, but there is something in my personality, a resilience maybe (some might say a stubbornness), that I developed early in my life and that kept me going in those weeks when the campaigning was the hardest.

I kept telling myself that I was representing thousands of people—and not just immigrant families, but other parts of the Arlington community too—who didn't have a public voice or the opportunity to use it. I couldn't let down the people who were supporting me, and so I bit the bullet. I met with the people I needed to meet with, the precinct captains and many others. I found ways to let them know why I was running, and I asked for their support.

My campaign committee met every Sunday at my house on Military Road, usually ten to twelve people, including a local high school student who would sit at my computer and write thank-you notes to donors and a teacher who was also a graphic designer and took charge of creating the mailings, fliers, and other printed materials for the campaign. I held my first campaign event at the Salsa Room on Columbia Pike, which is a big room, so you need a lot of people to fill it. We did.

Meanwhile, the other candidates were saying outright, "She isn't qualified." Despite my thirty-two years of experience as an Arlington educator, some people thought I was too emotional and didn't know anything about being an elected official in a school system with an annual budget of a half billion dollars. I'd be in over my head, in other words.

In politics, you must break through and surmount whatever obstacles people are throwing in your path, to gain endorsements, to convince donors, and ultimately to persuade the voters. I did. And there was one more factor in my favor. Barack Obama was running for president, and the entire country felt the electricity of this moment—especially in a blue county like Arlington, so close to the center of power in the United States, geographically and otherwise. Obama's campaign slogan, "Yes, We Can!" drew from the same well of inspiration as "If it can be done, it must be done." For me, the timing couldn't have been more fortunate.

When the time came for the Democratic caucus, I received more votes than any of the other five candidates, including Libby Garvey. When the election was officially "called" on election night, it felt like the day I was accepted at Radford, or when I was elected freshman class officer. It felt like getting the Fulbright award or graduating with a doctorate in education. Except this was better; the feeling was much stronger, and not just for the obvious reasons.

Years later, Walter Tejada and I were the guests of honor at another event at the Salsa Room, just a few months before it closed, celebrating the fact that the first Latino to chair a board of supervisors and the first Latina to chair a school board in Virginia were both serving, simultaneously, in Arlington County.

With this election, I was once again making history.

When I was sworn in a few weeks later, I was fresh and green and untested, the most junior member of the board, and still two years away from the chairmanship and the authority it carried. But I could see the road ahead, and it was paved with opportunity.

I thought: *I have a seat at the table now. My voice will carry far more weight and across greater distances than it ever has before.*

Which also meant the weight of responsibility on my shoulders was greater than ever.

I thought about my parents that night. I thought about Al Giddings. I thought about my sister Anneliese in Bolivia, who had recently been elected congresswoman, representing La Paz. I thought about the mothers and fathers who had worked to create Escuela Bolivia and Project Family. I thought about Walter and Alfonso; about Andres Tobar; and most of all, I thought about the man who had just been elected president. "Sí, Se Puede!"

Spanish-language newspapers here and in Bolivia wrote about my election in the same context as Barack Obama's. It looked like the times really had changed.

I would meet President Obama later, but for now, I savored what had just happened, a change so simple and yet so monumental that it seemed beyond belief, even though we all knew it was real. Which made me think about the many things that had once seemed impossible in this country—and about what another, very different kind of outsider candidate had practically screamed from the stage during his inauguration speech as the new governor of Alabama thirty-five years before: "Segregation now, segregation tomorrow, segregation forever."

No más! His evil words blew away like smoke. A new day had arrived, and I was part of it. I felt hopeful in a way I hadn't for a long time. I felt some of the deepest gratitude I'd ever felt. I saw a dream beginning to take shape, though I couldn't make out what that shape was. Yet.

And so, here it was again, that old familiar question. For better or worse, I was putting on the mantle of power. *What can I do? What must I do?*

But I'd save those questions for tomorrow. I was tired; I lay down on my bed and slept the sleep of the blessed.

Doing justice to the experience of serving on Arlington's school board would take a book of its own. It was a tumultuous time, when schools throughout Virginia and in other communities across the country were feeling pressure from many directions, political and otherwise. There was not much tranquility to be found.

My ninety-two-year-old mother was present, along with my children, when I took the oath of office at the Arlington Public School Board room in January 2009. It was a joyous occasion, but by then the Great Recession was in full swing, playing havoc with local and state tax revenues. A mood of anxiety seemed to hang over even our most routine deliberations.

We had to deal with issues of overcrowding in the classrooms, an uptick in school violence (that was not unique to Arlington), a continuation of the anti-immigrant rhetoric that was born in the rubble of the World Trade Center, and a sharp decline in the civility of public discourse in the United States. The country was slowly splitting down the middle, along ideological lines.

The Tea Party movement was born in 2008, a mix of libertarian, right-wing populist, and conservative activism that stood in vocal opposition to the very *idea* of government. In 2010, the national midterm election gave Republicans solid control of the US House of Representatives, effectively tying the president's hands when it came to passing legislation that would, for example, offer a pathway to citizenship for several million young people—"Dreamers"—who had been brought to this country as children, outside the established immigration channels.

Hundreds of these students were attending Arlington Public Schools.

In Virginia, demographic shifts were concentrating legislative power in the crescent that included Northern Virginia, metro Richmond, and Hampton Roads. This did not mean that Northern Virginia legislators got their way in Richmond, necessarily. But it did draw a sharp dividing line between the urban and more rural parts of the state, at least politically, creating suspicions and resentments that flowed both ways and pouring fuel on the fires of culture wars. Some "downstate" Republicans started referring to our community as "the People's Republic of Arlington." And they didn't mean it as a compliment.

Nationwide, the country wasn't finished arguing about what kinds of books should be available to school-age children; about the proper measures of classroom success; or about the things public schools should and should not be teaching about American history. Meanwhile, a surge in the growth of digital technologies was revolutionizing every facet of public education, creating immense budgetary challenges in the process.

We addressed many of these issues at the school board level; we often had no choice. But other times it was like background noise, an unstated presence moving through our deliberations about things like the capital improvements budget, textbooks and curricula, boundary changes, personnel issues, the next state or federal mandate being handed down, or what actions we should take—or not take—in response to the latest round of SOL test results. I found it exhausting some days but also rewarding because it gave me a platform from which to speak about things that had been overlooked or intentionally hidden before, like the statistics about dropout rates.

I was elected chair in 2010, the same year the Dream Project was founded. Three White board members were planning to reelect Abby Raphael as chair of the board. Abby had argued strenuously that I didn't have the experience needed to serve as chair. With a five-member board, it seemed that her reelection was a *fait accompli*. But I thought the board needed a different vision and a different kind of public face. So I called a meeting at my home.

Walter Tejada was there, along with several other Latino community leaders, progressive activists, and James Lander, an African American who had been elected in 2009 and was furious because the other board members had reached their decision about the new chair without consulting him. I can't say if the movement to reinstall Abby as the chair had the thread of race running through it, but the appearance wasn't good, and we decided it was worth the fight.

At the chamber of commerce meeting a few days later, a respected community leader in Arlington sought me out to ask what was going on and told me that he supported my election as chair and would talk to his friends. A local newspaper published an editorial about me, and a letter went out to the Arlington Latino Network, written by another friend, Gabriela Uro. They were asking whether the board's behind-the-scenes maneuver was designed to ensure continued White control of the school board. The question hit home, and a day or two later, the board's vice chair, Sally Baird, came to my house.

Sally told me she had been planning to vote for Abby but that she and one of the other board members had reconsidered and were thinking about changing their votes. She said she didn't want to have a large group of Latinos advocating for me during the meeting when the elections took place. I told her I couldn't tell people not to show up for a public meeting.

With a large group of Latinos present in the audience, I was elected chair. But during the entire proceeding, and for months thereafter, I felt Sally watching my every move. She would call me at home to tell me all the things I wasn't doing well. It was stressful to say the least. I developed a new round of stomach problems that I'm sure were a direct result of what was happening within the board.

Later that year, attention shifted to the thousands of Arlington County students who walked to school instead of taking the bus. This too proved to be a divisive issue within the community, with some people thinking we needed more intervention and control by the government to protect the safety of these children and others arguing just as forcefully that we needed less.

I took it upon myself to visit these places personally, to see for myself how far the children had to walk, especially in the poorer neighborhoods of South Arlington. We had a large group of parents at one of the school board meetings where this issue was discussed, so I decided, more or less on the spot, to create a special working group composed mainly of parents, whose sole task would be to review these travel routes and make recommendations.

What we found was that many young children were having to cross the streets during rush hour, at busy intersections; and that some parents, mostly Black and Latino, had to walk more than a mile—in an intensely urban area—just to get their kindergartener to school. On the surface, the problem was a transportation policy issue; underneath, it was about disparities, the extra burdens that poor people carry, and about the unspoken privileges that come with wealth.

I requested that the board hire a professional to help us in discussing race and cultural competence. The other members agreed. We hired an excellent consultant, and the conversations helped. The superintendent was supportive because he knew that another priority of mine was reducing dropout and increasing graduation rates. It felt sometimes like eternal vigilance is not just the "price of liberty" but of basic human dignity for all.

―――

There were some major challenges and a few disappointments during my years on the board. Aside from the normal stresses inherent in politics and public service—working with antagonistic and sometimes overtly hostile colleagues, for example—there were some boundary changes I disagreed with; and we did find evidence of systemic discrimination against Black and Latino families, which we quickly took steps to address.

We also decreased the dropout rate and achieved a 98 percent rate of high school graduation. We introduced Spanish-language instruction at all elementary schools. We created Advanced Placement (AP) and International Baccalaureate (IB) classes that were open to all students and eliminated the fee required to take the AP and IB tests.

At our urging, Virginia created a special seal for high school diplomas of students who reached a level of bilingual proficiency. I argued publicly that bilingualism is an educational, economic, and social asset. I also worked hard to increase salaries for the lowest-paid employees and enhance salaries for teachers at all levels; and we succeeded in providing funding for teaching assistants to enroll in courses that would lead to their teacher certification.

We also introduced two weeks of paid maternity *and* paternity leave, a step that was long overdue; and we formally recognized the historic importance of Stratford High School (now Dorothy Hamm High School) as the first White public school in Virginia to admit Black students during the desegregation era.

These are a few of the tangible achievements and successes. Others can't be measured or quantified, but they are no less important: the scores of public appearances where I was given a platform to speak about pressing issues like the achievement gap, why it matters, and what to do about it; advocating for the importance of using local history and local stories as entry points to the study of Virginia and the United States; the small but important opportunities that arose on an almost daily basis, to speak up and speak out and know that people were *listening*, if only because it was the school board chair who was speaking. The list goes on.

My presence on the board and my chairmanship shattered a glass ceiling once thought to be impregnable. I never fully broke that ceiling in Bolivia, but I broke it here. And now other women with roots in Latin America—Tannia Talento and Christina Diaz-Torres—have also had the opportunity to serve on the board, and to lead it. The door is open to us, and it won't close again. Our voices will no longer be excluded or confined to the margins. *No más.*

Finally, one of the highlights, the most meaningful and beautiful outcomes, of my time on the board was the introduction it gave me to young Latino leaders in Arlington. I met scores of these inspiring young people, many of them Dreamers, like Karen V., Natalie M., Henry M., Hareth A., and others.

Karen graduated as high school valedictorian, went to law school, and years later became the first full-time executive director of the Dream Project. Natalie was accepted to Stanford's medical school and became a member of the Dream Project board. Henry was a high school valedictorian who graduated from Bucknell with a degree in mechanical engineering. Hareth is a nationally known poet and one of the most effective advocates for social justice I've ever met.

So, in the end, this part of the story too, like all the others, is about service and relationships. My (relatively) brief time in the political arena wasn't as much about achievement as it was about influence, support, opportunity, service, about representation and identity, about breaking glass ceilings. I was simply stepping out of one arena into another. It was just another way of answering the question "How can I serve?"

CHAPTER XX
The Dream and the Shadow

You can see the whole story in their faces. Sunlight and clouds; clouds broken by sunlight. The dream and the shadow mixed together. Soaring hope and uncertainty. Anxiety that can degrade like a radioactive isotope at a moment's notice into fear. Fear of even simple things: Is my taillight broken? Did I slip and say the wrong thing to the wrong person? Should I answer the door? Where is my dad? Should I have given them my home address?

The American Dream is part of who we tell ourselves we are, as a nation. It's a shared dream of hope, opportunity, an unobstructed pathway for pursuing happiness; the chance to live as we wish, free from persecution, to go as far in life as our talents and aspirations can take us.

This dream has never worked for everyone; we know that. But if we were born and grew up in this country, we might take it for granted, like a birthright. For many young Americans, it doesn't look like a dream so much as a road that beckons—toward education, a career, a good and meaningful life, whatever we want that to be.

Meanwhile, for those who come here from another country, without the right documents, the dream is often brighter and more vivid on the one hand; and on the other, it can seem too far out of reach, like the moon. Not so much an inviting path as an obstacle course strewn with dangers. You could be rounded up by agents and sent away to the place you supposedly came from, even if you don't remember that place—even if you were an infant or not yet born when you came. Or it could happen to your sister, your mother, anyone in your family. Imagine what that feels like.

You want to dream, and you hold on to the dream, even in the shadow places where the fear lives. You go on with your life the best you can. The dream can feel like wings sometimes. But there's that story about Icarus, who also wanted to fly and who thought he could make his own wings using beeswax. And in this story from the Greeks, he did fly, but when he got close to the sun, to the light and warmth he was longing for, the wax melted, and he fell to earth.

So, you ask yourself: *Is this my story too?*

It's neither fair nor accurate to blame it all on 9/11. The resentment of "foreigners" and the false prophets of "America First" were here long before the planes hit the towers on that beautiful September morning in 2001. They're part of the American story too, those resentments. But it was like the shock and horror of the September 11 attacks opened the lid of a poisoned box, and the spirits hidden inside came screaming out into the sunlight. Anti-immigrant hatred and a different kind of fear surged forth, curled back on itself, and struck again like a rattlesnake. And the snake is still among us, all these years later.

After September 11, it became not just easy but commonplace to talk about sealing off the borders of the United States, denying entry, denying asylum, denying even the basic humanity of those who come here for no other purpose than to drink from the sweet fountains of the American Dream. It became routine to declare them all terrorists and criminals, even the children.

I saw it happen. I saw what was coming. But in some ways Arlington and its public schools in particular were a protected place, or at least they seemed that way at first. We were a progressive community, after all; and in those early days post-9/11, we were receiving many students whose families had fled their homes, especially in Latin American countries, but from other places too. We welcomed them and did everything we could to respect their cultures, to honor their stories, and provide them with what they needed most: a supportive learning environment where differences were acknowledged and every student was given an equal shot.

The story of the Dream Project starts with political paralysis and frustration at the federal level, and with an attorney general in Virginia who made his own bias against immigrants and the migration of "undesirable" people to this country the centerpiece of his time in office. His name is Ken Cuccinelli, and his hostility to undocumented people living in Virginia is important to the story of how the Dream Project came to be. But so were developments in Washington.

It was 2010. Congress had been wrestling for years with the question of what to do about the thousands of undocumented migrants who'd been coming into the country for decades and settling in under the radar. Barack Obama was in his first term as president. He'd made immigration an issue in his campaign, but during his first two years in office, his more immediate priorities were health care and repealing the "Don't Ask; Don't Tell" policy regarding the service of gay and lesbian soldiers in the US military.

The House of Representatives had passed the Dream Act, providing a pathway to citizenship for people—many of them now high school students or young adults—who'd been brought to this country as children. In the Senate, the bill had bipartisan support and was introduced by two of its most powerful and longest-serving members, Richard Durbin (D-Illinois) and Orrin Hatch (R-Utah). But the legislation failed by six votes, leaving the so-called "Dreamers" and their families in limbo.

Two more years passed without further progress on the issue, and then in 2012, Secretary of Homeland Security Janet Napolitano issued and the president signed the now-famous executive order on Deferred Action for Childhood Arrivals (DACA). It was never meant to be a long-term solution. It was intended as a stopgap measure, to secure the protections the Dream Act *would have provided* until new legislation could make its way through Congress and to the president's desk.

To qualify for DACA, applicants had to have arrived in the United States before their sixteenth birthday and lived here continuously since 2007. The other stipulation was that applicants approved for DACA had to refile their applications and renew their DACA status every two years. It was a tenuous, imperfect solution that provided minimal comfort to these young people and their families, but it was better than the threat of deportation.

The problem was that deportation still loomed over every person without "documents," and for younger immigrants, the uncertainty of their status presented major barriers to their dreams of education beyond high school.

Ken Cuccinelli was elected attorney general of Virginia in November 2009 and took office in January 2010. As a state senator, he'd opposed bills that would have allowed undocumented immigrants to pay in-state tuition rates at Virginia's state-supported colleges and universities. He also called for a "Convention of States" at the federal level. One of its purposes would have been to rescind the Fourteenth Amendment's guarantee of birthright citizenship, and he was aiming these efforts squarely at the US-born children of undocumented immigrants.

In one of his first acts as attorney general, Cuccinelli lent his support to a bill working its way through the *Arizona* legislature that would have allowed police officers to question the immigration status of any person based on "reasonable suspicion" that they were in the country illegally. In Virginia, he issued an opinion that authorized police officers statewide to check the immigration status of any person at any time for any reason and to arrest people they suspected of violating US immigration law, effectively turning Virginia's state and local police into agents of US Immigration and Customs Enforcement (ICE).

Also in that first year, he explicitly advised colleges and universities in the state not to admit undocumented students at all. He'd supported similar legislation as a state senator representing Fairfax. It's significant, too, that five years before Donald Trump made immigration the centerpiece of his 2016 presidential campaign, Cuccinelli was already talking about an "invasion" by illegal immigrants and calling for swift and strict measures to stop it.

Against this backdrop, I joined a small coalition of parents and supporters in conceiving the Dream Project, also in 2010.

My friend Angela Guzman was a member of the Arlington Young Democrats (AYD), which sponsored a screening of a documentary film titled *Papers* at the main branch of the public library. I think everyone who saw the film that night had a strong emotional reaction to it. I did, and afterward I invited members of the audience, most of whom I knew anyway, to come to my house for a post-screening conversation. Walter and Robin Tejada were there; so were parents, students, educators, and community members. We wanted to talk specifically about higher education and the barriers to it that undocumented families faced.

Besides being a member of the school board, I was also chair of the scholarship committee of LULAC's Arlington branch. The national LULAC organization had matching funds available for college scholarships, but they refused to provide these funds to students who did not have "documents." The Arlington Community Foundation (ACF) was another potential source of support for young people in the county, with a large scholarship budget, but they were unwilling to award these funds to students who could not complete the Free Application for Federal Student Aid (FAFSA), which requires social security numbers.

FAFSA is the most widely used measure of a family's financial status when applying for student loans and scholarships, but it's not the only one. I'd argued with members of the ACF board, asking, "Why not use some other measure of a family's financial situation?"

Their response was that, being "undocumented," these students would have trouble finding work even if they did graduate from college, and there were other students with similar needs who would *not* face these same impediments.

Attorney General Cuccinelli had just issued his infamous memorandum stating that Virginia would not allow "undocumented" students to attend its state-supported colleges and universities, *including* the two-year community colleges. Up to that point, undocumented students could be admitted but had to pay out-of-state tuition at the same rate as students from other states or countries. Prior to the Cuccinelli memorandum, Northen Virginia Community College, George Mason University, and Virginia Tech were making exceptions. They admitted some students who were not permanent residents of the United States and charged them the higher tuition rates.

I knew one young man, Brian Marroquin, who was waiting for his permanent resident visa to be processed. He'd been denied admission to Virginia Tech, and attorneys from the Mexican American Legal Education Fund sued the Commonwealth of Virginia, successfully challenging the decision; but he still had to pay the higher fee.

Many of the Salvadorans who were then living in Northern Virginia had been granted temporary protective status (TPS), which is a special designation given, usually en masse, to people fleeing war and genocide in a particular country. NVCC initially admitted students with TPS but charged them out-of-state tuition rates.

In response to a legal challenge, Cuccinelli acquiesced, ruling on July 1, 2010, that students with TPS could be admitted, though they still had to pay out-of-state tuition. It was a small victory within an ongoing struggle that affected many immigrant students in Arlington and the neighboring counties.

Meanwhile, at NVCC, I confronted a stunning lack of sensitivity to the issue among the board and staff. NVCC had a progressive president, Robert Templin, but any progress he tried to make was squelched by the board. How could this be? I argued that as a board, we should be taking the lead, advocating in the General Assembly on behalf of these students, pushing for in-state tuition for immigrant students who graduate from Virginia high schools and pay federal and state taxes like everyone else. In my mind, ours was the kind of institution where anyone involved should be able to see how the number of immigrant students was growing and to feel their need.

But my colleagues refused to support a resolution. It was all politics. And fear. They simply didn't want to openly oppose the policies of the statewide community college board or the attorney general. They gave me the runaround constantly.

Within Arlington Public Schools, at least, there was more openness. APS always included in-state tuition proposals as part of its annual legislative package to the General Assembly. But in those days, there was very little support within the legislature for changing the status quo; that is, until Alfonso Lopez was elected, and the tide of our decade-long battle began to turn.

Alfonso was elected to the Virginia House of Delegates in November 2011, after working for several years on the staff of US Senator Tim Kaine. As soon as he took office—in his first act as a new legislator—he introduced a bill to secure in-state tuition for Dreamers, but the bill languished and died in committee.

I'd known Alfonso and his family for many years and was especially close with his mother, Carole. Carole worked as a counselor at Washington-Lee High School, where she was a much-beloved advocate for the school's immigrant students and worked hard to find good matches for those who wanted to attend college. She welcomed students into her home. She was fiery but also gentle and caring, a true servant in her life. When she was diagnosed with cancer, she took leave from the public schools while she was in treatment.

She responded well but had some long-term effects from the

chemotherapy, and the counseling director used that as an excuse to demand that she retire. The way it was handled by the school under his direction verged on cruelty. I supported Carole as best I could in those months; and by then, I'd come to know Alfonso well. When the time came, I was an active supporter of his campaign.

Alfonso continued to introduce the Dream Act in Virginia every year until it finally passed in both houses of the legislature and was signed by Governor Ralph Northam in April 2020. But in the fall of 2010, that day was a long way off, invisible from where we stood and hard to even imagine back then, considering the roadblocks we were experiencing.

Four of Arlington's most courageous students who were undocumented at the time, Antonella C., Henry M. Karen V., and Hareth A., were in Washington in the Senate gallery that day in 2010, watching as the bill was defeated. They were discouraged and angry (so was I); but they were also energized and unwilling to give up.

I invited them and several other students to my home. It was clear to all of us that, for the time being, the door to tuition relief was shut tight—in Congress, in the General Assembly, with LULAC, even with the Arlington Community Foundation.

When I looked into their faces and into the faces of their parents, I saw the dream and I saw the shadow. These were some of the most talented and motivated young people I had ever known. It was a waste of time to be discouraged. We couldn't afford that. These were not wealthy families; they needed and deserved help to give their children the opportunities they wanted and had earned. But the help we were asking for simply wasn't there yet, so there was only one path forward. It was as clear as the trees outside my window where the leaves were just starting to turn color: We would have to do this ourselves.

So, I began making calls. I mobilized friends and colleagues, parents who offered to cook, and we hosted the first holiday dinner at my home to raise money for scholarships. Within a few weeks, we'd raised $14,000. We put out the word and received a handful of applications; and in the spring of 2011, we awarded four scholarships of $2,000, with the promise that each one would be renewable for up to four years.

This was an act of faith on our part because it meant we had to keep raising money year after year, but we made the commitment. We were on the path. We created a 501(c)(3) organization to be the vessel for our work. We called it the Dream Project.

The first four scholarship recipients were Jose V. from El Salvador (Arlington Community High School); Henry M. from Bolivia (Yorktown High); and Hareth A. and Antonella R. C., both from Bolivia (and both from Washington-Lee).

Jose came to the US as a nineteen-year-old, on a tortuous and risky journey with his girlfriend, who was pregnant at the time. When he got to Arlington, he worked during the days and took classes in the night-school program we'd established at Arlington Community High School. With the funds from his Dream Project scholarship, he earned an associate in science degree from Northern Virginia Community College and eventually started his own successful business.

From the beginning, it was important to us to honor and support the ambitions of these young Dreamers, whatever form it took, and that didn't necessarily mean a four-year college degree.

Antonella was also an excellent student and was accepted at two universities in New York, but her parents couldn't afford the tuition; so, like Jose and many other Dreamers since then, she went to NVCC. She went on to get married, rose rapidly in the business world, and became a US citizen.

Henry came to the United States from Bolivia when he was eight years old. He was the valedictorian at Yorktown, with an exceptional transcript. The only B he received in high school was in AP Calculus. He was accepted at Bucknell University in Pennsylvania, where he majored in mechanical engineering. He received DACA and now works with an engineering firm in Colorado. He was one of the first board members of the Dream Project.

Hareth also experienced a harrowing journey. She and her younger sister came by plane from Bolivia without their parents, who were planning to join them soon after. This was in the summer of 2001. Tourist visas that were relatively easy to obtain before 9/11 were heavily restricted for years after, and so her parents had to come through Mexico, over land, not by plane. It was three years before the family was reunited. Meanwhile, Hareth and her sister had to make their way alone. They were detained in the Miami airport by immigration and customs officers, hammered with questions, but eventually allowed to proceed. Then they got lost in the airport and almost missed their connecting flight.

Hareth excelled at APS, showing herself to be a gifted writer, in English as well as Spanish, and graduating near the top of her class. But when the time came, she wasn't even allowed to take the test for admission to NVCC. When she was finally admitted, the college wouldn't issue her a school ID because she didn't have a "valid government ID." She couldn't pay her tuition with a credit card because neither she nor her parents had one. NVCC (where I was still on the board) refused to accept payment from her parents in cash. It also refused to accept a check from the Dream Project.

There were obstructions at every turn. Eventually, Hareth graduated from community college, then from Trinity University with a degree in international relations. She became a business owner and an activist, working on a wide range of political and social justice campaigns. And she continued to write exceptional poetry.

Her story winds through that of the Dream Project, and the power she exuded felt like a fresh breeze or a spring tonic. It empowered all of us.

Roadblocks, yes. We weren't strong enough yet to remove them. But we had to keep trying to change minds and policies, even as we worked around them. I learned about a training opportunity in Los Angeles, offered by a man named Kenneth Wong, that was designed to give Dreamers the tools and skills to advocate for change. It was a paid internship, but you had to apply.

I recommended this program to Hareth and Antonella, and they were both accepted. They went to LA in the summer of 2010, and when they came back from the training, it felt like they'd both caught fire. They came to see me in my office the next day to propose what they were calling a Dream Summit, a public event at Washington-Lee to be sponsored and hosted by APS.

There was a phrase they'd learned at the training, and they kept repeating it: "We're undocumented, unapologetic, and unafraid." They knew exactly what they wanted to do: to tell their stories so that the people who needed to hear them would hear them, and to embolden other students to tell theirs. To come out of the shadow, into the open.

I helped them develop a plan for the summit and get other Dreamers involved; and I arranged for them to meet with Patrick Murphy, the APS superintendent at the time, so they could present the case themselves. This was very important, the cornerstone of empowerment—that the students should speak for themselves. I did meet with Superintendent Murphy in advance to let him know the purpose of the meeting and bring him up to date on what was happening with the Dream Project, specifically our efforts to raise scholarship funds.

The superintendent was supportive and open, which was the first good sign. In the meeting, Hareth and Antonella explained that they wanted to cast the net broadly, to invite APS staff, faculty, parents, and students. Murphy was concerned, naturally, about their intentions to publicly announce their undocumented status. The event would be publicized in advance, and he worried that ICE agents might show up and arrest them, and their parents too. This was a real possibility, and I didn't blame him for being cautious.

He asked his chief of staff to work with the students and me, to prepare. We agreed that every student who was planning to participate had to obtain explicit permission from their parents in advance. The parents were almost uniformly supportive, another good sign; some of them even offered to provide refreshments at the event. Gabriela Uro, who was then chair of the Arlington Latino Network, shared Pat Murphy's concern about attracting the attention of ICE. But the parents and students insisted. And the school's principal was enthusiastically on board.

Henry M. would present a PowerPoint about the needs of students who wanted to attend college but faced challenges due to their immigration status, with the song "The Impossible Dream" playing in the background. Hareth would tell her story about arriving in Miami, parentless, with her little sister. There would be a panel discussion.

The summit was after school. About seventy people showed up. Henry had prepared well, and his PowerPoint was impressive. It moved everyone. When Hareth began telling her story, she was overcome with emotion and ran from the stage in tears. Her boyfriend and I followed her outside, and I told her that if it was too difficult, she didn't have to speak. But she pulled herself together and said, "No, I have to do this."

When she came back into the room, she got a standing ovation. From there on, she spoke beautifully, with composure, and I saw that many people in the audience—including the superintendent, who usually held his cards close to the chest—were deeply moved.

Soon, other students in the audience were standing and telling their stories. I remember thinking at the time that it was like a "coming out" from the shadows and standing in the sunlight for the first time. They were releasing some of their trauma by speaking about it. You could see it in the way they stood at the microphone. You could feel it in the room.

At the end, the students all stood together and proclaimed; "I am undocumented, unapologetic, and unafraid." For the educators in the audience, it was transformative. Several promised to help by mentoring students. And luckily, there were no incidents. As far as we ever knew, there were no ICE or other law enforcement agents present. It was an important moment in the struggle, one that galvanized and lit the fires of activism in these Dreamers in a way I have rarely seen.

Hareth ended up attending the training course in Los Angeles three times—in 2010, 2011, and 2012; Antonella once, in 2010; and Lizzette A., who later became the first paid executive director of the Dream Project, took the training in 2012.

Lizzette and Hareth were there in Los Angeles on the morning of June 15, 2012, when President Obama issued the executive memorandum creating DACA. The Dream Project had already received its nonprofit status by that time, and we were busy raising funds.

I knew the announcement was coming. My niece Angie, an immigration attorney who was then serving as an advisor to staff in the Obama White House, called me the day before to say that she and others had met with the president, urging him to accomplish through an executive order what Congress had been unable to do through legislation. She told me to watch the TV news the following morning but not to tell anyone else.

As soon as the announcement came, I started calling the Dreamers I knew and their families. When I reached Lizzette and Hareth in California, they were still sleeping, and we all started crying on the phone. I cried with their parents too. It was a moment of release that I still have trouble describing: the joy, the relief, the exhilaration, the gratitude. Gratitude to President Obama for taking the step, but also to be living in a country—flawed though we are—where such things can still happen.

Another door began to open when Terry McAuliffe was elected governor in 2013, defeating Cuccinelli in a race that attracted national attention, and when Mark Herring was elected attorney general.

In January 2014, I was working closely with Alfonso and Virginia state senator Barbara Favola, a friend and another highly effective member of Arlington's General Assembly delegation. I met Barbara when she was serving on the Arlington Board of Supervisors, where she struck me as an exceptionally well-informed and forceful voice, especially on issues related to education and human services. I supported her when she first ran for state senate in 2011.

Barbara and Alfonso were our chief sponsors of the Virginia Dream Act, which was being submitted for the third year in a row. The prospects were not much better than they'd been in previous years, but we all agreed that we had to keep trying until the bill passed and was signed into law by the governor, however long it took.

I'd invited them to a holiday party at my home a few weeks earlier, along with Stuart Raphael and his wife, Abby, the previous chair of the school board. Stuart had just been appointed to the post of Virginia's solicitor general. I introduced them to Dreamers Karen V. and Nataly M., both IB students at Washington-Lee High School, where they were classmates of the Raphaels' daughter.

Stuart was interested in hearing more about the impact of the Cuccinelli decision and about the reasoning behind the argument that undocumented students were not eligible for in-state tuition. The Raphaels became supporters of the Dream Project that night, and we all agreed that we should meet again soon, to talk about options and a path for moving forward.

At my urging, Barbara invited Stuart, Alfonso, and me to her home soon after the New Year, just before the General Assembly session opened. Stuart asked some excellent questions, and we provided as much background information as we could. It was beginning to seem not just possible but likely that Attorney General Herring would overturn Cuccinelli's ruling. I told Stuart that if this were to happen, it should be done prior to May 1, which was the date when most college-bound high school seniors had to decide which school they were going to attend.

Meanwhile, Hareth, Lizette, Giancarla K. R., Dayana T., and several other students had founded a separate organization called Dreamers of Virginia. DOV's purpose was to advocate for policy changes, so its mission complemented the Dream Project's but did not compete or overlap with it. Hareth and Dayana had met Mark Herring a few weeks earlier at a conference.

Alfonso was chair of Terry McAuliffe's inauguration committee, and he asked all of us to attend the inauguration parade. He also asked Dayana to come to the General Assembly in the early days of the 2014 legislative session, to meet with delegates and senators and help him lobby for passage of the Virginia Dream Act bill. Dr. Ángel Cabrera, George Mason University's president, attended the inauguration and cheered us as we went by. He became one of our strongest advocates.

Momentum was building; the right people were together in the right place at the right time; and on April 29, 2014, Herring made his announcement. After a thorough review, it was his opinion that undocumented immigrants who met certain other criteria, such as a two-year state residency requirement, were in fact eligible to receive in-state tuition at Virginia's state-supported colleges and universities, including the community colleges.

He mentioned Dayana T. in his speech. US Senator Mark Warner and other prominent political figures welcomed the decision publicly and declared their support. The press release announcing the decision was issued in five languages—Spanish, Hindi, Vietnamese, and Korean, as well as English—and included these words from the attorney general: "We should welcome these smart, talented, hardworking young people into our economy and society rather than putting a stop sign at the end of twelfth grade."

None of us could have said it better.

Almost immediately, the president of Northern Virginia

Community College began reaching out to Dream Project scholars, inviting them and their parents to attend an information meeting. Doors that had been tightly closed began swinging open. We had just won an important battle on the political front, but the war wasn't over; and it still isn't.

It would take eight more years before undocumented students in Virginia (DACA recipients and others) became eligible to receive state financial aid. But in that same year, 2022, Virginia Governor Glenn Youngkin also signed a two-year budget that redirected $10 million in funds previously earmarked to support tuition and other costs for undocumented college students. These funds, appropriated by the previous year's General Assembly, had been specifically intended to help immigrant students who, for whatever reason, could not receive federal grants or loans. Youngkin took those funds and instead made them available to the five historically Black colleges and universities in Virginia.

It was a cynical move that caught Black and immigrant students in a zero-sum political game not of their own making. And it's an old strategy, one often used in the past by those in power to set groups of people at the bottom rungs of the economic ladder against each other when they should be allies.

In September 2019, President Trump announced his intention to phase out DACA. In June 2020, the Supreme Court blocked its rescission. Barely a year later, the United States District Court for the Southern District of Texas ruled that DACA was an unconstitutional overreach by the executive branch. Back and forth. Light and shadow. Fear and uncertainty.

And so, it continues, a political contest that holds the fates of tens of thousands of young people and their families hostage. It's a contest that shows little sign of ending, maybe because immigration has been both central to the American story and a divisive force within that story almost from the beginning.

The stakes have always been high for those who migrate to this country, especially if they lack resources and political connections—as most immigrants and refugees do. But the stakes are also high for the nation as a whole. We've been told by some prominent political figures that immigrants are "poisoning the blood of our country," but the truth—and I've witnessed it in a thousand ways—is that immigrants nourish and reenergize the country. They enrich the "blood" of American society; they do not poison it.

Which is why we need these Dreamers and their dreams of becoming, of contributing, and we need their dreams of what America can and should be. It's also why many of us felt back in 2010 that we *had* to do something that would give Dreamers in Virginia a better shot at continuing their education beyond high school, to support their dreams, financially and otherwise.

The Dream Project was never *solely* about providing money for college, as important as that is. Mentoring is also an essential part of the organization's mission because, in many cases, these students are the first ones in their families to finish high school, much less to go on to college or a professional school. Beyond mentoring and financial aid, the project also offers coaching, legal referrals, technology assistance, mental health support, and emergency relief for families when the need arises.

All this is done on a case-by-case basis. There is nothing corporate about the work the Dream Project does.

The Dream Project's mission also includes helping others understand the challenges these Dreamers and their families face. I try not to use the word "undocumented," although I have used it here sometimes, for convenience, usually in quotation marks. Instead, I prefer to talk about students who face barriers because of their immigration status.

Why? Because immigration status is a temporary condition,

and labels can be insidious. "Illegal alien" is probably the worst, and "illegal" is almost as bad. These words trap human beings in a box with no means of escape. "Undocumented" seems more positive, but I still shy away from it whenever possible, to avoid painting or tattooing *anyone* with a scarlet letter.

The first Dream Project Board of Directors had little fundraising experience, yet they managed to grow the program from four scholarships in the first year to ten in the second; and both the number of annual scholarships and the amounts offered to each recipient have grown substantially since then, to 100 scholarships at $3,500 each in 2023.

It's also worth noting that in 2023, Virginia's Dream Project was still unique in the United States. A few other states have established programs to advocate for Dreamers and their families, and one or two of those have modest scholarship programs. But Virginia's was the only such organization in the country to offer scholarship *and* mentoring programs, along with a range of services to the Dreamers' families.

The work was never easy, but the organization moved steadily forward from its founding until Donald Trump was elected president after stoking anti-immigrant sentiment through a bitter and dispiriting campaign. Then, three years later, the world convulsed under the weight of the COVID-19 pandemic, which disrupted every aspect of public education throughout the country, further inflaming the xenophobia that was on the rise long before the 2016 election.

It was like watching two fires converge. "America First" became a rallying cry that only thinly concealed the anger many Americans felt toward "foreigners." At the same time, the pandemic hit hardest those students who could *not* pivot easily toward virtual learning and whose parents worked the kinds of jobs—childcare, restaurants, construction labor, cleaning houses, the lower rungs of the health-care industry—that non-English-speaking immigrants, with or without "documents," often hold.

When you're working with a group of people who are trying their best to stay invisible, almost everything is hidden, including their needs. During the early years of the first Trump administration especially, there was a pervasive fear of summary deportation, of DACA being canceled; and as a result, many people went even deeper into hiding. Ironically, it became harder to reach prospective applicants electronically, to let them know about the opportunities, at the precise moment when there were more funds available.

The one bright spot during the darkest days of the pandemic was a healthy increase in donations, which allowed us to continue paying staff salaries and scholarships while providing mentoring through Zoom. Then, as has been the case throughout the Dream Project's history, the organization's greatest asset was not the board or the donors or even the staff, as important as all those were. It was the parents.

Parents carry the burden of uncertainty, the never-ending contest between the dream and the shadow, just like their children. Their steadfast support and willingness to do whatever was required during that excruciating and confusing time, often at great risk to themselves, sustained us. Without it, we could not have survived as an organization.

When I think about the Dream Project, the word that comes first to mind is "inspiration." I've been inspired by the students, the Dreamers. And I've been inspired by their parents. I've also been inspired by the board as I've watched it grow in wisdom and capacity over time, and by the staff of the organization, past and present—people like Lizzette A. and Karen V., and forceful advocates like Hareth A.

I've also been inspired, and deeply encouraged, by the support and recognition that's come from all parts of the community in Northern Virginia, and from other parts of the state too; from friends like Alfonso Lopez, Barbara Favola, and other members of the Virginia legislature; from Governor Northam; Senators Mark Warner and Tim

Kaine, Congressman Don Beyer; and by the generosity of donors, large and small, that sustain the work.

On a personal level, the work has been profoundly gratifying. I think giving birth to the Dream Project is what I was preparing for throughout my career, even in childhood and as a young immigrant. It's part of the work I was born to do. Seeing the faces of the Dream Project scholars, hearing their stories, watching them step out of the shadows and soar with wings held together with far stronger stuff than beeswax, has opened my heart and uplifted my spirit in ways I can scarcely begin to describe. But there are discouragements in the work too, regrets that are seemingly wired in, hidden risks and dangers, disappointments, exhaustion, even casualties along the way.

I think about one of the most talented Project scholars in our history, Manuel M. from El Salvador. Manuel came to this country as a teenager, worked hard, excelled in math and science, and combined his Dream Project funding with other scholarship support to attend Virginia Tech, where he graduated in 2022 with a degree in aerospace engineering.

This field of aerospace is his passion; it's his American Dream. But what he found out is that to get a job in the aerospace industry, he needed a security clearance; and he couldn't qualify for even the most basic security clearance because he is not a US citizen.

We focus too much sometimes on the stories with neat, happy endings. We'd prefer to think that once these Dreamers are set on the path to higher education and they have a degree, doors will open for them. But that isn't always true. It's not as if they get the scholarship and suddenly everything is okay. That's just the beginning, a new chapter in a struggle that continues.

I also think about a beautiful young woman from Guatemala who does some of the finest embroidery work I've ever seen. She applied to the Dream Project, hoping to attend NVCC, but her application wasn't funded—not because she wasn't deserving but because there were other applicants whose needs were *even greater* than hers.

And I think of Hareth. Her courage and passion inspired me; it inspired her fellow students, their families, her teachers, all the way to the highest levels of county and state government, and beyond. She was—she is—one of the most committed and gifted activists I've ever known.

Soon after I met her, Hareth's father was targeted by ICE for deportation. Hareth led the effort to gain his release. She worked day and night for weeks. She asked me to go to court to support them, and I did. She fought the authorities and put herself at risk. She swallowed the stress. Her only thought was to keep her father from being deported; and she succeeded.

Word got around. She was becoming well known as an advocate for immigrants' rights. She was poised to move onto the national stage.

But then something happened. I've seen it happen often to young activists like her. After years of pouring their energy into a cause that also forces them to constantly relive their own trauma, they burn out, they reach the end of the line, and they have to step back. Some never return to the work, not because they don't want to but because they can't. When that happens, it's like losing a great warrior in battle or seeing a flower wither.

Other challenges are wired into the mission of the Dream Project. The costs of higher education are rising and will continue to rise. So is the cost of living for the Dreamers' families. Which means that the need to raise Dream Project scholarship levels must continue to grow. It's a treadmill that doesn't stop.

At the same time, more and more immigrant students and families need financial help, a sense of community, and a safe place where they are welcomed and loved. Which is the higher priority? To award more scholarships at the same amount? Or to raise the amount but keep the number of scholarships the same? There's no "right" answer to this question because something will be lost either way.

Already, 5,000 students from all over the world who face challenges due to their immigration status are graduating from Virginia's high schools every year, fleeing every imaginable trauma. It's hard to see the need, to see the potential, to see the dreams (and the shadow) in these bright, highly motivated young people and not be able to help every student, every family, who applies.

It's been a long road since we sat in my living room in the house on Military Road and said: "We have to do this ourselves." There has been great joy on this road, great satisfaction, and—considering everything—relatively few disappointments. The Dream Project emerged and began its work at exactly the right time.

I think sometimes that the work has hardly begun. The need for what the Dream Project offers certainly isn't going away, so the organization has no choice but to keep moving. The challenge is twofold: to keep the kinds of personal connections, the relationships, that have brought the Dream Project this far; and to keep the focus where it belongs, on the Dreamers and their families, and not just on "growing" the organization.

Because the work is not about this or any other organization. It's about service. It's about compassion and understanding, about individual needs and circumstances, not algorithms.

As the organization grows, as it must, systems will need to be upgraded to help manage the increased financial and communication needs. The natural tendency is to look to these systems for guidance, to invest them with greater and greater authority; and for "management" to replace relationships as the keystone of the organization and its daily work. For organizations to become more corporate in structure, in other words, and to adopt the values and "best practices" that are common in other successful nonprofit organizations.

As the Dream Project changes, I hope it will never lose sight of its original mission. But I don't see this as a zero-sum choice. Instead, I believe there is a middle path, where systems that support the healthy functioning of an organization can coexist with the commitment—with a firm resolve—to keep relationships at the center so that the Dream Project will remain a haven and a place of refuge and belonging for students and families who have lived so long in the shadow of being told they don't belong.

I know burnout is a danger. I've felt it myself, and seen it, and the only antidotes I know are found in spiritual practice. That's what sustains my energy and keeps my focus where it needs to be—not *just* in relation to the work of the Dream Project but in family life, friendships, even the writing of this book. Because in the end, the only true cure I know for exhaustion, fear, and discouragement is love.

CHAPTER XXI
The Faces of Love and Loss

There is no way to write about the joys of my life and not remember the loss of people I've loved. My husband Al, my beloved grandmother, my sister Paty, my aunt Mecha, my parents, and in later years, my dearest friend and partner of twenty-one years, Jim Weber.

Death winds its way through life like veins in a piece of turquoise. The shudder, the emptiness, the sorrow and pain, the cold touch of grief—only the ones who leave this world when they are very young escape this part of the human experience.

Al Giddings was twenty-three when he entered the vortex of the war in Vietnam and saw too much of death all at once, so hideous and overwhelming that it broke his heart and his spirit. At least that's what I've come to believe. I experienced the trauma of his death by suicide for more than forty years. It was a long, complicated grieving process that was confined beneath the surface for too long.

I visited Vietnam in November 2023, and it brought a measure of peace. I went there to bring his spirit home after all his suffering and mine. I look at death in a different way now. The spirits and the energies of the people I have loved and lost continue to be with me. I feel their love and protection.

Grief has many faces. It takes different shapes. It can be long or short. On the surface, grief seems more like a wounding than a healing. The death of loved ones cuts new channels in our psyches, the way a river in flood stage cuts away pieces of the embankment, and the river never flows the same way after that. But we grow through our grief. It makes us stronger. It gives us tools to understand and perhaps ease the suffering of others.

It's one of the most profound ironies of life: Loss creates an emptiness that is never filled completely; but it can also make us whole.

My sister Paty was living in the United States when she was diagnosed with stage-four breast cancer at the age of forty-four. The diagnosis came on the same day she learned her application to become a US citizen had been approved. I was there at her townhouse in Arlington when she got the news.

There's a photo of my sister and the other members of her family celebrating the day she took the oath of citizenship. She looks radiant, even though she was gravely ill. She was happiest because of what US citizenship would mean for her children, the doors that would be open to them now without question—the stability and opportunities it would provide.

She enrolled in an experimental treatment program at the National Institutes of Health in Bethesda, Maryland. She remained hopeful about the prospects of remission. She had a bone marrow transplant that was not successful; and a second one wasn't possible because, by then, the cancer had spread too far.

When we knew Paty's illness was terminal, all six sisters spent a weekend at Susy's house on Virginia's Northern Neck. The end was coming fast, and we all knew it; still, the days were full of joy. We laughed, we sang, we told stories. The love that filled the house that weekend was palpable, and to this day, the memory of that time fills me with happiness, not grief: because of what we all experienced together.

I still remember Paty's courage and composure in those final days.

When she entered hospice, one of the attending priests was from the NOVA Catholic Community. He gave her last rites. He took her last confession. Then she stopped talking. She'd already chosen the music she wanted to hear in her final hours. It was a celebration of life, and I know she heard it, even though she couldn't speak or open her eyes anymore.

What does it mean when a woman in midlife dies, leaving three children, a husband, and a loving family behind? It's the natural question, but I've come to believe it's the wrong one. The question is, what does her death mean to the ones who survive, who must find a way to carry on the work of life, the joy of life, without her?

For me, Paty's death showed that peace is possible, even when facing the end of life. She looked it in the eye, and she did what was still in her power to do: She chose, and she accepted what was not in her power to change.

Paty was part of the genesis of Escuela Bolivia, in the same way that her cheerful nature and her courage in her final days will always be part of me. No one ever knows how far his or her influence will extend, what lives we touch and inspire, or what doors we open without ever knowing it. This has been a lesson worth more than gold: that we are all connected, and no one's life matters more than any other.

My mother came to live in Arlington to be near Paty in the months following her diagnosis. She'd been living in our family home in Cochabamba with Paty's oldest son, Juan Cristobal, a talented filmmaker. She loved Cochabamba, the open-air markets, the pace of life, and the closeness to family and friends.

She was in her early eighties then, but she still took great pride in keeping the house and garden. She had a car, a Volkswagen that my sister Anneliese and her husband, Pedro, had given her; and she loved to drive, even with the loss of sight in one eye decades earlier. Whenever the children and I went to Cochabamba, she insisted on picking us up at the airport, which was one reason I never forgot how to pray.

It took a while for her to adapt to life in the United States. Arlington was a different kind of urban environment than the one she'd known in Cochabamba, but she adjusted, meeting Bolivian friends for lunch, playing bingo, and taking exercise classes during the week.

Still, she was homesick sometimes; and in the years after Paty died, she went back to Cochabamba often, to see her house, her friends and family. But she developed macular degeneration in her "good" eye, and even though she was vigorous and active, she was an elderly woman and thus an inviting target. One Sunday, she went to church as usual, and when she came back, she discovered two men she'd hired to paint her house trying to break in.

They ran when they saw her, but it was a wake-up call. I begged her to sell the house in Cochabamba and come back to Arlington permanently. She resisted at first—partly because Juan Cristobal was still living there, working on the script for a now famous film called *¿Quién Mató La Llamita Blanca?* (*Who Killed the Little White Llama?*). She agreed to come back to Arlington; but she kept the house.

My mother was a proud Bolivian from Tarija, a *chapaca* through and through. On her ninetieth birthday, we celebrated in a Bolivian restaurant, and the only thing she asked me for was to find a friend from Tarija who could dance *cueca* with her. She told me no one could ever dance *cueca* the way they did in the city where she was born. She also chose the menu and handpicked the guests to be invited and the music—a live band *and* a DJ.

At the age of ninety-one, she decided she wanted to become a US citizen. Her English was poor, and she failed the written test. But then she took it a second time, in Spanish, and she passed. Her resilience and determination never failed her, even in old age.

Sometime around my mother's ninety-eighth birthday, my daughter, Julie, noticed that her breathing was becoming difficult. She had to be hospitalized. The doctor told us she was terminally ill, had less than two months to live, and that we should take steps immediately to get her into hospice care at home.

I decided she should move into my house and arranged a room for her. The hospice care was excellent, and her condition began to improve. Six months later, hospice ended their service: It seemed my mother was not dying after all, at least not yet. I used to joke with her that she was the only person I ever knew who had "graduated" from hospice.

As things turned out, my home was the very best place for her. I was taking care of my first grandson, Victor Luis, during the day while his parents worked. My mother loved him, and he loved her. It was a big, comfortable house, family and friends coming in and out constantly, and we could celebrate all the holidays there easily. It was hard for my mother to travel, but by then she'd recovered much of her energy, and she wanted another party, this time to celebrate her ninety-ninth birthday.

My sister Susy organized it. All the family members came, and my mother's grandsons Mauricio and Juan Cristobal decided she should record songs and a message for her family, which she did. We all got copies of the CD, and I still play it often. To still hear the voice of a loved one who is gone is a gift.

My mother's dream—and she set this as a goal—was to live to be 100. She wanted to have a big party, and just like she'd done ten years earlier, she dictated her guest list and reviewed it often, adding, subtracting. My sister Julia bought her a new dress, new shoes; and my mother was determined to dance a *vals* (waltz) with her son-in-law Pedro, Anneliese's husband.

In Bolivian tradition, *vals* is the first dance in a wedding celebration. My mother chose the vals that she and my father danced at their wedding. She loved Pedro; he arrived early for the party so they could practice together beforehand. The entire family gathered, and we celebrated her 100th birthday in the way she wanted, on September 1, 2018, with seventy-four family members and friends at the country club in Arlington.

As the next few weeks went by, her condition worsened, and on December 20, I had to call an ambulance. I rode with her to the hospital. The doctor didn't expect her to survive more than a few days at most.

But it still wasn't time. She suddenly got better, just like before. She asked for a McDonald's cheeseburger and told the doctor she wanted to go home to celebrate Christmas, and that they couldn't keep her against her will regardless. Which was true except that I had her power of attorney and her medical directive, so it was my decision. I hesitated—asked myself what the right thing to do was; but it was obvious. I told the social worker it was all right. My mother would come home with me, and we'd get hospice services (for the second time) at my house.

And so, my mother celebrated her final Christmas at home. Anneliese came from Bolivia, and we made my mother's favorite Bolivian soup, *picana,* for Christmas dinner. It was a joyous time—children, grandchildren, great-grandchildren, all surrounding her with love and music.

I was nervous and anxious after the holidays, knowing that the end was not far off. One night, she had a vision of herself as a little girl who needed milk. She was anxious about a treasure that was hidden, about a debt that needed to be paid.

She told me she would soon meet her parents again in heaven and was excited to see what her mother looked like. She was only one year old when her mother died, had no photograph, and did not remember her face. It was heartbreaking but also beautiful, feeling the power of my mother's faith, knowing the hardship she had overcome in her life and that she was about to be set free.

She would sing to Victor Luis. He would climb on her bed and tell her he loved her.

In those final weeks, she gave us clear instructions: She wanted a blessed sheet to cover her body when she passed. We couldn't find one in the United States, so we had one sent from Bolivia. When the sheet arrived, she wanted us to make sure it fit her body, so we measured it. She chose songs from Tarija to be sung at her funeral Mass. She also told us what dress she wanted to wear when she was placed in the coffin. She wanted to be buried with a rosary and with a little doll from my sister Paty. She instructed her caregiver, Flor, to put in her dentures and put on lipstick. She was meticulous and wanted to be sure everything was done properly. She wanted to look her best.

She said we could use the 100th birthday guest list for her funeral. She paid all the funeral expenses herself. She made Juan Cristobal swear he would become a US citizen. When he came to the house to show her the document proving he'd done it, my mother told him: "Mi misión está cumplida" (My mission is accomplished). "You are a US citizen. Now it is up to you."

She stopped talking soon after that. I knew there would be no sudden rebound this time. It was almost over.

On the night of March 16, I called the hospice nurse to say my mother was having trouble breathing. He came right away and said, "Yes, it will happen tonight" and that I should notify anyone who could come in time to see her. My sisters Julia and Maria Eugenia were there; so were Mauricio and Juan Cristobal.

We sang a song to her, and she stopped breathing. It was 2 a.m. I called the hospice nurse, and they said they would come in the morning to get the body. James and his fiancée, my sisters and nieces, Flor, and another friend, Gilda, were all there to sing as her body was carried out to the funeral car. I was numb until I spoke with my daughter; then I began to sob.

I asked a Bolivian singer, Julio Cuellar, to sing at her funeral; he knew all the songs she'd requested. Father Jose, one of the priests from the NOVA Catholic Community, helped us to plan the liturgy. My mother had asked Gilda to sing "La Vidita San Lorenzina." Anneliese came back from Bolivia for the funeral. Another grandson, Paul, produced a video with family photos, incorporating songs she'd recorded.

In the end, it was like we were all standing in a shower of love and gratitude for the richness of her life. We wrapped her coffin in a

Bolivian flag. We stood in a circle around it with a Tarija *cueca* in the background and began to raise handkerchiefs. It was a dance of honor and celebration of her love of music, the love she had for her family and for her home city of Tarija.

After the burial, everyone left, and I was alone in the house for several weeks. There would be no more boisterous visits from family members. No more "I love yous" from Victor Luis. No more television news in Spanish turned up loud. Only silence.

I wanted more than anything to feel her presence, but her spirit had left the house. The smells of her hair and clothing lingered, though. And the music. And the memory of her telling me, "Come home" when home was what I needed most. And gratitude. For all she had been, all she had seen and known in her life, the good and bad, the joy and pain, the things she loved and the things she had lost. All of it.

And this is what I took with me, as a blessing, from my mother's death. Her life was long. It was full. She knew her share of suffering, but she drowned it in joy, in celebration, and in love. There is no greater gift anyone can give to the people they leave behind.

In 1995, the Fulbright Fellowship in Bolivia gave me precious time with my dad. We had some of the best conversations we'd ever had. He acknowledged the pain and confusion the divorce from my mother had caused all of us, and he apologized. He was happy to have me back in Bolivia and that I'd brought my two children with me. My mother was still living in Cochabamba then, and we would visit her often. I know that he respected my mom and was grateful that she had been such a good mother to their six daughters.

My father and I became closer than we'd been since I was a child. He had bladder cancer, and my sisters and I found a way to bring him to the United States for treatment. This was in 1997. He stayed in

Richmond with Susy, preparing for surgery, but he also visited me in Arlington, which was where he received that precious Communion at NOVA Catholic Community.

Those weeks he spent in Virginia, preparing for the surgery and recovering from it, also helped my dad reconnect with my sisters. It was a time of healing for all of us.

In 1998, my dad was appointed ambassador to Egypt. His wife had a stroke on the airplane just before it stopped in Spain to refuel. They decided that he would go on to Egypt, and she would return to Bolivia, to Santa Cruz, and so for most of the four years he served there, he lived alone. He had all the amenities that come with being an ambassador, but I know he was lonely. I visited him once, and we had a beautiful time together, enjoying Luxor and Cairo. I loved my father dearly, despite the pain he had caused, and that visit brought us even closer.

When he finished his posting in Egypt, Dad returned to La Paz. I visited at least once a year.

Jim Weber and his son came with me in June 2003, and my father welcomed them graciously, the way he always did. He had a way about him: charming, dignified, but also warm and open. I loved seeing this side of him. I was on the train to Machu Picchu when I got a phone call from Maria Eugenia that Paty's condition had worsened; her cancer was in its final stages, and I had to go back to Arlington right away. My father came with us, and I remember that trip especially because he had to use a wheelchair in the airport. He'd been diagnosed with Parkinson's disease by that time, and walking long distances was difficult.

It was a blessing that my parents were both there, together, when Paty died. As painful as it was to lose their youngest daughter, they always seemed to rejoice and gather strength from being with each other. It was never awkward or strained. I know that on some level, my mother never stopped loving my dad, that he was the love of her life; and I think he still cared deeply for her. This time of grief also brought healing to our family.

I've thought many times about how rare this is, and how lucky for the family, when divorced parents can maintain not just a level of civility but a warm relationship throughout their lives. I remember one occasion when it just happened that my mom, my dad, and my aunt Mecha were all in Virginia at the same time, and I got everyone tickets to a performance of tango music at the Kennedy Center. My dad was sitting to my right, my mother on my left, and Mecha was next to her. When the musicians started playing, my mom and dad both got excited and started talking loudly, remembering the time when they danced tango.

Mecha was telling my mother to be quiet, and I told Mecha she should let my mom and dad enjoy the show. I think we caused an uproar, but the moment was so joyous; and I marvel to this day that as soon as they began to feel the excitement, Emma and Adalberto turned immediately to each other. I'm surprised—and still relieved—that they didn't stand up and start to dance.

By 2003, my dad was growing weaker , but he was working on his book with the help of a historian. He lived in La Paz by himself now, his wife having moved to Santa Cruz permanently to be with her son. My father had a butler, Jorge, who paid the bills, took him to appointments, and tended to his needs. Jorge's wife cooked the meals, and they brought their two children to live at my father's house. It was a good arrangement; he needed the companionship.

But what my father needed most was love; he needed his family, but by then, everyone but Anneliese was in the United States. Still, he remained positive. His book (*Retorno al Mar con Soberanía: Una Negociación Frustrada*) about his efforts to negotiate a coastline for Bolivia was published in 2004, and he took great satisfaction from that.

I called him every day from the United States. I even hired a young woman named Maribel to visit him on weekends because Jorge and his wife only worked during the week. One Sunday, Maribel came to the door, and no one answered, so she called Anneliese, and my father was taken to the clinic. When they called and I heard his voice, I knew I had to go to La Paz right away.

By the time I arrived at the hospital, my dad was unresponsive. He had tubes everywhere. It was horrible to see. The doctor told us there was little chance he would recover.

All my sisters came. We sang songs. I held his hand. After two days, his wife arrived, and he died shortly after. Maybe he was waiting to see her one last time; maybe there was something he wanted to say to her even though by that time he'd lost the ability to speak. I don't know.

He had asked to have his casket placed at the Ministry of External Relations (Bolivia's equivalent of the US State Department). We had Mass for him, and many people came to tell us about his kindness and generosity and what a gift his service to Bolivia had been. It was painful but uplifting.

We had a band, his funeral was in the plaza near the ministry, and then we went to the cemetery. His wife was in the car with me, insisting that I send her some china that was in my dad's apartment; then she left for Santa Cruz as soon as the burial was finished. It was clear she didn't love my father, even though—as frail as he was—he'd gone to see her just two weeks before his final illness. He wanted her love and affection.

My father was a complicated man, worldly, charming, sophisticated, generous, and kind. He also left my mom and his daughters when we were very young. He loved his country as intensely as my mother did. He also served in the administrations of a repressive dictator, but the affection and admiration that so many of his fellow Bolivians expressed for him in the end was real.

My father craved love. It's ironic that as charismatic as he was, he was alone in the final years of his life. And it's ironic, too, and tragic that the person who loved him most deeply was the one he betrayed.

I wish my dad had felt the same joy that surrounded my mother in her last days. I do believe he knew we'd forgiven him and that his country was grateful for the many ways he'd served. He was—and always will be—my role model for public service. In some ways, I've served all these years in his shadow. He taught me so much about life. And yet . . .

There was a sadness when he passed from this world that was

different from the grief I felt in losing Paty or my mother. The feeling of a wound, an emptiness somewhere in the heart. It was too deep to pinpoint, much less to heal, but I felt it there even in happy times.

Because death teaches this too: that what is left unresolved when a person dies remains unresolved; and that sometimes, the thing a person spends most of his life looking for is what he rejected or denied in the beginning, by his own choice.

There are times when I wish I could have my mother back again, for my sake; but I never wish she'd lived any longer. When she died, her life was complete. With my father, it's different. I wish I could have him back for my own sake but mostly in the hope that he could find the love and resolution I know he craved.

My aunt Mecha was a powerful force in my life. When she moved back to Bolivia permanently after living for more than a decade in the DC area, she was elected to the Bolivian senate, representing Tarija. She worked with women in prison and with the elderly. She taught aspiring teachers at the Normal School in Sucre.

My own decision to enter the field of education was inspired by her. Like me, she established organizations to do the work she believed was most important. She could be a fierce presence, but she also had a loving and nurturing side.

In 1995, when I was in Bolivia with James and Julie, we celebrated her ninetieth birthday. The next time I saw her, two years later, she'd lost sight in both eyes after a botched surgery that was supposed to cure her glaucoma. She was confined to her bedroom and needed round-the-clock care. She also suffered from recurring nightmares.

We were close in some ways, but in other ways, Mecha's life remains a mystery. She was admired and respected, but she had a remoteness, a formality about her; hers was not the kind of personality that invites intimacy or inspires affection.

I wonder what it was like for her, going back to Bolivia after living for so many years in the United States. She was the first in our family to gain US citizenship, but I don't think she ever assimilated. Did she feel acceptance when she came back home? Or did people in Bolivia think of her as an American, the way they thought of me? I also wonder about her doubts, her fears, about those recurring nightmares. What demons haunted her? I wish I could ask her. I wonder if she would tell me, or if she even knew the answer.

In her final months, Tía Mecha was cared for by amazing women. She was not alone. And yet the celebrations of life that attended my mother in her last years were not possible for Mecha. She had no children, no grandchildren. No two-year-old to climb into her bed and say, "I love you."

What does it mean to die alone, without loved ones nearby singing; to have no one to lift you and dance the vals one last time? Is this also the wrong question to ask? Maybe. Because Mecha's life had an impact, a meaning, and her legacy is strong in the world—in Bolivia where she did so much of her best work, but also here.

Wherever I go, whatever I do, everything I've accomplished, even the fact that my sisters and I and our children and grandchildren are citizens of the United States—all this is the result of Mecha's influence. After all, it was because of her that Julia, Susy, and I came to this country in the first place. It was a "good opportunity": She was right about that.

Without Mecha's urging, and without her help, we likely would have stayed in Bolivia. And if you trace the linkage out far enough, both my parents had access to the best medical care in the world as they were aging because of Mecha; and my mother died in my home, in Arlington, surrounded by three generations of a loving family—also thanks to Mecha.

And so, the lesson once again is that we are all connected. Mecha lives in me, as an educator and advocate. She lives in the families that were lifted up by Project Family and Escuela Bolivia and in the achievements of hundreds of Dream Project scholars. And still, I regret that I couldn't be there for the death of this woman who set my life on its course, opening so many doors for me and others in the process—some of which even she never knew existed.

Sometimes, it's the mystery that matters. Sometimes, the mystery is what stays behind.

In the early days of the pandemic, Jim Weber was diagnosed with lymphoma. He had chemotherapy, which compromised his immune system further, and he needed to stay isolated. I would go to his house and bring or cook meals for him, always wearing a mask.

When the doctors said his cancer was in remission, he started coming to my house again. My mother had passed by this time, James was living with his girlfriend, and I lived alone.

We started eating dinner together every night; we'd cook steaks.

Jim would arrive at 5:30 "on the dot." He always brought a bottle of Charles Schwab pinot grigio and a half bottle of milk. We'd listen to music while we cooked and then watch a movie pulled from a list of "100 Great Comedies" that he'd gotten somewhere. He had no interest in movies with darker themes.

One night, he didn't show up on time. I called him at 6 p.m. and he seemed confused. He said: "Do you want me to pick up pizzas?" I told him no, and he said he'd be right over.

He still wasn't there at 7, which was completely out of character, and when he finally showed up at 7:30, I knew something was wrong. It was a Thursday night, we cooked dinner and turned on the movie, but I could tell he wasn't fully present. When he left, I texted his daughter, Jennifer, to tell her what I'd seen. She saw him the next day and told him not to drive.

On Friday night, I brought dinner to his house, but once more he seemed distracted and upset. He said the microwave didn't work. I tried it, and it did. He said the computer was broken. I could see he was entering the wrong password.

Jennifer had scheduled a medical exam for early the following week, but I called her and asked, "Should you take him to the emergency room? He needs to see a doctor. There is something wrong. Maybe he had a stroke." The next morning, Jennifer found him lying on the living room floor and called the ambulance.

We got the diagnosis on March 14, 2022. Jim had an inoperable brain tumor. He went immediately into hospice care at Jennifer's home and died three weeks later, on April 18. The woman Jennifer hired to help care for him spoke Spanish, and when she saw that he was failing, she called me to say, "Jim is dying." I rushed over, but by the time I got there, he'd already passed. The night before, we'd both said, "I love you." They were the last words we ever said to each other.

When I went back to my house on Military Road, it felt vacant, like no one lived there. It was the same feeling I had when I first learned about Al's death, fifty-three years before. The same feeling I had after my mother died.

Jim was my partner. He knew me, and I knew him. What I had with Al was pure and innocent. Our love was youthful; it was never spoiled, its surface never marred and twisted by the harshness of the world. With Jim, our love was suffused with the wisdom gained over a lifetime, with the sweet and bitter herbs of sorrow, loss, joy, acceptance, understanding, peace. The wearing away of the riverbanks that comes with time.

From Jim Weber I learned that love is trust, responsibility, companionship, friendship, respect, and independence. Loving and losing Jim changed me. It helped me understand that after death there is grief, there is emptiness, confusion, sorrow, pain; and this is natural. But there is also an enduring love that transcends death.

Later, Jennifer gave me Jim's high school ring, which I wear constantly now, as a symbol, a way to remember the love for that person who was in my life for twenty-one years, which is a long time but also briefer than the flickering of a candle. Besides the ring, his son gave me CDs of songs Jim had recorded—John Prine, Iris Dement. I play the music and I remember dancing with him.

Picturing Jim now, I see him wearing his glasses on his chest, and I remember how he wore the same single pair of shoes; and if you gave him a new pair, he would thank you and just give them away.

Jim wasn't a writer, but I still have an essay he gave me, something he wrote in 1985, years before we met, titled "Now." Its message is simple but profound in ways I'm only just beginning to understand: The one thing we can control is not the past or the future but how we choose to live in the present.

Jim met and honored life in the present through his actions. He didn't want to spend time thinking about it. My own path of mindfulness—the Buddhism of Thich Nhat Hanh mixed with threads of Catholicism—is similar, but it's also different.

And so, the final lesson is that I will carry the love I have for Al Giddings, Patricia Violand de Mercado, Emma Sánchez Rossel, Adalberto Violand, Mercedes Sánchez Rossell, Jim Weber, Abuelita Julia, and all the other friends who have transitioned to a new life. I remember them and will remember them as long as I live—and beyond. Their spirits survive, and I feel their energy, their protection, and a love that is far more powerful than grief.

CHAPTER XXII
Spiritual Journey

"What seeds have I planted and nurtured in others that give meaning to my life?"

This is the question my dear friend Etta Johnson asked in a brief reflection she wrote to me and other members of our Joy Group when she was nearing the end of her life. It's a question many of us ask ourselves, in one way or another, as we confront our own mortality.

What has been the purpose of my life? What are my greatest accomplishments? What is my legacy, and to whom am I leaving that legacy? What do I regret? Whom have I injured? Whom have I nourished and lifted up?

Where have I found joy? Pain? Am I ready to take the next step; to meet whatever or Whoever lies beyond? Are there messages I'd like to send? Are there gifts I hope to leave? Are there things I've learned or come to understand, and how can I share those with the people I love?

Etta Johnson was my colleague at Arlington Public Schools. We worked together in the ESOL/HILT program for many years. She was the elementary specialist, and I was the supervisor.

After retirement, she was deeply engaged in building a community of learners. Together, we tried to reshape a system of public education so it could respond to the needs of *all* the children who'd been placed within the realm of our stewardship. She was a true servant in life.

Etta Johnson was born in Austria in the 1930s but left at the age of six, fleeing for the safety of England with her four-year-old sister on a train full of other Jewish children. She understood what the life of an immigrant is and what it means to be a child coming of age in a strange land. We bonded in that way.

When my mother died, Etta and another former APS colleague, Isabel Hoyt, gave me a copy of *The Book of Joy*, which is a series of conversations between His Holiness the 13th Dalai Lama and South African Archbishop Desmond Tutu—a Buddhist and an Anglican, two men recognized internationally for the work they were doing to try to heal and repair the world. I learned from them that suffering is inevitable. It is our choice how we respond to our suffering and confront the obstacles of grief, stress, fear, illness, and death, affirming joy at every stage.

This same concept of repairing the world appears in *tikkun olam*, a cornerstone of Jewish teaching. In Hebrew, "tikkun olam" means, literally, "to repair the world." It begins with the recognition that the world is broken, but it doesn't stop there. According to rabbinical teaching, it's the responsibility of Jewish people—of *all people*—to repair what is broken, first by confronting darkness and naming it for what it is and then by working toward the light of reconciliation, healing, and "repair."

The Book of Joy helped me see exactly what the English poet William Blake proclaimed in *All Religions Are One*, a book he printed and first published in 1794: When you get past the doctrine and dogma that define many religious traditions, surrounding them like a carapace, there is a place where they are all connected, all drinking from the same living springs of truth.

How much difference is there, really, between the Jewish concept of tikkun olam and the Buddhist Eightfold Path that prescribes right thought, right intentions, right understanding, right speech, right livelihood, right actions, right effort, and right concentration (which could be read as right mindfulness)? Perhaps not very much.

Here were these two men, world-renowned figures, spiritual giants, bantering with each other, laughing with each other, finding common ground on every page. I was enthralled. I had an idea: What if we were to all read the book and talk about it together? We recruited three other friends, and everyone bought or borrowed copies of the book; we read it, came together one afternoon to talk about it, and the Joy Group was born.

Later, I introduced a short group meditation as part of our gatherings. As time went on, we read *Tuesdays with Morrie* by Mitch Albom; *True Refuge* by Tara Brach; *The Second Mountain* by David Brooks; *Braiding Sweet Grass* by Robin Wall Kimmerer; two books by Thich Nhat Hanh, and many others.

Etta started sharing her drawings, reading poems she had written. She encouraged us all to collaborate on a "curriculum guide" for aging, each of us contributing whatever seemed most meaningful to us personally. I wrote an essay about Al's death. I called it "Lifequake." Etta wrote about preparing for her own death, which by then she knew was not far off.

She also wrote a book of her own called *Finding Home*, which was published after she died on January 20, 2023. It's partly about the joy she found in this group of women, and she wrote this for the cover: "An aching heart, a missing love, and unanswered questions united six friends to share the sentiments of loss, compassion, and gratitude that led them to a writing adventure."

For me, Etta Johnson was the heart and soul of the Joy Group, its spiritual center, and when she died, there was a deep and abiding sense of loss. I felt her absence almost as strongly as her presence. She was gone from us, but she wasn't. The group has continued to meet, to share the losses endured in our lives, the suffering, and the hopes too, trying simply to be there for each other, like companions on a journey, helping and encouraging one another, another form of faith in action.

When I was six years old, I was standing in Plaza Colon in my hometown, on a mission I only dimly understood, wanting to repair the world I was seeing, the injustices heaped on Indigenous Bolivians and on the poor. When Etta was six, she was on a train filled with Jewish children, many of whom would never see their families or their homes again. I imagine she felt fear and sadness. But I know her heart was open and that it never closed. I loved her. Our spirits were connected. They still are.

I began my spiritual journey as a Catholic, and a pious one at that. As a young girl, my grandmother was my role model. I can still close my eyes and see her praying in her bedroom, attending Mass, taking Communion, talking to God; and that is the foundation of my faith. Prayer is how I connect with spirit. I continued to pray, even through the years when I was angry with God and estranged from the Catholic Church. These days, I meditate more often than I pray, but that doesn't mean the connection has been lost—just the opposite. I've always had the feeling of someone, something, a presence that exists beyond the material world but not apart from it, protecting me, loving me, always there.

Like most other Catholics I know, and many Protestants, I've struggled with the idea of sin. Can a child sin? Did I sin when I lied to my mother? Or is it just something that children do and (hopefully) learn not to do? Maybe that's why I loved confession; it is a release from sin, an act of cleansing. But in strict Catholicism, confession requires a priest, and the priests were all men.

How could they understand what I was telling them? Was it really God's wish that women be excluded from the sacrament of ordination? And what about those priests who behaved badly in confession, the one who tried to kiss me, and the others? I think many young Catholic women, then and now, have these same questions, and many have had similar experiences. I may have been bolder than most about expressing what I felt, but this kind of confusion is wired into every form of organized religion, the Catholic Church especially.

As my own ideas took form, I became less comfortable with church doctrine: with denying Communion to those, like my father, who've been divorced; with its intractable opposition to birth control; and with subtler ways the church exerts its influence, like inspiring guilt for not going to church on Sundays.

What spoke to me in those early years was the action that arises from faith. I identified strongly with the theology of liberation that was moving through the church like an electric current when I was in my twenties. Liberation theology prescribes a strong role for the church both in service to the poor and in advocating for social change, the path I chose for myself. I wanted the kind of faith that works for justice and breaks down the structures that support injustice, including those ingrained within the church itself. Liberation theology sees Jesus as the greatest liberator, and it prescribes that role for those who would follow Him. I've been inspired by this thought.

In Bolivia, throughout the 1960s and '70s and even well into the '80s, priests and nuns from the United States came to serve the poor. People like my dear friend Sister Ruth Payne, the Dominican nun who directed the education department at IBEAS. Working with three other nuns, Sister Ruth started a free health clinic to serve the poor; they also funded a small library for children. Eventually, she left the convent and married a leftist Bolivian senator from Potosi, Enrique Bachinelo. This woman was the essence of what it means to put faith into action, to move beyond the dogma of the church into the free air of unapologetic service to others. I loved her, and I still have an inscribed copy of the book she published in 2012 titled *They Make Us Dangerous: Bolivia, 1964-1980*.

I believe that faith and spiritual practice are about empowerment, whatever form that takes. As a young woman, I created Un Maestro Más, serving teachers in the rural parts of Bolivia. Later on, I became involved with another organization, called Bread for the

World, whose mission was to help Indigenous communities apply for development grants.

My own faith, too, is expressed through action—the founding of Escuela Bolivia; the Dream Project; Project Family. Through the prayer beseeching God to make us ever mindful of the needs, and the pain, of others.

Perhaps for that reason, I've been inspired by the words of a song called "Solo Le Pido a Dios" by Leon Geico. For me, it's like a prayer, asking God not to make me indifferent to suffering, to injustice, to war, to corruption in human affairs and of the heart and spirit.

I don't want to be indifferent to the suffering of others. I know the pain that war can cause. I know what the talons of injustice feel like. I understand the despair that makes people decide to leave their homes, their families, and their cultures behind.

Who knows? Maybe I'll ask for this song to be played at my funeral when that time comes, as an affirmation of the way I've tried to live.

Suffering is something all human beings have in common. So it's not surprising that both Christianity and Buddhism hold the idea of suffering at their cores. The cross is a symbol of suffering, but it's also a symbol of love, the love of God that gives our suffering a purpose.

My Catholic upbringing was suffused with this idea, and I have always been aware of the suffering around me. I saw it in the way Nestor Paz died. In the struggles of my own family, my mother and father. In the rural teachers I was serving. And with the death of my beloved Al Giddings in Vietnam. I saw it in my sister Paty's death. In my mother's blindness. In my children who were growing up with an alcoholic father and then grappling with their parents' divorce. I saw it in my son, with his ADD. In my struggles with a painful divorce from Jim Hainer, who has not seen his children in many years and has never held his grandchildren.

And then there was the immense suffering of people who came here on boats from Southeast Asia or on foot from countries throughout Central America, and from my own country too. They were all pointing in the same direction, one my Catholic faith had not equipped me to imagine. A shift was coming, a beautiful upheaval in my spiritual life. It was just over the horizon, and I'd been preparing for its arrival for years, without knowing it.

In 2013, my daughter Julie was living in Toronto, and she invited me to join her in a five-day retreat with the Vietnamese Buddhist teacher Thich Nhat Hanh. The retreat was designed specifically for educators, and I was eager for the chance to spend time with my daughter, so I happily said yes.

It was a transformative experience, to put it mildly. Revelation followed revelation. Challenge followed challenge. I was overwhelmed by Thich Nhat Hanh's presence, his gentleness and strength that seemed to come effortlessly. I learned that it's possible to live happily in the present without being lost in regret about the past or anxiety about the future. To live mindfully, in other words. I learned that through mindfulness, we can transform suffering by extinguishing desire, attachment to outcomes. It's a way to create peace within the self and with the world.

In the teaching of Thich Nhat Hanh, mindfulness is not just a concept. During the retreat, we experienced walking meditation and group discussions. It didn't merely focus on the problems (of anxiety, clinging, craving, and regret); it offered practical solutions. Being with this gentle but brilliant man, I saw the path to my own peace unfolding. I understood that peace can be attained in a very practical way that does not involve removing oneself from life but instead requires living more fully within it.

The essence of this approach is to "let go and let God," which is also one of the foundational precepts of Al-Anon and other similar twelve-step programs. I'd been involved in Al-Anon for eight years prior to the retreat, trying to understand my ex-husband's alcoholism and its impact on our family, the children especially. All that immersion in the philosophy of Al-Anon had been like rain softening the ground, and when the seeds from Thich Nhat Hanh's teachings fell there, they grew like magic.

And so, when I heard "Let go of worries, fear, and anger," I was ready; and I had plenty of all three to go around. After all, I'd spent years in a difficult marriage to an abusive alcoholic who was charming but completely untrustworthy, trying to be a good mother and somehow keep the marriage together, all the while knowing in my heart that it wasn't possible.

Mindfulness helped me understand that being in the present moment—fully, consciously, mindfully—dispels suffering and stress. I had to let go. I had to stop trying to please others and fulfill their expectations and needs. Al-Anon had taught me to understand and accept that I was not in control of Jim's drinking. But during this retreat and in the weeks and months that followed, I was lifted to another level.

Thich Nhat Hanh showed me that the kind of mindfulness I so desperately needed and wanted to bring into my life is not passive. You still take action, but with a different, more conscious relationship to your efforts—an awareness of who it is that is taking this action, and of what can and cannot be accomplished.

An engaged Buddhism emphasizing the hard work of incorporating spiritual practice into daily life is not esoteric or theoretical. Nothing about it is incompatible with my Catholic faith, with prayer, with the ideal of service or the path of activism. It doesn't require you to believe anything; mindfulness is just a way of being in the world.

I have a beloved spiritual advisor, John Mooney, who guides me toward a greater understanding and appreciation of the love of Jesus Christ that is always present in my life. I have NOVA, a progressive and inclusive Catholic community committed to social justice, to caring for God's creation, and to peacemaking; a community that has dispensed with hierarchies and recently celebrated fifty-five years of communal worship and faith in action.

My spiritual life also includes respect for Pachamama, Mother Earth. Pachamama is the web of life, the perfection of God's creation, the interconnectedness of all living things. It's the earth giving life and the sun giving energy. It's what sustains us.

Common among Indigenous peoples of the Andes region and in other parts of the Americas is the belief that everything that lives is part of us—and we are part of everything that lives. There is no separation, no "higher" or "lower" in the order of creation; and it's our duty, our responsibility, to honor and care for the earth and for all those who dwell on or within it.

The spirituality I practice is not this earth-centered spirituality, although I respect that path. But it *is* rooted strongly in relationships, especially with those friends who are there for me and with my family.

I live alone but I am not lonely.

Thanks partly to the influence of Thich Nhat Hanh and his teachings, thanks partly to the beliefs I still carry from my Catholic upbringing, thanks partly to the joy I feel in being with my children and grandchildren, and thanks partly to the simple act of living, my spirit grows stronger and my experience of life grows richer now with each passing year.

I'm still keenly aware of suffering, but I've come to see that suffering and joy are really two sides of the same coin; there is a strong, indelible connection between them.

What is it that transcends suffering and impermanence? I think the answer to that question is to be found in mindful living. The reflection Etta wrote as she was preparing for death put this beautifully:

> I am aware that everything matters. I appreciate the here and now, valuing the intricacies of nature, being curious about my surroundings. I've regained my childlike sense of wonder.

I look at the palm of my hand and see the lines, the blood flow, my nails and how they grow, the veins and age spots on the top of my hand. I am ultra-aware of the sounds in nature, a bird singing, the wind blowing, the rain on the window. I marvel at an ant's shadow and the translucent wings of an insect, a dandelion's vibrant color.

Mindfulness also helped me to be more present, less judgmental, and less controlling in my relationships with my children. My daughter used to say to me often, "No *más* consejos, Mam*á*" (No more advice, Mother). Thanks to mindfulness practice, the way I relate to her and to James is more peaceful now (I hope), with fewer demands, and therefore with less room for conflict.

I still hope to be an influential presence in their lives and to give help and support where it's needed; I'm still who I am. But the relationship is different.

One of the places I see the power of spirituality most clearly is in how I relate to my grandchildren, Victor Luis, Diego, and Jaimito. I'm simply there to be with them and be a loving presence. What matters is the love and joy I feel in spending time with them, and I'm grateful beyond words to have this time.

I want them to know I love them, to know that their *abu* is there for them, that she's Bolivian and she's proud of who she is. I speak Spanish to them, and I want them to remember this, but the past and future matter less than the time we have together now. The family that holds me now might look different from the one I knew when I was young, but it is still my rock.

In Buddhism, there is no death, only a transition at the end of life. In Catholicism, that transition means ascending, being lifted up to enter the realm of eternal life. I don't see a conflict between these two beliefs. Aging doesn't interest me so much as the transitions that come with aging. Retirement. The passing of friends and loved ones. Letting go, not just of possessions but of familiar ways of being in the world; of physical strength, independence. Death itself, the certainty of that.

What are the relationships we should cultivate as we near the end of life? Family is one obvious answer, relationships with children and grandchildren, great-grandchildren. And friendships: These have been and remain for me a source of boundless strength, along with the pride I feel in being an immigrant.

But, for me, part of letting go is realizing that my own acculturation process as an immigrant continues. I'm only beginning to learn how to be a senior citizen in the United States.

In Bolivian culture, grandparents are usually brought back into the family. Older Bolivians don't normally *choose* to live independently, by themselves. I think of my own mother, who came to live with me in the last years of her life. I think about the gift of being able to die at home, with loved ones close by, in the presence of familiar sights and sounds and smells—where the last thing you hear in this life is your family singing you through the portal, into whatever comes next.

Will this be possible for any of us when the time comes? In this culture, we don't know. It often isn't. But I do know I want to be like my mother, celebrating each birthday with dancing and singing among the people I love most.

I have the anchor of my family. I also have my Joy Group—Evelyn, Isabel, Maria Teresa, Carol, Sarah, and Etta, whose spirit is with us whenever we meet. We're united and inspired by the reality of joy after loss. And I have the large extended families of the Dream Project and the NOVA Catholic Community. All of these are gifts.

And so it comes down to gratitude, and it's always a choice to be grateful. It's foolish to be blind to the darker sides of human nature—our capacity for cruelty, for inflicting wounds, for willingly exploiting, taking advantage of, or destroying others to assuage our jealousies, ambitions, and greed, or for the sake of an ideology; the part of human nature that hates and divides the world into "us" and "them."

I must never overlook evil, much less accept it. To repair the world, it's necessary first to see and acknowledge the darkness and to name it for what it is. But spirituality has helped me realize that I can't control these things, any more than I could control my former husband's drinking. What *is* within my power is to live my life as an antidote, with an even stronger commitment to service, to healing, and to planting seeds of compassion and gratitude wherever I can.

When I was a teacher, I wanted to change the way public education is understood and delivered, from the classroom to the administrative offices to the halls of state and federal government. I wanted a transformation in our schools, one that would focus on the whole student and not on test scores.

But I was still thinking about the work of education in a conventional way: getting students to learn what you teach them. Now I'm more inclined to see education as the process of motivating students and empowering them to learn from their experience, to trust in themselves as they're learning, and to apply what they're learning to their lives.

I used to be completely comfortable leading others in doing whatever needed to be done. For many years, I thrived in that role. But less so now. There comes a time when you must step back and let others lead.

I think about the world I've known and loved and all the people in it. I wonder what my beloved Al Giddings would say about this path I've taken since his death. I wonder what that little girl in the Plaza Colon thinks about the journey we've been on together all these years. And I think about my parents, and about my dear friend Etta.

When she was writing her final testament, Etta wrote about acceptance, forgiveness, mindfulness, gratitude, and the seeds she'd planted. And most of all, she wrote about joy.

She wasn't interested in holding on to regrets. She advised her friends to put them on a piece of paper, tear the paper to pieces, and then "breathe deeply and let it go."

EPILOGUE
Transformations, Lessons Learned

How did I move from shadows to light as a young immigrant searching for the American Dream? It was not an easy answer or a straight road that led me from Bolivia to Virginia. My life has had many ups and downs, but now I feel at peace and am grateful because my hope and love are anchored in the soil of family and community. These are what sustain me.

My life's deepest shadow lifted in the fall of 2023 after I returned from my painful trip to Vietnam. Being there, I felt like the trauma of Al's death was being cleansed and that I could finally bring his spirit back home. I understood, not just intellectually but in a much deeper way, how his sensitive mind and soul had been shattered by what he saw and experienced in the war. Knowing this, I can now accept the truth—that he died by suicide—in ways I never could before. I don't need to torture myself anymore by asking why he did it: I know.

I loved him so deeply. It took fifty-four years, but my suffering has been freed, like his spirit—to be transformed by love, to move from darkness into light.

My life as an immigrant began when I was only sixteen, transplanted from my native soil of Cochabamba and La Paz to a place called Virginia. I left my mother and my youngest sisters in La Paz. I left my friends, my school, my church, and I had to restart my life in a foreign land. It's a familiar story, but one that is always new to those who live it.

I was like a tree that is transplanted and must find a way to resume its natural growth in a new place. It's not easy to reinvent oneself; but this is the challenge that all immigrants and refugees face when coming to a new land. For me, it was difficult, leaving my family and being separated from my ancestors, from my language, values, and culture; but I found a new way of being in the world. I also found ways to hold on to these things and not leave them behind completely.

It's clear to me now that my own difficult passage as a young immigrant planted a seed. As that seed grew, it gave me the capacity to understand how it is for others who come here, and not just to understand but to identify with their suffering—and resolve to do what I can to ease it.

There were times in my life when I felt alone and abandoned. Like when I was sent to Argentina to study in a boarding school at the age of twelve. But those dissipated like thistle seeds on the wind when I was sitting in a classroom and being uplifted by some new knowledge; or when I went to church, saw Christ on the cross, and knew in my heart that I was loved by God. In this time of deep loneliness, my faith and my love of education were drawn together, becoming inseparable, and they remain so to this day. Sometimes, loneliness can be a gift in disguise.

As a high school senior in Fairfax, Virginia, I was lost at first. But as I learned English and continued studying Spanish, I tasted success in new and stronger ways, and my dream of a university education came within reach. The dream was realized, partly through my own perseverance but also through the support and encouragement of mentors and the full scholarship I received from Radford College—a monumental gift whose value has continued to increase in the years since.

My wish to repay and to replicate the gift I'd received led to the formation of the Dream Project, created with immigrant parents, students, and other supporters. My spirit is guided by *ayni*, the principle of reciprocity that is so common in Native societies, and by a mission to serve. I was blessed to pursue my career as an educator at a time when so many doors were open to me.

I'm very proud that my son, James, and my daughter, Julia, are teachers. Their challenges are different from the ones I faced, but in other ways, they are the same.

I'm also grateful to have lived so much of my adult life in Arlington, Virginia, and to have the feeling of belonging here. I'm proud to have played a part in shaping a public school system—Arlington Public Schools—that continues to welcome new immigrants and refugees and to treat them and their families with respect. It was a blessing to work with dedicated teachers and educators who shared my conviction that family engagement is essential for classroom success.

My eight years as an elected school board member were challenging, but we succeeded in making a difference in the lives of thousands of students and educators.

My personal life has also had its joys and upheavals. I struggled to readjust to life in Bolivia following the death of my first husband; and I suppressed the trauma of my loss in the way that many trauma survivors do—just so I could live and keep going. The pain of two failed marriages, both ending in divorce, still lingers; and I continue to regret and struggle to understand the way my third husband seemingly forgot his children, our children, afterward.

I learned firsthand the damage that an alcoholic parent causes within a family and how stubborn and insidious addiction is. I know the ways that trauma implants itself in the body and stays there, over years, over decades, an entire lifetime in many cases. But I also know that the effects of trauma can be healed through therapy and support, through the power of love, and through actions that address the source of the trauma in an honest and loving way.

I grew up as one of six daughters and in the presence of two strong women who stood as lifelong examples of strength and faith, my mother and my grandmother Julia. I love my sisters: July, Susy, Maria Eugenia, Anneliese, and Paty.

I've learned that wherever she lives, a woman needs to own her power. As a young girl and later as a female educator working in Bolivia, I experienced the glass ceiling women in my own country have always faced and still face. There were more opportunities for women in the United States, and I'm grateful to have had them; but even here, women in positions of leadership face challenges their male counterparts do not. We work under a different set of mostly unspoken rules. Too often, we must still fight our way uphill.

As a young woman, I felt abandoned by my father and then by a husband whose pain was too much for him to bear alone but who never shared it with me. As an immigrant I faced disrespect and false assumptions about who I was and what I could do. I felt the wound of being silenced. And then, as an educator and advocate, I confronted the pain and suffering of young people and their parents who faced legal and institutional barriers in the search for higher education, jobs, and other opportunities solely because of their immigration status. From all these experiences, I learned that when we come together as a community to empower ourselves and each other, we can transform suffering into hope.

There are shadows and barriers in my life as a Catholic too, knowing that the church does not recognize the full equality of women and still does not allow women to become priests. This flaw in my beloved church is painful, for me and for every woman who experiences it. But who suffers most in the end when we place these obstacles in the paths of human beings? It is our community, our church, our country. It is the future that suffers, along with the present.

On the other side, my spiritual life continues to be reinforced by NOVA Catholic Community, an intentional community that focuses on social justice, and by the mindfulness teachings of Thich Nhat Hanh. These are blessings that can't be measured. They are too vast and powerful for that because they do their work of transforming and uplifting mostly in small, ordinary ways. I can only say I'm grateful for these too; they're part of what I see and feel whenever I think of "home."

As I get older, I'm reminded about suffering whenever a friend or loved one dies; and of how suffering and love are joined. Along the way, I lost my husband, sister, parents, partners, and many dear friends. Each of them has left an imprint in my own life—and I hope my work has created and is still creating imprints in the lives of others.

I believe that love and life transcend death.

It is a joy to be eighty years old, to have reached such a milestone, and to still be physically healthy, enjoying the precious time with my beloved grandchildren and family. I'm grateful to have dear friends to talk with and who support each other in good times and bad. I recognize the privileges and blessings I've been given—some of them clear and straightforward, others hidden inside the experience of loneliness and suffering.

I know of no greater blessing than to extend my hand to those in need. Giving is receiving; and the more I learn to take one moment at a time, to meditate and pray constantly, even while doing the most mundane tasks, the more I understand that I am not—I never have been and I never will be—alone.

ACKNOWLEDGMENTS

I am very grateful to David Bearinger for writing this book with me. *Dreams and Shadows* would not have been possible without this talented writer. After David retired from Virginia Humanities, he said to me, "Emma, you have a story to share." I said I would love to, but I felt insecure about my ability to write. I asked him directly, "Can you help?" He said yes. David not only has a gift for writing, but he also values my complicated journey and deeply understands me. We are not only collaborators; we are friends. I trust him and respect him. I opened my heart to share my deepest sorrows, and he brought a light to my shadows and dreams.

I wanted to share my personal story as a legacy to my children, James and Julia; my grandchildren, Victor, Diego, and James (Jaimito); as well as my sisters and other family members; and with other immigrants who share a common struggle to start a new life in the United States. I am forever indebted to my mother, Emma Sanchez, for modeling the love and fortitude of a mother who can overcome adversity and make the most difficult decisions to ensure a better future for her children. I'm also grateful to my father, Adalberto Violand, for modeling civic engagement and service to one's country. Thanks to my abuelita Julia, my religious guide who showed me that our Catholic faith can sustain us in life. My tía Mecha taught me the value of education and the joy of being an educator.

Thanks to the Koehler Books team, including Greg Fields, John Koehler, Adrienne Folkerts, Danielle Koehler, and Hannah Woodlan.

Thanks also to Girasol O'Neill for the initial cover artwork.

I am also thankful to have had the opportunity to work in Arlington Public Schools for thirty-two years, with amazing educators and friends who were committed to providing the best instruction and support services to immigrants and children of immigrants. My greatest blessing has been working with other parents, students, and supporters to create and sustain the Dream Project, a nonprofit organization whose mission is to provide scholarships, mentoring, and support to students whose immigration status creates barriers to higher education. The Dream Project is a supportive community made up of students, their families, board members, volunteers, and donors. I am grateful to have had the opportunity to be of service in this way.

I would not have reached my goal of graduating from university without Radford University's scholarships. I'm also grateful to Dr. Martha Rashid, my George Washington University graduate advisor, and to the American Association of University Women for the fellowship to finish my dissertation.

Thanks too to my dear friend Mark Habeeb, who read the manuscript and offered me guidance and encouragement in writing this book, and to the other reviewers of this book.

I also acknowledge my dear friends of the Joy Group—our beloved Etta, Isabel, Evelyn, Carol, Maria Teresa, and Sarah—for listening to my lifequake and supporting me in writing about it. My coach, Lisa Ling, also encouraged me to write my memoir and showed me how to find the love within. It is difficult to name all my dear friends, but you know who you are; and I thank all of you for your encouragement and support. Muchas gracias.

PHOTOS

Emma as a baby

Abuelita Julia with Julia, Emma, and Susy as children

Emma and sisters with their mother as children

School in Argentina in 1958

Family in Bolivia in 1961

Emma with best friend Ana Maria at their school in Argentina

Emma with Al Giddings at Virginia Tech

Wedding day with Al, July 22, 1967

Circle of Joy friends

Emma visiting Hogar Salomon Klein orphanage in Cochabamba

A photo from a local newspaper article on Emma's school board victory

Emma celebrating her school board victory alongside county board member Walter Tejada and Delegate Alfonso Lopez

Senator Kaine celebrating his campaign event alongside Emma, county board member Walter Tejada, and Delegate Alfonso Lopez

Emma as school board chair and President Obama when he visited Arlington Public Schools

Emma with daughter, Julie, and grandchildren Victor and Diego

Emma with grandson Jaimito

Emma with Jim Weber, her partner of twenty-one years

Emma's adult children, Julia and James Hainer-Violand, in 2012

Emma with sisters Julia, Susy, Anneliese, and Maria Eugenia in 2021

Emma's mother celebrating her ninety-ninth birthday

Emma receiving the Arlington Community Foundation Spirit of Community Award with her 100-year-old mother and her daughter, Julia, at her side

www.ingramcontent.com/pod-product-compliance
Lightning Source LLC
LaVergne TN
LVHW041223080526
838199LV00083B/2304